UNFORGETTABLE OHIOANS

UNFORGETTABLE
OHIOANS

Thirteen Mavericks Who Made History on Their Own Terms

Randy McNutt and Cheryl Bauer McNutt

Black Squirrel Books™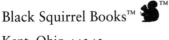

Kent, Ohio 44242

BLACK SQUIRREL BOOKS™ 🐿™
Frisky, industrious black squirrels are a familiar sight on the Kent State University
campus and the inspiration for Black Squirrel Books™, a trade imprint of The Kent
State University Press.
www.KentStateUniversityPress.com

LIBRARY OF CONGRESS CATALOGING-IN-PUBLICATION DATA
McNutt, Randy.
 Unforgettable Ohioans : thirteen mavericks who made history on their own terms /
Randy McNutt and Cheryl Bauer McNutt.
    pages cm
 Includes bibliographical references and index.
 ISBN 978-1-60635-235-9 (pbk. : alk. paper) ∞
 1. Ohio—Biography I. McNutt, Cheryl Bauer, 1953– II. Title.
 F490.M45 2015
 977.1—dc23
 2014049489

19 18 17 16 15   5 4 3 2 1

Dedicated to the memories of our parents,

Ruth and Frederick Bauer

Kay and William McNutt

CONTENTS

PREFACE

Ask any Ohioans to name five famous Buckeyes and they could probably quickly come up with Neil Armstrong, Orville and Wilbur Wright, John Glenn, and Thomas Edison. They also might be able to name a few of the eight Ohioans who have occupied the White House. The better informed might also list shooting expert Annie Oakley, poet Paul Laurence Dunbar, and Tecumseh, the Native American warrior who never surrendered. In fact, Ohio has such an abundance of famous people and history makers that it's nearly impossible not to know something about some of them; their accomplishments and quirks have been chronicled and passed down through generations until they've become almost legendary.

But Ohio is a large state with a long history and plenty of fascinating people who have been overlooked over the years. We wanted to find some unforgettable Ohioans who accomplished something—good or bad. To do so, we had to dig into our research a little deeper, visit more sources, and travel more back roads, but the project was worth it. You may have studied some of these people in school, heard about their legends, flown in their airplanes, read their books, and sang their songs without ever realizing their Ohio connection.

We chose them based on our own interests—and simply what we consider fascinating stories. To us, the story is everything, more important than race, gender, occupation, or anything else. So we went with the best stories we could find—we went with the entertainment. Our only criteria: the subjects had to live in Ohio for a significant time, or be attached to the state in a special way—whether artistically, professionally, culturally, or otherwise. And, finally, more important, any person included in our book must be dead.

Unforgettable Ohioans profiles the lives of an eclectic group of men and women from diverse backgrounds. Some grew up in rural areas; others came from cities. Some were formally educated; most of them were self-taught. A few were quite young when they experienced success; some did not excel until they were elderly. Several were prominent throughout their lives. One was so elusive that he is considered a frontier legend. The majority of them spent most of their time in Ohio. They were national—or in a few cases international—history makers. Their eras range from the late eighteenth century until well into the twentieth.

Not all of these people were "good guys." One of the most unapologetic traitors of World War II grew up in Ohio and—even more surprisingly—returned to live here after being imprisoned for treason. Not all of our subjects accomplished all of their goals. The commander behind one of the worst dirigible disasters in U.S. aviation history was a young Ohioan who died much too early while pursuing his vision. The composer of several famous songs died in his early thirties, before he could write more hits.

But all of these unforgettable people have one thing in common: their stories contain elements of wonder. At some point, you'll be amazed at their accomplishments, or determination, or just plain audacity. And you'll say, "I never knew he came from Ohio" or "I've heard of her, but I never knew she did *that*."

We hope that after you read their stories, these people will be as unforgettable to you as they have become to us.

CAESAR

Frontier Explorer

On Ohio's frontier, a legend grew around an escaped slave from Virginia known only as Caesar. Named, ironically or defiantly, after the powerful Roman emperor, he found war and freedom north of the Ohio River decades before Ohio became a state in 1803. Caesar's story was part myth, part truth. Now, roughly 175 years after his death, Caesar's name is still mentioned daily, yet no one knows exactly when and where he was born, who he really was, how he arrived in Ohio, and with whom he left, or why. He is a mysterious figure whose adventures were passed down through generations of Ohioans, leaving multiple, conflicting plots. As with a mythological creature, it was as if he inhabited four bodies—all the same man, but with different lives. This particular Caesar invokes the imagination and helps us understand more about the fate of escaped slaves.

In the late 1700s, the name "Caesar" was common among slaves. But this man was a pioneer in a sprawling, untamed region. His story is as much a part of Ohio history as any other pioneer tale, although it began a full quarter century before the territory gained statehood.

Two centuries of Caesar storytelling and retelling make it difficult to trace his lineage and timeline. Yet, his name lives on: at Caesar Creek State Park in Warren and Clinton counties as well as at several popular businesses, including the Caesar Creek Flea Market off Interstate 71 and the Caesar Creek Vineyards in Xenia. At the park's attractive visitor center, a display board tells Caesar's story—or what is known of it. "College students are interested in him, but the younger kids think he

Caesar as he might have looked in the 1780s. (Courtesy United States Army Corps of Engineers, Louisville)

is either Julius Caesar or else the pizza [chain]," said Kim Baker, a park natural resources specialist ranger with the United States Army Corps of Engineers. "We try to tell his story to them as best we can. But we may never know the true story behind this fascinating man."

According to the Ohio Division of State Parks, Caesar's Creek was named for a black slave who had been captured by the Shawnee during a raid along the Ohio River. The Indians adopted the young man and eventually presented him with the valley where the state park is now located. He lived there during Blue Jacket's days as Shawnee war chief, 1786 to 1795, and was said to have participated in raids against settlers.

In 1978, two hundred years after Caesar trekked through the early West, the federal and state governments built and opened the forty-seven-hundred-acre park that bears his name, as well as an adjacent twenty-five-hundred-acre wildlife site. The land and wildlife are preserved much as they were when Caesar lived there.

Warren County historian Dallas Bogan, once a Caesar skeptic, listed four different legends about the elusive frontiersman. The first is that he escaped from his southern owners and made his way to the North-west Territory, where slavery was banned in 1787. There he lived in a cabin on the banks of Caesar's Creek, about thirty-five miles north of the Ohio River. In the 1800s, some people of the area claimed Caesar had died by the stream and was buried there, but others believed he left for Canada on the Underground Railroad. Bogan's second legend, gleaned from George F. Robinson's 1902 history of Greene County, has it that in 1786 Caesar was the slave of an officer in an American army General Benjamin Logan had raised in that area to respond to the Shawnee's theft of horses. But before the army could attack the Indians, Caesar escaped along a scenic creek and then took Kenton's Trace, a route opened by pioneer explorer Simon Kenton that ran from Aberdeen on the Ohio River to the Shawnee's major encampment. When he arrived, Caesar informed the tribe of the army's intention. Indian leaders believed him, and soon after, as Bogan wrote, "the soldiers moved upon Old Chillicothe, destroyed crops, and burnt the village, but found the Indians had fled. . . . The creek afterwards was known as the creek where Caesar ran away. The General most certainly had slaves accompanying him, but was Caesar among them?"

Robinson noted that Caesar's Creek was named for Caesar and said he learned this from Thomas C. Wright, who claimed he had heard the story from Simon Kenton himself. Kenton, along with Daniel Boone and Caesar, lived to old age in an era when most people didn't—particularly on the frontier.

The third legend, Bogan wrote briefly, is that the creek took its name from the servant of an officer who served with the American army in the Warren County area in 1794.

Bogan's fourth legend recounts that when the Shawnee held fellow frontiersman Simon Kenton prisoner, Caesar was living with the tribe. When Kenton pleaded with him for help escaping, the unusual-looking Indian refused. But perhaps the former slave empathized with the white captive, because he did provide him with invaluable aid—an escape route along the creek, which would lead him to safety via the Little Miami River and on to the Ohio River.

"Whether truth or fiction," Bogan wrote, "this writer, while searching through the many sources regarding the Negro slave, Caesar, and the naming of Caesar's Creek, can say with all due respect, that ground for substantiation 'is in the eye of the beholder.'"

It's a fascinating puzzle. How did Caesar find time to live with the Indians, perhaps start a family, accompany an American army during the Revolution, and then leave for Kentucky to spend his old age? And why did he choose Kentucky—where slavery flourished—over a free state? Could it have been Ohio's old law that required free Negroes in the state to present a $500 bond?

Alabama author Wade Hall doesn't answer questions like these, but he does believe Caesar existed. During Black History Month of 1996, as a professor of English at Bellarmine College in Lexington, Kentucky, Hall wrote a story about Caesar for the *Louisville Courier-Journal*, in which he suggested that Caesar was a slave of an army officer serving with Colonel George Rogers Clark's western campaign during the American Revolution. Hall based his idea on the contents of an old letter, discovered earlier in the 1990s, which mentions an African American who served with General Clark's army during its conquest of Vincennes, a former French town in what is now Knox County in western Indiana. Henry Beard of Lexington penned the letter on March 28, 1836, to friend and business partner Thomas S. Hinde in Mt. Carmel, Illinois. He wrote: "We are all well thank God except an old Negro Man Ceasar [*sic*] who was with Genl. Clarks Army at the taking of Vincennes. This Winter & Spring has been to Severe for him & I think he must [be] . . . between 80 & 90. He is a Strict Methodist & I have no fear for his soul."

Military historians believe Clark's officers took their body servants with them, so the presence of a slave or servant on the journey wouldn't be surprising. If Caesar did travel with Clark's band, the letter puts to rest any idea that he was a fictional pioneer; rather, he was a participant in the American Revolution.

Hall mused: "Now Ceasar [sic] has stepped from the silent shadow of more than 200 years ago. We don't know whom he served. It was probably not Col. Clark. . . . But could it have been Capt. Joseph Bowman or Robert McCarty or Robert Todd or Jesse Evans? Or was it one of the young lieutenants—Anthony Crockett or John Roberts or Richard Brashares or Isaac Bowman? We may never know for sure. Maybe that's not important anyway. All we know is that he was apparently with this expedition for its entire mission." The entire mission ran over two years and led Clark's small army west through both hot and cold weather.

Hall surmised that Caesar—whether the name was spelled "Caesar" or "Ceasar" is anyone's guess—left Corn Island at the Falls of the Ohio near Louisville on June 24, 1778, with 175 officers and men under the command of the Virginian Clark, twenty-five years old and filled with courage and daring. Clark's little army was heading toward former French towns that the British had occupied since the French and Indian War ended in 1763.

The Proclamation of 1763, which set treaty limits between the French and British, forbade American colonists from settling on the lands west of the Appalachian Mountains, but they did so anyway. The British, who had taken over French forts on the western frontier, tried to enforce the proclamation. They used Indian war parties to kill any colonial settlers, including those in Kentucky, who ignored the terms.

Hall tried to imagine Caesar's fear of the unknown as the little group floated west toward uncertainty. British troops outnumbered the Americans, who had gathered short-term enlistees and volunteers. On the way, Hall said, Caesar probably had to work hard doing menial tasks for his master as well as chores for the army. During a total eclipse of the sun, the soldiers rode flatboats downriver toward the western British outposts of Kaskaskia, Cahokia, and Vincennes. The small American force would have had to float and later walk the 240 miles over boggy ground. Though Clark's group was low in number, it made up for any shortcomings in desire to guard Kentucky from more British and Native American attacks.

One can only imagine what Caesar thought as he trudged through the wetlands on his way to the Illinois country. He was a part of the small army of white men, one of them his own master, who wanted to kill Indians and British, who had not harmed him. Did he sympathize with the dark-skinned people who were losing their lives, culture, and homeland to white settlers? Or did he share the whites' fear of the Native Americans? Did he have a choice?

After traveling ten days, the American troops arrived at Kaskaskia on the Mississippi in the Illinois country, where the small band was able to defeat the well-entrenched British, thanks to Clark's tenacity and bravado. Assuming the invaders' numbers were far greater, the British surrendered on July 4. So too did those at Cahokia, about fifty miles to the north. No shots were fired. Then larger Vincennes, a former French colony won by the English during the French and Indian War, gave up too.

But the American victory there was short-lived. On December 17, 1778, the British retook Fort Sackville, and a grueling winter set in. Clark planned to return. He knew the weather worked in his favor because the British were suffering too, and they didn't know how large a force he commanded. They planned a spring offensive to regain control of their lost forts.

The town of Vincennes soon welcomed the Americans. Some French men joined the Revolutionary army, believing they would fare better with the Americans and have a better chance of hanging onto their land.

Clark boldly demanded unconditional surrender from the British troops inside Fort Sackville on February 23, 1779. Some fighting followed, but after negotiations the British surrendered again. Two days later, at 10:00 A.M., the red-clad garrison marched out of the fort; the West was in American hands. Clark quickly renamed the outpost Fort Patrick Henry. He also captured the notorious Henry Hamilton, the British lieutenant governor based in Canada, who had organized the retaking of the fort. The despised Hamilton was nicknamed "Hair Buyer" because he paid Indians for settlers' scalps in Detroit.

Caesar witnessed and participated in the unlikely American victory in the West, which hindered the British and Native Americans in their attacks on colonial pioneers in Kentucky and other remote areas. Three years later, the new land would become America's Northwest Territory. Congress would pass the Ordinance of 1787, prohibiting slavery and involuntary servitude in the territory. But Caesar would not be there to enjoy it; he would move to Kentucky, where he lived the rest of his life. Nevertheless, according to Wade Hall, there was a "kind of long-term, cosmic justice that Caesar had helped set in motion. He and his unnamed black brethren who had served bravely alongside their white masters . . . had helped prepare his way to freedom for all people, black and white, whether north or south of the Ohio River."

When Lebanon, Ohio's former librarian Dennis Dalton decided to fight the federal government over a missing "'s" in the name "Caesar Creek," some people told him he should find a hobby. He told them he already had one—history—and it is the reason he will preserve Caesar's story. "Someone has to do it for the people who come after us," he said. "This man—one of the early nonnative explorers—should be remembered. Enslaved by white people as well as the Indians, he was caught between two worlds, trying to make a place for himself in a new land. I'm not surprised that he's nearly forgotten. A lot of whites of the 1800s overlooked black people. So we have to preserve what we do know of him."

Dalton believes he might as well be the man to rediscover faded historical figures. After all, he has been interested in genealogy and history since his boyhood in Waynesville in the 1950s, and he is a direct descendant of Joseph Boone Sr., Daniel Boone's uncle.

For decades, Caesar's legend has fascinated Dalton, who has always believed the man was real. "He's a little hard to pin down," Dalton said with a laugh. "I keep at it, though." Dalton's genealogical search takes him through country cemeteries, small-town libraries, and the back pages of history. When he's not working on another history project, the retired nursing-home activities director studies state and regional history, making him as qualified as anybody to find the trail that Caesar left cold in the early 1800s.

Though Caesar didn't make it into *The Ohio Almanac,* he is not a myth. Allan Eckert wrote about him briefly in *The Frontiersman,* claiming that Caesar, who lived with the Indians, warned captive frontiersman Simon Kenton that the Indians planned to kill him. The almanac did list Kenton, who was "captured by the British and Indians, ran the gauntlet eight times, was tortured, thrice escaped burning at the stake, saved Daniel Boone's life, and died at 81—in bed."

Dalton's best guess is that Caesar came down the Ohio with his white family when the Ohio Country was wilderness. Caesar's black skin saved him when a group of Shawnee warriors killed the whites and either rescued or captured him.

Exactly when he came into the Ohio Country is open to question. Opinions have varied. "We think he arrived in the bloody sevens—1777," said the Reverend Fred Shaw, of Neeake, a minister of the United Methodist Church and an official storyteller of the Shawnee Nation, United Remnant Band. "When the flatboat was taken, he became a part of the tribe. We don't know a lot about Caesar, but there are references to him by Indians and colonists of the period. I think he was a strong man, well respected, but he was not a warrior."

Dalton surmises that Caesar's time with the Indians came after he had served in the military campaigns in the 1780s. "Very little was ever written down about him," he said. "A lot of it was passed on orally through the generations. Probably it is something that will always remain a mystery." The Shawnee either invited Caesar to move into Old Town, their big community that stood near the present city of Xenia, or ordered him to do so. Later, according to some stories, they supposedly gave him property on a small tributary, now known as Caesar's Creek. Perhaps that is when Caesar left the Shawnee.

"At some point he became a servant to the military and he came through with Clark's army, which camped along the Little Miami River," Dalton said. "People have found swords and other army pieces buried along there over the years. I believe this is where Caesar first learned of the beautiful area in what is today Warren County."

Later, Dalton said, Caesar took the first name Charles and moved to Lexington, where he did indeed die at an old age. "I am still trying to find his grave," Dalton said. "My guess is that it is unmarked and around Lexington. Because he was a former slave, I doubt if he had a marked grave, and I doubt if anyone would even consider bringing him back to Ohio in . . . the 1830s. I won't stop looking. After all, he was one of our state's early explorers. He showed Daniel Boone escape routes to flee from the Indians. They were valuable then. But finding Caesar has been difficult; he had only one name early in his life, so it was tough to trace his descendants. Then I remembered that classical slave names like his were changed about 1800. That made the search a little easier. Caesar became the last name. I found a Charles Caesar living in Lebanon in 1825. I'm convinced he was a descendant of our Caesar."

Each year, Dalton uncovers more clues in brittle courthouse records, eighteenth-century histories, and dusty genealogies—and in telephone directories from southern Ohio and North Carolina. Dalton contacted Nancye Caesar Donaldson, her family's historian, who has been tracing Caesar for years. They became a team; they are convinced that she is Caesar's great-great-great-great-granddaughter. "When I was young," she said, "people used to tease my family about being named after him. We didn't know much about our background. Many years later, a friend told me about the black man named Caesar, and how there is a park named after him. I was fascinated. I tried to connect him to us. Going back several generations, I ran into trouble. Dennis helped."

Dalton—with assistance from fellow Warren County historians—compiled a dossier on Caesar, based on hundreds of hours of research. While he was writing a pioneer history for the Caesar Creek State Park Visitors Center decades ago, he became more interested in Caesar. He was not satisfied with gathering only dates and names. With Donaldson's help, he organized a Caesar family reunion at the park in July 1996. Dressed in a colonial town crier's outfit (he was then the town crier for the village of Waynesville), Dalton addressed fifty-three family members about Caesar the explorer.

A patch of Caesar's wilderness still exists at the state park, which opened in the late 1970s, after decades of preparation. The United States Army Corps of Engineers dammed Caesar's Creek to create the park's 2,830-acre recreational lake, between Waynesville and Harveysburg. The corps obtained the land and leased it to the state. Later, Caesar's Creek Pioneer Village Association—its members had no problem with apostrophes—subleased a tract and obtained and preserved log buildings to display authentic pioneer history. Today, Caesar Creek State Park is one of the state's larger nature preserves, protecting bountiful forests in the gorge overlooking the Little Miami River. While city people fish and boat on the lake and play on the park's miles of bridle, hiking, and snowmobile trails, park rangers protect a microcosm of Ohio wildlife that hasn't changed much since Caesar walked through the ravines and rolling terrain.

All seems right, except that missing "'s." In its zeal to open the park, the government somehow changed "Caesar's Creek" into "Caesar Creek." Many maps misspell the name, adding to the confusion. That rankles Dalton. "I've always wanted to correct the grammatical error," he said. "But I'm told there's no way now. Officials have told me that too many things—from letterheads to signs—would have to be changed. I said, 'So? We squander enough on other things.' That didn't go over very well, though. The shame of it is, some people think the park was named for Julius Caesar. Can you imagine the red tape involved in changing the name from Caesar Creek to Caesar's Creek? I'd settle for a bronze marker to set the record straight. Caesar should be possessive. It was a mistake when it happened in the 1970s. Officials admitted it to me."

Though they encouraged Dalton and others to preserve the area's history, they told grammar-conscious historians to forget about changing the park's name. "That would take a congressional order," said Vinnie Ewing-Gibbins, a park spokesperson. "It wouldn't be feasible."

Dalton insists that government employees originally told him they would have added the "'s" to Caesar's name, but they erred. But it is also possible that they didn't add it because of a nineteenth-century presidential order prohibiting apostrophes from being added to post office names and other places affiliated with the federal government. Nevertheless, Dalton persists; he considers circulating apostrophe petitions to park visitors, but he wonders how he might present them to Congress, if the Army Corps of Engineers and the state of Ohio won't willingly add the "'s". He knows that circulating the petitions would be a lonely job. He won't receive much help from the older members of the Caesar clan who attended his family reunions. These folks, the ones who were interested in Caesar's genealogy, are dying off. In addition, few people at all seem interested in erecting a historical marker to commemorate Caesar.

"The time is now, before we lose more history and everyone forgets," Dalton said. "Of course, I'll probably end up in jail for doing all this." Then he added with a laugh, "What is the penalty for rabble-rousing these days?" Whatever the penalty, he knows it would be worth it to focus more attention on one of Ohio's most enigmatic pioneers. Like many frontiersmen, Caesar left no written records. No one else wrote down his legend until decades later, which added to the confusion. To his contemporaries, he may have been just another man on the frontier, struggling to live, but being black, he also had the constant challenge of staying free. Even in the free Northwest Territory, bounty hunters had license to track down and retrieve slave owners' "property." Whether Caesar entered the Northwest as a slave or servant, he must have been a capable, intelligent man whose services were needed by army officers or the Shawnee—depending on the legend. He had to be tenacious to have survived slavery in the first place and then to survive life with the Shawnee during a rigorous military campaign.

If Caesar could come back to life, he might be stunned to learn that historians have been trying to piece together his story for more than two centuries. And it's also likely that he would be quietly proud of all the attention. For he is not just Caesar, black man and former slave, but Charles Caesar, Ohio pioneer and legend.

2

BENJAMIN R. HANBY
Christmas Composer

Few people in New Paris, Ohio, know the Reverend Benjamin Russel Hanby or his music. Occasionally travelers will stop to inquire about his historical marker, but the villagers have let Hanby and his song-writing career rest in obscurity. After all, in this town Hanby was just another rejected sojourner on a walk through time, a man who never believed he had reached his goal. He stayed briefly, wrote the enduring Christmas folk song "Up on the Housetop," and left. His is considered among the oldest American Christmas songs and the first folk piece written about Santa Claus.

Hanby's life began the first time he heard melodies in his head, made by various musical instruments that he longed to play. He plucked the tunes from his mind, matching them with words that came to him in quiet moments. Songs flowed from his pen, and by the late 1850s he was one of Ohio's most successful songwriters—but not the wealthiest. The only thing rich about him was his creative and happy spirit.

During the Civil War, Hanby's songs entertained weary Union and Confederate soldiers. Afterward, his holiday tunes created Christmas traditions for millions of children and churchgoers. In his brief life, he wrote an estimated one hundred songs, of which seventy-nine were published—for any songwriter, in any time, a 79 percent publishing rate is impressive. Though most of his songs are now a forgotten part of Victorian history, three are still sung regularly: the sentimental prewar standard "Darling Nelly Gray," the hymn "Who Is He in Yonder Stall," and, of course, the Christmas carol "Up on the Housetop."

Benjamin Russel Hanby, probably in the 1860s. (Courtesy Ohio Historical Society, Columbus)

But Hanby did more than just compose enduring songs. He used his positions as minister and, later, sheet music editor to campaign for musical accompaniment in churches. In a time when most congregations wanted to hear only human voices, he believed that instruments of many kinds could enrich Sunday services. He also supported the temperance movement and wrote anthems for its followers, including "Heroism," in which he lauded moral strength. He also wrote for the prominent Dayton-based Ohio temperance newspaper, the *Christian Repository*, and supported the antislavery movement in the days before the Civil War.

Of all his works, the Christmas song is his legacy; it has long entertained children and adults, and it added a touch of modern Santa Claus to America's brand of Christmas. Hanby borrowed from his early—and busy—childhood to craft the song's lyrics. He was born in Rushville, Fairfield County, Ohio, on July 22, 1833, the oldest of eight children of the Reverend William Hanby and his wife, Ann. The elder Hanby, a saddler and a bishop in the Church of the United Brethren in Christ, was an abolitionist who volunteered on the Underground Railroad, helping escaped slaves find their ways to Canada. ("We may be bound by a man-made law," he said of the Fugitive Slave Act of 1850, "but we are more bound by a Lord-given conscience.") His children lovingly referred to him as The Old Crusader, for his zeal to end slavery and other injustices.

In 1854, the elder Reverend Hanby moved his family to Westerville, where he became one of the first trustees of the new Otterbein College. School literature described his position as "Pioneer Advocate of Colleges for the United Brethren Church." He and his family left behind their original log cabin and moved into the simple frame house that is now a state memorial managed by the Westerville Historical Society. He knew that by accepting the advocate position, he was making it possible for his children, if they worked hard, to receive a higher education.

Young Hanby toiled to pay for his schooling. He had started working at age six folding papers for his father, and at ten he became a paper carrier and collector in the family's print shop. (The family also owned a harness shop.) At fourteen, Benjamin bought his first flute with money he'd saved working as a newspaper delivery boy. In those days, flutes were still made of wood; his was made of mahogany, with ivory mountings and German silver keys. He crafted his own wooden case for his new treasure, woodworking being a craft he learned from his father. The case was walnut, lined with brown flannel. His flute became his constant companion, and he stored it in his workbench or carried it in one of his saddlebags everywhere he went. He was always ready to play and compose music.

Enrolling at the college in Westerville at age sixteen, Benjamin followed his father's path to the Church of the United Brethren, religious music, temperance, and the Underground Railroad. But the younger Hanby had a cause of his own—writing and performing songs. He had started playing music at nine years old when first he took up the flute, and later he added the organ and other instruments to his repertoire.

Hanby might have led an easier life if his calling had been strictly secular music. But he wanted to serve the church by combining music and the ministry. In fire-and-brimstone days, this was no easy task, for many denominations forbade musical instruments during worship.

In 1854, while still living in his parents' overcrowded house on the corner of Grove and Main Streets with his siblings and grandmother, he wrote songs and studied. (In 1937, the house was moved to 160 West Main Street and dedicated as a historic site.) Patriarch William Hanby bought the children a Hazelton Square piano, and sweet melodies echoed from the parlor. Of course, the younger Hanby took up that instrument, too.

A lack of money prevented Benjamin from graduating from college in four years, so he alternated work and study over nine years. While he was a sophomore at Otterbein in 1856, he put his antislavery sentiments into words by writing "Darling Nelly Gray," a song based on the true story of a runaway slave named Joseph Selby, who had died at the Hanby home in Rushville in 1842 while fleeing to Canada. During his final hours, Selby had explained that he once hoped to earn enough money to buy his sweetheart's freedom someday. The day before they were to be married, however, Nelly Gray was sold at auction. Selby lost her, but he never forgot her.

As a child, Hanby heard the escaped slave's story as his family retold it. It touched him deeply. The Hanby children performed "Darling Nelly Gray" for Hanby's music teacher, Cornelia Walker, who convinced Benjamin to send the piece to the Oliver Ditson Company, a Boston music publisher with national distribution. Hanby received no reply. Without notifying him, company owners published it under his name, filed for a copyright under their names, and printed and distributed the sheet music. When Hanby heard his creation performed in a concert, he realized it must be a success. So he wrote to the company, seeking payment. "He couldn't understand why he didn't get paid," said Larry Pryfolgle, a docent at the Hanby House museum. "The publisher wrote back and said, 'You didn't sign the papers.' He sent along a dozen copies of the sheet music and added, 'We have made the money, you the fame. That balances the account.'" With a lawyer's help, Hanby eventually received $100 for the song. The lawyer took $50; Hanby kept the other half. The publisher did grant one favor: the sheet music was dedicated to Miss Walker.

The song was typical of the era's sad love songs. A century later, ABC Radio broadcaster Ted Malone described it as "not just fictitious sentiment. It was real-life drama, a page torn out of Ohio and Kentucky history. . . . The song caught on like a flame and swept across the nation and the world. Translated into foreign tongues, it sold millions of copies."

"Darling Nelly Gray" became popular two decades before the invention of the phonograph and seven decades before radio swept the nation. It was called the "*Uncle Tom's Cabin* of songs" for using a true story to acquaint the public with the evils of slavery. It also tugged at Americans' collective heartstrings, regardless of region.

There's a low green valley on the old Kentucky shore
Where I've whiled many happy hours away
A-sitting and a-singing by the little cottage door
Where lived my darling Nelly Gray.

Chorus:
O my poor Nelly Gray they have taken you away
And I'll never see my darling anymore
I'm sitting by the river and I'm weeping all the day
For you've gone from the old Kentucky shore

When the moon had climbed the mountain,
And the stars were shining too
Then I'd take my darling Nelly Gray
And we'd float down the river in my little red canoe
While my banjo sweetly I would play.

In those days before the war, when many Americans wanted to learn more about slaves and their possible mistreatment, Harriet Beecher Stowe wrote *Uncle Tom's Cabin,* which she claimed to have based on stories she heard about slave trading in Kentucky while she lived in Cincinnati. Like the slaves in her book, Selby escaped across the Ohio River and pushed deep into the Buckeye State. Both Stowe's book and Hanby's song caught on quickly in the North.

Hanby entered the prewar music business just as it was leaving minstrel and torch songs for more patriotic music. With the success of Stephen Foster's sheet music a few years earlier, the business was expanding to tap a growing market for families who wanted to sing and play piano in their parlors. Sheet music was fast becoming the main source of song distribution in America, and it would remain that way until the phonograph developed commercially in the late 1890s.

To Hanby's surprise, "Nelly Gray"'s sheet music remained a major hit for several years. At the start of the Civil War, Union soldiers sang its melancholy melody around campfires. Confederate soldiers enjoyed the song so much that they changed the lyrics and sang it too. "The song had phenomenal sales," historian Charles B. Galbreath wrote in 1925. "It was published in many forms and the tune was arranged for band music. The publisher must have made a small fortune out of it; Hanby had the obscure notice accorded to the songwriter and what to a man of his taste and sensibility must have been far greater—satisfaction of knowing that he had reached the popular heart and conscience in the support of a worthy cause."

Hanby appreciated Ohio's abolitionist congressman J. R. Giddings and various antislavery proponents, who sang the song as an anthem of their cause. Some claimed that it had more influence on the public than *Uncle Tom's Cabin* because it was sung for free. But Hanby realized that popularity and worthy causes could not pay for food. He would have to work, and the ministry was a natural course.

In 1858, one month shy of his twenty-fifth birthday, Hanby graduated with honors from Otterbein College. He began working there to help the school obtain endowments, but the pay was low and he longed to preach. He also could have left for New York to try the songwriting business, but he had love on his mind—and the object of that love was Mary Katherine "Kate" Winter, one of two women who had graduated in Otterbein's first class a year earlier.

Kate liked Ben because of his optimism, good humor, and talents. He talked three male friends into going with him to her house to sing her a love song he had based on "Mary Had a Little Lamb." She was embarrassed, but eventually she realized how much she enjoyed being with him. He shared with her his songs and articles, and he always kept her laughing, even when his subject was food:

> By merciful Providence," he once wrote, "man is so constituted that he may eat, think and talk, all at the same time. Here the table is often the scene of animated and interesting conversation, provided love is there. How beautiful is the arrangement by which members of a household are morning, noon and night (I pity the folks who eat only twice a day!) brought around the family board. Would it not be well for modern times to take a hint here? Had I been appointed architect of the Capitol at Washington, I would have constructed a couple of immense dining rooms with all the necessary appurtenances. . . . Imagine, if you can, a congressman helping himself to a batter cake, and at the same time calling his brother member a liar!

Kate Winter must have smiled when she married Ben Hanby on June 25, 1858, and thereafter every time she set the dinner table. They had love in the house. The following year, she gave birth to a son, Brainerd, in Westerville. Their own family was set.

But their plans for a growing family pressed Hanby to earn more money. In 1860, he accepted the job of principal at Seven Mile Academy, a private school in that small village, near Hamilton in Butler County, Ohio. He ran the school and also taught. With no pastor's job available, he worked at the academy for two years. Finally, he received the call from the Brethren Church in Lewisburg, a small Preble County town where the main occupation was, and still is, farming. Although the rural congregation liked Benjamin and Kate for their kindness and good-natured ways, they had expected a preacher filled with hellfire. From the start, they saw Hanby was not going to offer that style of preaching. They could see by his appearance that he was a positive thinker, a man who would rather talk about music than hell. They could see kindness on his face—his curly dark hair fell across the tops of his ears, and his beard was moderately long, with no mustache. His eyes were penetrating.

When he suggested using musical instruments in the church, members didn't exactly sing his praises. A few parishioners began to doubt his commitment to the sacred rites. Meanwhile, the Hanby family added a second child, a daughter named Minniehaha, born in Lewisburg in 1862.

Benjamin and Kate were an outgoing couple who enjoyed joking and talking with neighbors and congregation members. People liked the new preacher because he was down to earth and enthralled with life and its possibilities. Setbacks did not deter Hanby; neither did poverty.

As parishioners wished him well, he tried to explain to them the joys of using music in church services. They didn't like his idea. To try to prove his point, he played his flute in the sanctuary. People frowned; some told him that such devices were "instruments of the devil." Patiently, he said the instruments were not evil, but because good people refused to allow musical instruments to be played in churches, others took them into dance halls and barrooms, where anyone with a fiddle and flute could entertain. He said church services didn't have to be bleak and repetitive, not when such music was available. Children responded to music, and he predicted that they would come to church willingly if instruments were played. Church members didn't agree. They threatened action if musical instruments were introduced into services. They went so far as to say that music threatened the sanctity of church services. As one writer would explain later, "the Reverend Hanby was treading on dangerous ground . . . the austere element of the Puritan spirit was then still dominant," and many people believed music "was one of the insinuating devices of Satan himself."

Hanby backed off temporarily, trying to fulfill his songwriting needs through a new part-time job he had taken with the John Church Company, a music publisher with offices in Cincinnati, Chicago, and New York. When he no longer could resist sharing music with his congregation, he came up with an idea: Present a church play for the children showing the three wise men visiting Jesus. Unfortunately, that rankled important members of the church. They shunned the young minister and his play, and finally, they asked him to resign—he did. The Brethren Church transferred him to a small church in New Paris, a neighboring Preble County town, and to another small church in Darke County. The jobs offered hope for the heartbroken minister.

In New Paris today, the only reminder of Hanby is a marker erected by the state, declaring this is the town where he composed "Up on the Housetop" in 1864. "The children of New Paris were the first to sing the song," said Barbara Brower, a local teacher who researched Hanby's life. "A few years ago we tried to promote him and the song, but really there's not much left here to remember him by. Everything has changed."

His wooden house at the corner of Pearl and Washington streets burned long ago and was replaced by an insurance agency. In December, village workers hang big green wreaths and red bells all along the business district, but that's as close as anybody comes to proclaiming New Paris as Ohio's Christmas song capital. "This thing about Mr. Hanby," postmaster Hugh Hart once said, "is not something we bring up in town that much."

Despite the changes, New Paris is still much like the farming community of Hanby's time. Small town. Honest people. No theaters, no shopping centers, no fancy buildings. Just a collection of old homes, stores, and churches. Barbara Hutchison, a librarian at the county seat in Eaton, recalled that New Paris used to have a Christmas celebration in honor of Hanby, "but that was years ago. Now, we don't even have much information on him here at the library."

When Hanby arrived in New Paris in 1863, the region's economy was sinking and people were worried. As the Civil War continued, neighbors in southern Ohio towns argued about whether the fight was good for their state and the nation. Businesses found their vital southern markets cut off, and antiwar activists called Copperheads grew in strength in neighboring Butler County. Yet Benjamin Hanby still had music to make him happy; he continued to write secular and religious songs in his spare time. In a letter dated September 14, 1864, he told the owner of the Philip Phillips & Company, a song company in New Castle, Indiana, that he wanted to buy one of the firm's songbooks. Apparently Hanby was personally acquainted with Phillips. In the letter, now on file at the Smithsonian Institution, Hanby revealed his aspirations and good humor by ending, "I hope I shall prove a formidable, but always honorable, competitor. Good luck to you (whenever it don't cost me too much!)."

At the time, the Brethren Church in New Paris needed a minister. Hanby accepted the call. At first, things went well; shortly after moving his family to town, however, he brought an organ to the church services. Members immediately split over such an innovation. "The majority stood behind the young minister," wrote historian Dacia C. Shoemaker of Westerville, "but his gentle and sensitive soul could not bear division of opinion in his little congregation. When his pleas for more beauty and brightness in the lives of young people failed, he made it known that if he could not take music into the church he would take the church into music and serve outside the pulpit. With anguish of heart, he quietly resigned."

Hanby knew only two things — preaching and songwriting. He didn't know how to combine them and create a full-time occupation. So he rented an empty store, moved in his organ and books, and opened a singing school for children. He taught them songs and how to sing together, and he preached to them. The country town reacted indifferently to his venture. Meanwhile, his health and income declined. He believed he was a failure. "The days ahead were dark and difficult," Shoemaker wrote in 1941. "Hanby stood before the world a misunderstood and misjudged man, his income gone, in frail health and in debt. But he kept a song in his heart and went forward."

In the gloomy days of December 1864, he tried to tell himself that he was useful, but his circumstances told him otherwise. His school was failing financially. He had no money to buy sheet music for his few students, so he wrote out their parts on a blackboard. His only commission was his promise to provide entertainment at a Quaker Christmas dinner for orphans in Richmond, Indiana, a larger town not far away. One day he remembered that he had no new song to sing. So he sat down and wrote these words:

Up on the house, no delay, no pause,
Clatter the steeds of Santa Claus;
Down thro' the chimney with loads of toys,
Ho for the little ones, Christmas joys.

Chorus:
O! O! O! Who wouldn't go,
O! O! O! Who wouldn't go,
Up on the housetop, click! click! click!
Down thro' the chimney with good Saint Nick.

Look in the stockings of Little Will,
Ha! Is it not a "glorious bill"?
Hammer and gimlet and lots of tacks,
Whistle and whirligig, whip and cracks.

Snow-white stocking of Little Nell,
Oh, pretty Santa crown it well;
Leave her a dolly that laughs and cries,
One that can open and shut its eyes.

The images were borrowed from Hanby's memories of childhood Christmases—Little Will was his younger brother. But even with such a store of recollections to draw from Hanby didn't have time to complete the song before Christmas 1864. The children of the singing school didn't mind, though. They liked what they heard of it, and later the orphans in Richmond gleefully took up the refrain. Still, Hanby didn't know what he had in the Christmas song. For years he didn't even consider publishing it; he didn't think it was important enough.

Before 1864 ended, the John Church Company rescued Hanby by offering a full-time songwriting position. Of course, he accepted. For once, Hanby worked for someone who nurtured his talent. He composed temperance songs; religious songs; pro-Union songs; and jubilees, which he wrote in Negro dialect (he was one of the earliest composers to do this). The job enabled him the freedom to write and publish more songs, including the temperance pieces "Revellers' Chorus" and "Crowding Awfully."

By the time the war was ending in 1865, Hanby's songs had attracted interest from the music business, particularly from George F. Root, a famous Chicago composer. Root, the mid-Victorian equivalent of Irving Berlin, asked Hanby to be his children's music editor. Hanby couldn't believe his sudden turn of luck. Root was a partner in Root & Cady, the Midwest's largest music publisher and an instrument distributor. The company, established by his brother, Ebenezer Root, and his business partner, Chauncey M. Cady, had more prestige than John Church. George Root had already composed some successful Civil War songs, including "Tramp, Tramp, Tramp, the Boys Are Marching" and "Just Before the Battle, Mother." Impressed that the company's founders had all started as music teachers, Hanby gathered his family and moved to Chicago to write and promote songs for children.

When George Root listened to Hanby's material, he heard something original yet commercial. He wanted to teach the young minister how to further develop his composing style. Both men loved music, and, thirteen years Hanby's senior, Root took on the role of older brother. By then, the highly respected Root had played organ at the Church of the Strangers in New York and taught music at the Abbott Institute for Young Ladies. In 1850, he had toured Europe, and when he returned he took a job as an assistant at Boston's Academy of Music. Soon the lure of entertainment took him to New York, where he became a writer of minstrel songs and a collaborator with such successful songwriters as the Reverend David Nelson, composer of "The Shining Shore," and Frances Jane Crosby, who wrote "There's Music in the Air." In 1859, Root moved to Chicago to join his brothers in their sheet music publishing company. In 1863, he wrote "The First Gun Is Fired" and other war songs, making the company even more successful.

At Root's urging, Hanby collaborated on songs and edited songbooks for several months. Hanby wrote now-forgotten tunes such as "Little Tillie's Grave," "Ole Shady, the Song of the Contraband," "Terrible Tough," "The Nameless Heroine," "Chick-A-Dee-Dee," "In a Horn," "Over the Silent Sea," "Willie's Temptation," "The Robin," and "Now Den! Now Den!"

Finally, Hanby had found his real calling. He responded with total commitment. During his stay in Chicago, he wrote more than sixty melodies and lyrics for about half of them. It seemed he knew he had to make the most of his short time. He also toured the Midwest, lecturing on music. In 1866, he wrote his last song, the Christmas hymn "Who Is He in Yonder Stall," in Chicago. The five-verse piece is still sung today and is included in the United Methodist Hymnal. It includes these lines:

Who is he in yonder stall
At whose feet the shepherds fall?
Tis the Lord, O wondrous story!
Tis the Lord, the King of glory!
At his feet we humbly fall
Crown him, crown him, Lord of all!
Lo, at midnight who is he
Prays in dark Gethsemane?
Who is he in Calvary's throes
Asks for blessings on his foes?
Tis the Lord, O wondrous story!

Tis the Lord, the King of Glory!
At his feet we humbly fall
Crown him, crown him Lord of all!

One day in 1866 while working in Chicago, Hanby remembered his old "Santa Claus." He polished and finished the song with a little help from a friend known only as Pauline, who added two stanzas that included the characters Lazy Jim, pa, ma, uncle, and grandma. "These two verses Hanby liked and retained," Shoemaker wrote a century later, "but he rearranged the poem so as to allow Rover, the dog, to create the story's and wag his 'Thankee' in the last verse, as originally written."

Although Pauline's identity remains unknown, Shoemaker noted that the mysterious songwriter could have been a friend, the wife of P. P. Bliss, a musical evangelist who knew Hanby in Chicago. The Blisses died in an 1876 railroad accident in Ashtabula. Pauline, whoever she was, did not receive credit for her small but important contribution to the lyrics. But this was not unusual in the 1800s and early 1900s.

In the autumn of 1866, Hanby featured the newly revised song in Root & Cady's quarterly *Our Song Birds,* edited by Hanby and Root. The song's popularity spread quickly.

Sadly, Hanby had little time to enjoy his good fortune. While on the road, he caught a bad cold. After he climbed three flights of stairs at a hotel in Wisconsin, his lungs hemorrhaged. Kate came to nurse him. Three weeks later, she helped him get back home to Chicago, where physicians diagnosed him with tuberculosis. With his family and Root by his bedside, Hanby died, at just thirty-three. Adding more frustration to his early death, his traveling trunk—packed with new songs and other works—was lost.

Root was shaken. "He died," he said of Hanby, "at the commencement of his career." Kate Hanby said, "If to be a good storyteller is to be a king among children, he certainly deserved the title." His body was taken to Westerville for burial in Otterbein Cemetery. Honoring one of Hanby's song titles, his grave marker read, "Over the Silent Sea Passed Benjamin R. Hanby, March 16, 1867, aged 33 years."

Fortunately, his most popular song did not die with him. Thanks to children across the nation, "Up on the Housetop" continued to be sung without benefit of songbook. After his death, the song began to take new form—its stanzas reversed, its text slightly altered, its title changed—depending on the memory and accuracy of the one who handed it down. The composer's name, meanwhile, was forgotten, and the song marked "anonymous." During its lost period, the tune was known under five titles: "Santa Claus May Be Recognized," "Santa Claus," "Good Saint Nick," "Saint Nicholas," and, in Hawaii, "Up on the Housetop." Ultimately, sheet music publishers settled on the latter title.

Hanby's death came eleven years before Thomas Edison invented the phonograph. Ultimately, the so-called talking machine gave Hanby and all songwriters the most prominent distribution for their creativity in the history of entertainment. Thanks to Edison and the people who refined the phonograph, "Nelly Gray" and "Housetop" were heard by succeeding generations of listeners. If Hanby had lived forty more years, he could have been a big success writing secular and religious songs. The new phonograph performers could have recorded his latest songs, and his music might have revived. Death had ended the prolific Buckeye storyteller's career just a little too soon.

In 1968, Merrill C. Gilfillan of the Ohio Department of Natural Resources researched "Housetop's" long history and concluded in a state-published magazine story, "Hanby's name was forgotten, but the jingling Christmas tune he gave to the world lived on in the hearts and minds of little children. For years the song was out of print. During those years it was handed down from generation to generation. . . . As a folk song it underwent some changes, most of which improved the original version."

The modern opening stanza became

> Up on the house-top reindeer pause
> Out jumps good old Santa Claus
> Down through the chimney with lots of toys
> All for the little ones' Christmas joys.

The rest of the song remained about the same, except for the second stanza, which reflected a change in toys available for children. Hammer, lots of tacks, a ball, and a whip that cracks replaced hammer and gimlet and lots of tacks, whistle and whirligig, and a whip that cracks. Over the next half century, Hanby's Christmas song became jumbled—the title was changed at the whim of music editors, and some words were changed. The composer's name continued to be forgotten.

But in 1940 Shoemaker discovered some old papers that proved Benjamin Hanby, not Stephen Foster, wrote "Nelly Gray" and also "Up on the Housetop." Shoemaker had heard this claim fifteen years earlier from Hanby's sister, Elizabeth and from Kate Hanby, who died in 1930 at age ninety-five. So Shoemaker started writing to publishers who sold the sheet music, asking them to credit the song to Hanby and offering to prove that he did write it. Most of them agreed to use his name. "Perhaps no other American song," she once said, "has had a more varied record from its inception, has been more altered in text and title, and still holds an unassailable place in the hearts of little folks."

Shoemaker's own story is so firmly connected to the songwriter's that they have become one; it was though she was destined to know and appreciate him. It all began on May 21, 1873, when Benjamin's brother, Dr. William O. Hanby (the Little Will of Hanby's Christmas song), delivered a baby—Dacia Custer. She would grow up in Westerville and graduate from Otterbein in 1895. Fittingly, she was the class historian. The following year, she married banker John Shoemaker. An old Hanby House brochure noted: "While writing a pageant for the seventy-fifth anniversary of Otterbein's founding, Dacia reached a turning point in her life. In doing her research for the pageant she walked into the Hanby House and there found Ben. She fell in love with his sensitive spirit, and never again would she be able to forget him." Shoemaker recalled: "In 1922, while doing research, as co-author of the historical pageant 'Spirt of Otterbein' . . . the story of Bishop William Hanby . . . and of his son, Benjamin, fell into my hands. So fascinating and so diverse were the circumstances that shaped their lives that, from the start, I could not let the story go. When further study disclosed the fact that many incidents of historical value had been neither published nor preserved in any form, the impulses came to me to collect and record them for future generations."

In 1926, the Hanby House, now dilapidated, came up for sale. Dacia and her husband purchased it for $1,500 and announced her plans to restore it as a memorial to Ben. She convinced state fire officials to rescind their order to tear the house down, and she developed her own plans for it. Through her diligence, she helped make people aware of Hanby's talents and importance. He became the focus of her life's research, which she continued for years. Meanwhile, she sought and received help from the Ohio State Archaeological and Historical Society (as it was then called) and the Works Project Administration. She also helped organize the Benjamin Hanby Memorial Association, which raised money to move the house to West Main. She used proceeds from the sale of the property to help establish a museum. After the house was dedicated on June 13, 1937, she became its first curator. She served until 1950, while working on a history of the Hanby family. When she died in 1973, at age one hundred, the book remained unfinished. With assistance from two editors, however, *Choose You This Day* was finally published in 1983. It is still in print and offered for sale at the Hanby House.

In the 1980s, as the Ohio Historical Society could no longer afford to operate the old house, Emmeline Miller, curator from 1981 to 1988, developed a program that allowed the Westerville Historical Society to operate the place on its own. She also found volunteers to act as tour guides and helpers, and she trained them. Her work has enabled the Hanby House to continue.

In modern times, Hanby's songs continue to be recorded and published. Jazzmen Emile Barnes and Louis Armstrong once collaborated on a version of "Darling Nelly Gray," which was reissued on compact disc. Two songbooks written by Hanby are still in print: *The Robin: A Collection of Music for Day and Sunday Schools, Juvenile Singing Classes, and the Social Circle,* and *Chapel Gems for Sunday Schools,* which was a collaboration between George F. Root and Hanby. A few of the famous performers who've recorded "Housetop" over the last sixty years include Reba McEntire, the Jackson 5, George Strait, Eddy Arnold, the King Sisters, Gene Autry, and Alvin and the Chipmunks. Most surprisingly, 141 years after he wrote it, "Up on the House Top" became a national hit. Singer-actress Kimberly Locke, a former contestant on television's popular *American Idol,* took the song to number one on Billboard's Adult Contemporary chart during the weeks between December 17, 2005, and January 7, 2006.

But Benjamin Hanby didn't need a hit record or a new songbook to assure his musical legacy's survival: his songs do that by themselves. It is unfortunate, however, that he died so young, never knowing that his songs would be sung a century and a half later or that his brief ministry would outlast even the harshest critics of the flute and the organ.

3

JAMES W. DENVER

American Adventurer

When he pulled the trigger that day in California in 1852 and killed a popular newspaperman in a duel, thirty-five-year-old lawyer James William Denver didn't realize he was also killing his future chances to be president. The shooting would convince many voters—wrongly—that he was a hothead Democrat with a hair-trigger temper and an ego as wide as the Mississippi River. Nevertheless, in time he overcame the negative perception to become one of America's top lawyers and a longtime American political leader who helped shape a growing nation.

Though Denver is a relatively obscure player in American history, his story could be the plot of a historical novel or an epic television mini-series. He helped establish western rails, published newspapers, taught school, led pioneers to the gold rush, was twice considered briefly for the presidency, ran Bleeding Kansas for the federal government, fought in the Mexican and Civil wars, was appointed a general, served in Congress and as the commissioner of Indian affairs, got rich, had a growing Colorado city named in his honor, and became the embodiment of Manifest Destiny.

To say James Denver was restless would be a gross understatement. The man simply couldn't stay put, which may have either rankled or satisfied his wife. She stayed at home while he explored the country and worked in other states. He once wrote to her, "I think I must have been born under the influence of some comet, which prevents me from remaining long in any one place." When he wasn't traveling, he was living in faraway states; for instance, he was one of the early California pioneers.

General James W. Denver during the Civil War. (Courtesy Wilson's Creek National Battlefield, Republic, Missouri)

He seemed more comfortable in politics than at any place he ever lived, including Wilmington, Ohio, where he owned a home most of his life. He represented nineteenth-century America: geographic expansion, love of country, faith in the Lord, and a desire for more of everything. Denver was larger than life, figuratively and literally. He weighed 270 pounds and stood six feet, two inches in a time when that height was considered towering. He had thick, dark hair; handsome features; and a brilliant mind.

James Denver did not enter this world in Ohio, but, no matter where politics took him, he would always be a Buckeye from Clinton County. He called Wilmington home for much of his life, regardless of how far away he wandered or how important he became in other states. Most years, he spent only his summers and winter vacations at home, traveling or working the rest of the year.

The oldest of eleven children of Irish immigrants, Denver was born on October 23, 1817, in Winchester, Virginia. In 1831, at age fourteen, he moved with his family to Wilmington, the Clinton County seat, a small farming town in southwest Ohio. When he was old enough to work, he performed hard labor, but rheumatism convinced him to seek less strenuous employment. He attended grade school, but his family could not afford to send him for additional education. So he studied at night, educating himself in the law. He realized that Wilmington offered limited possibilities to a young man with unlimited ambitions, so he enrolled in the Cincinnati Law School. After earning a law degree in 1844, he went to Xenia to edit a Democratic newspaper called the *Thomas Jefferson*.

In 1845, Denver moved to Platte City, Missouri, to publish a newspaper and practice law with partner Bela Hughes, another man with high ambitions, who later would start the Pony Express and join Denver in the Colorado Hall of Fame. In only three years, they attracted a large number of clients, but, like the young nation, Denver could not contain his restlessness. At the outbreak of the Mexican War, he joined the 12th Regiment of the U.S. Infantry. When Captain Denver left Missouri to take command, Hughes told him: "You are a fool!"

Yet Denver never considered himself anything but smart, even when he contracted yellow fever in Mexico and had to return to his parents' home in Wilmington to recuperate. The small town's limited scope must have frustrated him, but the convalescence gave him time to think more about the West, which he loved.

After he recovered, he returned to Platte City to continue his law career—until he heard more about the gold rush in California. He said goodbye again in 1850, organizing a party of thirty-four pioneers on an overland trek to Sutter's Camp in California, and dreaming of gold. Along the way, eight people in his party died.

What he accomplished in 1850—at the age of thirty-three—would have taken most men a decade. The California air seemed to invigorate his capacity for hard work. Though he didn't make a lot of money in the gold fields, he did find a political career. Later that year, he won election to the California state senate as a Democrat, and he soon earned a reputation as tough leader who took politics too personally.

In 1852, Edward Gilbert, California's first congressman, a veteran, and well-known and fiery Whig editor of the popular *Alta Californian* newspaper, repeatedly attacked the Democrats and their governor, John Bigler. Bigler was California's third governor (1852–56) and the first to be reelected. Denver demanded that Gilbert retract several stories criticizing the state's Democrats and the governor. Gilbert refused. After exchanging heated comments in the newspaper and a few "ghastly formalities," Gilbert challenged Denver to a rifle duel—not a pistol duel, mind you. Colleagues and friends warned Denver not to accept the challenge, but he ignored their advice. They told him it would either kill him or haunt him. He refused to listen and lived to regret the decision.

Such extreme action was not unusual in California of the 1850s. One San Francisco newspaper of the period printed on its masthead: "Subscriptions received from 9 to 4; challenges [to duels] from 11 to 12 only." A Boston newspaper noted in 1852: "An American editor is a dangerous man to be trifled with." Writer William Secrest once called California's newspaper leaders the "fighting editors" because they were apt to do battle over anything. Two San Francisco editors, William Walker and W. H. Carter, fought a duel in 1850. Walker was wounded, yet he had enough nerve to fight another one that year with editor Will Graham, and he was seriously wounded.

California's editors apparently enjoyed challenging politicians. The newsmen had more than ink in their veins—they had nerve. They also were called hot-tempered, hotheaded, and hot-blooded. Gilbert seemed one of the most easily riled editors in the state. He would die for it.

Denver said Gilbert tried hard to gain any advantage he could, going so far as to push Denver to duel him the next morning, giving Denver no time to prepare. Denver also claimed that Gilbert wore a green suit so that he could blend with the trees and bushes at the duel site. At sunrise, both men walked forty paces and turned to face each other. They fired Wesson rifles without success. Gilbert tried to kill Denver, but Denver fired his rifle into the air and then walked away. He wanted to end the argument and move on. Gilbert wanted to continue it, however, so Denver obliged. "I acted as my judgment and sense of honor prompted me to do," he wrote.

Writer Henry Austin succinctly described what happened on the day of the duel: "Within five minutes, the leading journalist of California—statesman, warm friend, and stainless gentleman—was a blanched corpse." And Gilbert's opponent received the blame. "My God," cried a repentant Denver, "I have killed the best man in California for that infernal Bigler."

Democrat Bigler was a lawyer who served two gubernatorial terms. He supported many programs for immigrants and encouraged immigrants to come to California. But he had many political enemies, particularly in the newspaper business. When the *Alta Californian* printed mean-spirited things about Bigler, Denver in effect became Bigler's surrogate duelist.

In those days, "a violent resolution for libel was always a possibility when the language of *Code Duello* was referred to by an offended party," observed Ryan Chamberlain, a Wilmington native who wrote *Pistols, Politics and the Press: Dueling in 19th Century America*. He said dueling wasn't considered murder then and also "not merely combat"; it was an honor ritual, used to intimidate as well as silence critics and editors alike.

Gilbert's challenge was in character with his record and proud nature. The former Mexican War combatant, lawyer, and onetime congressman could not stand to be dishonored in the newspaper he had founded. His death sent shockwaves rolling through San Francisco. Though such shootings occurred from time to time, the city was surprised that two such prominent community leaders would stand before each other and fire guns over words printed in a newspaper. Out of respect, stores were closed on the day of the funeral.

Nationally, Americans soon began to reexamine the merits of dueling. The practice all but ended a few years later, when it was deemed barbaric. In a way, by calling more attention to it, Denver helped bring an end to dueling—but at a high price to his conscience and ultimately to his national political career. A quarter of a century after the famous duel, a usually tight-lipped Denver wrote to a friend: "Mr. Gilbert had been the aggressor and, as soon as he got me involved in it, he challenged me. I was a stranger to him personally . . . we had never before had any misunderstanding or controversy of any kind, on any subject."

Because the duel was one of the last major ones ever fought in the United States, it received much attention over the next forty years. Denver's reluctance to participate should have shown the public that he was not a hothead after all, yet many people persisted in believing he was. In 1895, Austin wrote a magazine story called "Famous American Duels—General James W. Denver and Hon. Edward Gilbert." His piece in the *Illustrated American* noted that the clash was one of the most "regrettable, terrible duels of modern times, and all on account of [Governor Bigler], who . . . did not deserve to have even a couple of mongrel curs fight in his quarrel."

No charges were filed in Gilbert's death, which turned Denver into a political spectacle, receiving attention he didn't want. Surprisingly, Gilbert's death didn't stop Denver's rising career: he was appointed California secretary of state in 1853. He used his position to push through a law allowing women to control their own estates—a move that shocked a lot of men. In 1855, he was elected to Congress, where he helped set up federal mineral-rights legislation and the Pacific railroads. These acts helped solidify America's Manifest Destiny, the expansion from coast to coast.

People soon stopped talking about the duel and started focusing on California's—and the nation's—future.

When Denver wasn't traveling and making political deals, his mind wandered back to Ohio and Louise Rombach, the daughter of a successful Wilmington banker and one of the town's elites. In 1856, at the "old" age of thirty-nine, he returned to Wilmington to marry her. They would later reside—at least when he was in town—at Rombach Place, a brick Greek Revival home at 149 East Locust Street. It was, and still is, considered a mansion. Now, it is the home of the Clinton County Historical Society and a county museum that contains Denver's personal library, items from his military and governmental careers; portraits of the couple; and the general's beaver tophat, military belt, Indian relics, military uniform, and other items.

After looking through the house, the visitor realizes that Denver's success came at a price: he had to live elsewhere most of his career, while his wife and four children remained in Wilmington. He once said she did not feel well enough to live away from her hometown.

He did not have such a restriction, though he did stay home often enough to father four children: Katherine, in 1861; James, 1863; Mary Louise, 1868; and Matthew, 1870. In 1865, he wrote to the family and said he missed them. "And I am left alone today—my mate and little ones away," he said. "But dreams of peace and . . . pleasure tell, my spirit with them still doth dwell."

On Main Street in downtown Wilmington today stands the General Denver Hotel, a monument to the roving man who helped forge the American dream. Most of its guests come to Wilmington—about fifty miles northeast of Cincinnati—for business or educational matters. The city of about twelve thousand people is the home of industries, Wilmington College, and a converted U.S. air base, where businesses operate. The hotel keeps Denver's name alive in town. But like the general's name, the Tudor hotel has been around for so long that it's practically invisible to many local people.

With civic pride running hot in the pre-Depression days, city residents decided their town needed a social focus, so they pooled $150,000 to purchase common stock and built the hotel. Its first reign lasted from 1928, when it opened, to 1978. Facing large operating losses, the hotel's last private owner closed it. Nobody wanted to buy it.

Then Barry Martens, a Dayton shopping center developer, arrived. The first time he saw the Pride of Wilmington, Ohio, he almost laughed. Offered to Martens as a "good" investment, the hotel looked anything but proud when he first saw it on that summer day in 1987. Yet he became intrigued with the shabby building's potential and history. Armed with only a developer's confidence, he decided to restore the chunk of English Tudor sitting among Main Street's typical turn-of-the-century storefronts. "The place came alive to me," Martens said as he showed a visitor around. "There is an aura—something old, something fascinating—about the hotel."

Though many of the hotel's windows were smashed and six to nine inches of pigeon dung covered the floors, Martens bought the building for $200,000 and spent about $1 million to renovate it for business travelers. "It took forty-five men about forty-five days just to clean out all the junk," he said. "We removed all the handrails from the halls and stained them three times. We cleaned the exterior brick with acid."

In December 1988, Martens reopened the hotel, intending to sell it to investors, but the deal collapsed. He ended up working eighteen hours a day to operate the place before selling it to new investors in the early

1990s. They found the original Warner elevator clanking again with its familiar glass windows and metal gate, and the lobby shining with the original brass letterbox. The hotel's twenty-eight rooms gleamed with coats of off-white paint and brown trim, and thick tan carpet covered the floors. General Denver might be proud to know that a hometown hotel has carried on his name for so many years, befitting a man of his prominence. Unlike other towns, whose heroes are forgotten, Wilmington remembers Denver and recognizes his accomplishments.

From the hotel, it is only a few blocks down to the museum, where director Joyce Thackston said Denver was once an important national Democratic figure—a man who commanded respect wherever he went. "Twice he was considered for the presidency by the Democrats' national committee," she said. "But he never made it far in the selection process, because committee members thought the killing of the newspaper editor might come up during the campaign. Despite that, he achieved many things in his career—statesman, successful attorney, business owner, and general. He lived from Washington, D.C., to Wilmington, to California. Our General Denver got around."

In early 1857, months after his defeat in a California congressional race, Denver received an unexpected appointment: U.S. commissioner of Indian affairs. In an era when some Indians were still foes, Denver treated the relocated tribes fairly and ordered whites to respect reservation boundaries. Some historians have criticized his brief term, however, saying he used the job to make favorable land deals for himself and his banker father-in-law.

At the end of that year, President James Buchanan named Denver acting governor of Kansas Territory, which included most of what is today the state of Colorado. Here Denver met a cast of roughnecks, renegades, and men determined to kill him and burn whole towns. Some of their leaders were former Ohioans. He told the fighting neighbors, "The majesty of the laws must and shall be maintained," and he used cavalry and common sense to enforce them. Several previous governors had failed to bring permanent order to the territory, called "Bleeding Kansas" because of turmoil over the slavery issue. Both North and South wanted the Kansas Territory for their own. This caused most of the deadly fighting. Because he brought some order to the territory, Denver won the affection of many residents.

But not all of them loved him. A Democrat named James Henry "Jim" Lane, a rabblerouser nicknamed "The Grim Chieftain," began stirring up trouble. He was a former lieutenant governor of Indiana who had moved to Lawrence, in the Kansas Territory. No one could say with conviction whether Lane was for or against slavery, but he once said he knew no difference between a Negro and a mule. He was all over the political map; he also said he was antislavery and would drive the slavers out of the territory. In 1857, he organized a militia and prepared to attack an opposing armed group under the leadership of George Washington Clarke, a Missourian and pro-southerner who led raids that led to the burning of pro-northern people's cabins. That year, an estimated hundred thousand immigrants—many of them from Ohio—arrived in the Kansas Territory. By this time the area was becoming free-soil, or antislavery, and new words were flowing from Kansas into the national lexicon. Denver learned them quickly. Newspaperman C. M. Chase explained their meanings to readers of his *True Republican and Sentinel* in Sycamore, Illinois: A Jayhawker was a "unionist who professes to rob, burn out, and murder only rebels in arms against the government"; a Bushwacker was "a rebel Jayhawker, or a rebel who bands with others for the purpose of preying upon the lives and property of Union citizens"; and a Redleg was a "Jayhawker originally distinguished by the uniform of red leggings. A Redleg, however, is regarded as a more purely and indiscriminate thief and murderer than the Jayhawker or Bushwhacker." The territory was filled with all sorts of violent people who wanted either slavery or freedom.

Immediately upon taking the oath of office in late 1857, Denver ordered U.S. dragoons to break up the two militias and stop the impending battle. Lane was furious. He wrote an insulting letter to Governor Denver, challenging him to a duel, just as he had earlier challenged Illinois senator Stephen A. Douglas. Douglas ignored him. No doubt Lane knew of Denver's dueling experience and how it had followed him. But this time, the more experienced and mellower Denver did not respond to the taunt. He simply laughed. The duel occurred only in Lane's vivid imagination, and through Denver's swift action the two militias did not clash.

But Denver's problems did not end with Lane. In 1858, the radical abolitionist John Brown and his followers arrived in Kansas, presumably to feud with slavers in the territory and possibly free some slaves in a violent confrontation. Knowing Brown's history, Denver worried. Brown threatened to burn down Fort Scott, in southeastern Kansas, because it had become associated with the pro-slavery faction. Instead, he ordered his followers to capture it, which they did. Brown lost one man, and so did the other side. When he started asking Kansas to invade

Missouri, Missouri governor R. M. Stewart asked President James Buchanan for help. Buchanan, a Democrat who had named a pro-slavery cabinet and appointed Denver, offered a $250 reward for Brown. Brown countered by placing a twenty-five-cent reward for the president. Denver held things together long enough to temporarily avoid disaster, and then Brown raided Missouri and liberated some slaves. Of course, Brown made his final and fatal crusade in the October 1859 attack on the arsenal at Harpers Ferry, Viriginia, where he had sought to arm and launch a slave rebellion.

Presumably fellow Ohioan William Clarke Quantrill did not share Denver's affections either. Acting Governor Denver's antithesis arrived in Kansas at nineteen years of age in 1857. These two men were ready to slide to the opposite corners of American history; Kansas would make them known, although Quantrill's fame would be dubious. Denver would become a man of prominence, while Quantrill, a former teacher from Canal Dover, would become an infamous terrorist. Fortunately for Denver, Quantrill remained peaceful until 1860, when he joined some ruffians in Lawrence, Kansas. Over nearly five years, he would become one of the territory's most notorious raiders. He and his gang went on to burn Lawrence, because he believed it was filled with abolitionist sympathizers. Kansas writer William Elsey Connelley described him this way: "His face was round and full, with piercing blue-gray eyes of a strange tint, the upper lids of which fell too low, imparting a peculiar expression which became very marked when he was in a rage. His forehead was high, his hair almost white (of the 'tow-head' variety), and his nose was curved and sinister."

Denver's time in the Kansas Territory served him well. He wrote that his Kansas appointees named the city of Denver in his honor. Because there was no county seat for Arapahoe County, he said in 1890, so officials had to create one. "So they laid out a town just below the mouth of Cherry Creek, and did me the honor to name it after me," he said. "This is about the whole story."

But it is not. According to a story in the *Denver Post* on June 23, 1901, many names were suggested for the new community in 1858, but none received enough founders' votes. Coincidentally perhaps, when Governor Denver arrived there for a visit that July, "in all his physical and mental magnificence," a faction suggested that the booming town be named Denver. The motion passed, although some participants claimed later that Denver was not present during the vote.

Tom Noel, chair of the history department at the University of Colorado–Denver, said the founders "named the city for him to curry favor so he would look upon their community as the center for government in this wild territory." By the time Denver received word of the town's name, however, he had already resigned as territorial governor.

He was moving on. Again.

In 1859, Denver felt the tug of the campaign once more, so he left Kansas for California. After running unsuccessful campaigns for governor in 1859 and the U.S. Senate in 1860, he seemed finished with public life. Then, at the start of the Civil War in 1861, Abraham Lincoln, a Republican, commissioned him brigadier general, despite Denver's strong Democrat ties. Briefly leaving politics, Denver bravely led Ohio volunteers at the battles of Corinth, Mississippi, and Memphis. Twice he was reported killed.

Though he was a leader on the field, he was nonetheless *on the field*. He would turn forty-four years old that grim year, in a time when forty-four was much older than it is in the twenty-first century. Yet, he rode with his men and camped out and served admirably.

In a letter to his wife written from Memphis on July 27, 1862, Denver said he saw "men sweltering in the hot sun, almost entirely exhausted by heat, dust and fatigue, eagerly snatch up and drink water from the ponds so thick with mud and filth that the thirsty horses would not taste it. Such water must, of course, breed diseases, and the only wonder is that the men hold out so well." He described the locals as "generally bitter secessionists—ready to cut our throats at all times when they could do so without too much personal danger, but equally ready to claim protection for themselves and property by demanding guards for their houses, gardens, etc."

He said Union troops were "pretty hard on gardens." They devoured all the vegetables they could find, and they particularly enjoyed eating onions: "I verily believe that they could nose out an onion anywhere within five miles of the camp." Denver also wrote that General William T. Sherman, who would soon become the hero of the North for his infamous march from Atlanta to the sea, preferred to allow deserters to escape without sending soldiers to find them. Denver said he begged Sherman to allow him to go after the deserters to teach the troops a lesson but Sherman refused because he did not want to lose more men to desertion. Denver said of the general in 1862, "He seems to have no confidence in anybody." Desertion was a problem for the Union; few people wanted to discuss it then, and it is still not addressed too often. With conditions so terrible, and so much killing, it is understandable that many wandered off. General Ulysses S. Grant was forced to disband a regiment because half of its members had deserted.

And at the same time, many Democrats, especially in the Midwest, in New York City, and in other scattered pockets vocally opposed the war. Ohio, in fact, had one of the nation's largest populations of Copperheads, Democrats opposed to the war. A loyal Democrat, Denver had to think of his constituents back home and what they thought of him for being one of Mr. Lincoln's generals. The party was split between pro- and antiwar Democrats (Copperheads). The latter group opposed the war for many reasons, including economic, moral, and philosophical ones—some were just sick of death. Many county political party conventions demanded an end to the war. Democrat newspapers carried on a war of their own against Lincoln and what they saw as his abuse of power.

By January 1863, growing disenchantment with military assignments and Lincoln's ever-expanding authority prompted Denver to consider resigning his commission. Lincoln suspended the right of habeas corpus, dropped protection against illegal detention, and arrested newspaper owners who dared criticize him. Denver, a Democrat fighting a Republican war, likely questioned the war efforts. Many besides Lincoln, to be sure, believed in saving the Union, but often they disagreed with the president about how much authority he could exercise to save it. On the Ohio home front, Democrat newspapers either supported the war only with stipulations or opposed it. The *Cincinnati Enquirer,* for example, attacked the war as unjust.

As a Democrat, Denver supported his country, but he did not believe the war was necessary. He was likely torn between party and country when on November 7, 1862, President Lincoln removed General George McClellan, a Democrat, as commander of the Army of the Potomac, for having been not aggressive enough. Then, in January 1863, came the final blow—Lincoln's Emancipation Proclamation, which Denver, a conservative Democrat, believed was unconstitutional. He opposed slavery, but he was a strict constitutionalist who believed in limited powers of the federal government; he declared that the proclamation provoked in him "huge disgust," and he had grown weary of dealing with politicians. He preferred to make peace with the South, but if that was impossible, he wanted to draft hundreds of thousands of additional soldiers to win the war faster. When he realized this would not happen, he resigned. By early March 1863, at age forty-seven, he had returned to Ohio. He was a brigadier general no more.

As the war entered its final phase in 1864, Denver left Ohio for Washington, D.C., and the next year he founded a law firm, Hughes, Denver, & Peck. (He continued to own the mansion in Wilmington, where his wife and family remained.) He was the perfect Washington lawyer; he had served in the government and he knew how it worked. As he once wrote to a friend, "There is nothing in the world more capricious or uncertain at times than the average Congressman." His firm soon became one of Washington's more prosperous, specializing in war property claims, Indian treaties, and national cases. Atlanta farmers hired him to sue the federal government for their shares of cotton that General Sherman had confiscated during the war; Tennessee farmers asked him to seek restitution for thousands of missing army mules. He even won a $15 million case against Great Britain for building the Confederate raider *Alabama*.

Hearing of his courtroom victories, his contacts in the Choctaw tribe sought his help in their stalled, fifty-year-old land-appropriation case against the federal government. The Choctaws maintained that under an 1830 treaty with the tribe the government agreed to pay $3 million for land in Mississippi. However, the government took the land and didn't pay. Denver pursued the case and won. Denver's insistence on taking on the case, despite public opinion, stemmed from his days as commissioner of Indian affairs. He sympathized with the Native Americans' plight, saying the white man had pushed them so far that there was no place else for them to go. The Chocktaws, he argued, must be protected from gamblers, alcohol salesmen, and greedy speculators.

Life in the U.S. capital suited Denver, for he enjoyed mingling with politicians and sparring with bureaucrats. He lived there thirty years, and he wrote his wife almost every day. Because she didn't like to travel, and he had to, she stayed at home. He missed her; he felt lonely. Yet he needed his career, like a second wife. In his room in the Globe House, he comforted himself with Robert Burns's poetry and Scottish songs.

In 1870, during tumultuous political reconstruction in the South, Denver decided to run for Congress again. He returned home and ran as a Democrat in the Sixth District, which was a mistake: Ohio was too Republican. Nevertheless, one of his sons, Matthew Rombach Denver, did get elected to Congress as a Democrat—three times during the early 1900s.

In 1874 and again in 1882, Denver visited his namesake city, as its residents had urged him to do for years. "The record shows that he could spare precious little time for the city," Edward Magruder Cook wrote in his Denver biography, *Justified by Honor.* "He visited it only twice and the citizens ignored him both times. The reception, for a man accustomed to acclaim, was humiliating." General Denver once told someone that he was mortified by the indifference shown him in Denver. But he did not let it affect him or his career. And in time, Colorado would make up for this treatment by installing his stained-glass portrait in the Capitol dome in Denver and later electing him to the Colorado Hall of Fame.

In 1884, friends encouraged him to seek the presidency. He wanted to run, but he knew what would await him: a grueling campaign, and, naturally, more gossip and negativity than he wanted. Despite his position, Ohio Democrats, who loved and respected him, published a booklet to promote his presidential aspirations: *A Democratic Nomination for 1884; James W. Denver of Ohio; His Life, His Services, and His Availability.* The Democrats quietly passed on him, however, preferring New York governor Grover Cleveland. In a close race, Cleveland defeated Republican James Blaine.

Shrugging off his rejection as a possible presidential nominee, Denver ran for Congress in Ohio in 1886 and lost again. Perhaps he had been removed from his Wilmington roots for too long. He was now a Washingtonian. Politically exhausted, he returned to the capital, where he counted among his law clients the famous and the powerful, the unknown and the powerless.

In early August 1892, he suffered from blood poisoning. While he soon improved and went out to make his usual rounds, he quickly complained of not feeling well. He may have had the gripe, or bowel cramps. On August 9, two days after these grumblings, he died at his apartment in the Globe House in Washington, at age seventy-five.

His body was sent to Sugar Grove Cemetery in Wilmington. On that final trip home, he was reunited—permanently—with his wife. His rambling days had ended. His epitaph should be that he lived as he pleased and accepted the consequences. As Edward Magruder Cook put it, "Certainly he made no secret of his dreams."

4

DAVID HARPSTER

The Wool King

In the late 1800s, when Ohio was feeding the nation's woolen mills as well as the lamb-loving population of the eastern seaboard, King David reigned over an empire of sheep. He needed a public relations campaign, however, for opponents painted him as ornery, remarkable, arrogant, stubborn—and a mysterious Mason. He was known as the only man who refused to take off his hat while visiting Benjamin Harrison's White House, where the dinner table possibly included a serving of his mutton; a windbag who claimed to own an entire county in Texas; and a businessman who enjoyed telling people about *his* town—the appropriately named Harpster in Wyandot County.

Opponents also claimed King David Harpster was looking out for the rich. But the one thing they could never say was that he was meek. The pioneer political lobbyist was Ohio's wealthiest sheep farmer—and one of America's. He knew practically everyone in politics and agriculture, from U.S. senators to county commissioners, and he wasn't afraid to share his opinions on tariffs and how to protect America's jobs. One of the late-nineteenth century's more influential lobbyists, he never failed to influence someone with logic and a handshake. He was the voice, soothsayer, and force behind the American wool industry.

In Harpster's day, Ohio was the nation's sheep state. Wool was an important commodity because so many things were made from it—baseball uniforms, military uniforms, carpets, dresses, trousers, sweaters, blankets, horse blankets, hats, pennants, coats, and even bathing suits and sometimes underwear. During wool's heyday in America, David Harpster thrived, and so did his small town.

David Harpster as he appeared in the 1880s. (Courtesy Wyandot County Historical Society)

When national and local newspapers referred to him as "the Wool King," they weren't always complimentary. Often they were hostile opponents of the country's controversial wool tariff, which Harpster protected like a sheepdog guarding his flock. One can imagine him thundering to fellow sheep farmers at their 1888 convention: "The wool-growing industry . . . cannot exist in the United States to any considerable extent in open unrestricted competition with wool production in Australia, South America, and some other countries."

His views came from observation. For decades, wool growing had been a poor occupation. Competition from imported British wool prompted a depression in the wool industry, which began in the East in 1826 and continued for years. When the American Civil War began in 1861, however, business flourished, as wool was used to produce military uniforms, socks, and blankets. When the war ended in 1865, Ohio had more sheep than people—8.6 million. More sheep lived in Harrison County per square mile than in any other place in the world. After the war, though, farmers and wool speculators lost money as the demand for their product diminished, and as they also competed with a healthy supply of cotton from the South and fine wool from the West and New South Wales. In 1867, when the price of wool decreased from $1 to forty cents per pound, wool growers and manufacturers called for government protection, and Congress responded by passing the Wool Tariff Act. But the damage had been done: as a result, Ohio's sheep population would fall from 7,688,845 in 1868 to 4,928,635 in 1870.

The tariff helped stop a disaster. As Harpster would say in 1888, "Under this wise legislation, both industries prospered, and the cost of clothing for all the people was reduced in price. The numbers of American sheep largely increased, the wool product grew vastly in amount." He added that farmers raised more sheep and that production of wool and related goods increased, giving jobs to "multitudes of men, women, and children" in factories, on farms, and in buying, selling, and shipping.

In the twenty-first century, wool doesn't sound too exciting, but in the 1800s it was a controversial and heated subject. The wool tariff was both celebrated and reviled, depending on one's perspective. Tariffs of all kinds were on most people's minds because they either protected or damaged livelihoods. Tariffs had contributed to the animosity that started the Civil War; because of tariff disagreements, South Carolina had considered seceding decades before 1861. In general, southerners, mostly agrarians, wanted low tariffs or none at all, and the industrial North, particularly New England, wanted protection for its factories. Unfortunately, when one industry received tariff protection, another often suffered when a trading partner retaliated by imposing a new tariff or increasing rates on an existing one.

Harpster, who was not afraid to speak out in favor of any tariff, became known in politics as the man who championed protectionism. He didn't mind criticizing the president, Congress, or anyone else who stood in his way of earning a fortune and saving the worker. "The ball has been set in motion, the line of battle has been formed, and we will fight it out on that line until victory crowns our efforts," he told the 1888 convention.

David Harpster wasn't born rich, but he always worked hard, and he knew business. His parents, George and Catharine Thomas Harpster, were of German American ancestry from Muffin County, Pennsylvania, where David was born on December 28, 1816. His grandfather had served in the Revolutionary War.

When George Harpster died, David was only eight. Two years later, his mother moved the family to Wayne County, in northeast Ohio. There, the family was so poor that young David could attend school for only fifteen months before quitting to work on a farm with his brother. Despite his youth and lack of education, David was smart. In 1828, at age twelve, he came to a small town named Bowsherville in Wyandot County to accept a clerk's job in Bowsher & Green's store. The community of Bowsherville was born of potent drink. Founder Anthony Bowsher knew the law prohibited anyone from selling liquor on the Indian reservation that occupied most of Wyandot County, so he opened a saloon next to the reservation and sold drinks to Indians and anyone else who could pay. A town grew around the saloon, including Bowsher & Green's general store, a hotel, a dry goods shop, a pottery, a hattery, and a racetrack, which attracted more drinkers. David did not appreciate Bowsherville's reputation, and he, like everyone else in town, was aware of its description in old newspapers as "the most ungodly place in the world." Perhaps in response, parishoners of the town's only church removed the building from its foundation, picked it up, and carted off to nearby Pleasant Grove.

After three years of hard work in the store, at just fifteen, Harpster became a partner. In 1836, he sold his interest in the business and began raising cattle with partners Thomas Hughes and James Murdock. From 1838 to 1840, he drove cattle to Detroit, and then he joined new partner David Miller in raising cattle in Illinois and driving them to the East.

Harpster earned his money the hard way—with back and brain. He also did it against all odds of economics and common sense, especially when he became a wool man.

A small part of Ohio's sheep industry—called mutton raising—continued to make money, despite what most people, who favored beef and chicken, thought of the meat. Butchers had been selling mutton for years by calling it "venison ham," to make it more more appetizing to customers, who believed mutton was a tough meat.

But wool was soft, warm, and necessary, and it had definite insulating advantages over its major competitor, cotton. So wool was bound to come back, and Harpster knew it. Although the early 1850s seemed a poor time to jump into the sheep business, David Harpster took a giant leap and brought other entrepreneurs along. If the business turned sour again, of course, he could simply buy more cattle and use his grazing land for that endeavor. He was always thinking ahead, gauging the political temperatures.

In the mid-1850s, Harpster bought land one half mile north of tiny Fowler City, in Wyandot County, and started a sheep farm. Over the next few years, he bought an additional 3,100 acres—a large farm, even by today's standards—in Wyandot County's Pitt Township, 1,300 acres in that county's Mifflin Township, another 4,000 elsewhere in Ohio, 240 acres in Iowa, 600 acres in Nebraska, and 2,240 acres in Illinois. And he planned to buy more.

At the same time as he progressed professionally, Harpster focused on his personal life as well. On April 6, 1847, he married Rachel S. Hall, whose father, James Hall, had been a soldier in the War of 1812 and a settler in Pickaway County. The couple had three children: Sarah; Ivy; and another child, who died young. During his marriage, Harpster spent many nights driving cattle. He worked with Miller for six years and then continued on his own for a few more. Then he started spending more time raising sheep. He began shearing nine hundred a year, and he increased that number annually until the early 1880s, when he was clipping as many as eighty-two hundred sheep in a single year on his Wyandot farm.

The nearby town was named for C. R. Fowler, a local landowner, but that name didn't last long. David Harpster partnered with John Wood, who owned most of the town's land; they started building houses, and they renamed the community Harpster. The Wool King cofounded the Harpster Bank with John L. Lewis, opened a general store with Cyrus Sears, and started other businesses too. He sold lots and occupied himself with the community, when he wasn't worrying about wool. Locally, he became a very influential citizen. Nationally, he was known as a self-made millionaire who influenced politicians, started new firms, and charmed or chagrined everyone with whom he did business.

When Harpster's wealthiest citizen heard rumors that the railroad planned to come through Wyandot County, he offered the Columbus, Hocking Valley & Toledo Railroad Company a free three-and-a-half-mile easement through his farm—plus an annual wool clip. "It was a hefty bribe considering that [his] wool production . . . averaged about 40,000 pounds a year, enough to fill six rail cars," writer Gene Logsdon—a Harpster resident—wrote in *Ohio* magazine in 1991. "The bribe was extolled as public-spirited generosity, and, of course, accepted." The offer probably wasn't worth the railroad's time, but its executives reconsidered when the King, just to be safe, bought $10,000 of the firm's stock. (Ultimately, he received $23,000 for his efforts—a fortune in those days.) Today such an offer would be considered bribery and more, but back then, to Harpster and other wealthy business people, it was just plain good sense.

The railroad's arrival in Harpster doomed old Bowsherville, where young David had first started out. The town had no rail connection, and the community had already been slipping, because of intense commercial competition from Harpster and Little Sandusky, which local people referred to simply as "Little." By 1880, Bowsherville would no longer appear on the county map, a fact that would please Mr. Harpster and others ashamed of its liquor-fueled bad behavior; and by 1900 the town would disappear into a dark corner of history.

When Rachel died in 1867, Harpster stayed sane by focusing on increasing his land holdings and raising sheep. Work was his salvation. Ten years later, he married Jane Maxwell, whose grandfather had edited the first newspaper published in Cincinnati. Twenty-six years younger than Harpster, she was described as "a refined and accomplished lady, and a member of the Baptist Missionary Church." He didn't mind a little Baptist fire: he was a Methodist temperance man, and proud of it.

Just when everything seemed to be going well, the sheep industry's recent financial success began to reverse itself. The decline could be traced to one infamous day—March 3, 1883, when Congress reduced the tariff on wool and on woolen and worsted goods. One year later, at the Ohio Wool Growers' convention, Harpster could say, "The results have been disastrous." Farmers cut back on their flocks. Wool imports, including carpet wool, increased significantly. So King David went into action, battling Democrats, free traders, malcontents, the uninformed, the unenlightened, rogue Republicans, and anyone else who stood between him and profit. He wanted workers and farmers protected from cheaper foreign competition.

The 1884 *History of Wyandot County* described David Harpster as "a strong Republican without political aspirations." Although he was never interested being a political candidate, he enjoyed entering politics as a combatant. If Congress hadn't tinkered with the tariff, Harpster might have remained an obscure figure in American politics, but as it was, he spoke his mind.

In truth, Harpster had political aspirations aplenty for himself and the Ohio Wool Growers' Association. In 1884 he had just been elected president of the group, and he wanted to expand its influence throughout the nation. It didn't take long. Soon more newspapers around the country were referring to him as the Wool King of America, and Democrats were attacking him personally for supporting tariffs. He didn't mind; he wanted to give sheep farmers and wool manufacturers a strong voice far beyond the borders of Ohio.

In the 1880s and 1890s, Republicans generally supported tariffs, and Democrats did not. One lifelong Democrat, John Stalter, of Cowley County, Kansas, for example, changed his registration to Republican in 1884 because he was a sheep farmer who wanted protection. "What difference is it to a farmer if the clothes for his family under protection cost him $25 a year more when he gets $100 to $1,000 more for the products of his farm [as a result of a tariff]?" Stalter told the *Winfield (Kansas) Courier.* "I am in favor of protecting American labor, American factories, American farmers, and American stockmen against unreasonable and degrading foreign competition, and as the Democratic party is not, I am henceforth a Republican."

Harpster supported such determined men as Stalter, a former Ohioan who changed parties the same year Harpster succeeded Columbus Delano as president of the Ohio Wool Growers' Association and turned it into a national lobbying group. Stalter was a mini Harpster, the top sheep man in his township, having nine hundred head as early as 1875. He maintained in his 1884 Wool Growers' speech that "every wool grower in the United States is convinced that a further reduction of the tariff on woolen goods and wool would destroy the domestic sheep business."

His prediction was halfway correct.

In Logan in 1891, the *Ohio Democrat* rebuked Harpster and two important wool-growing lawyers who often worked with him to influence national policy on tariffs. The other two men are all but forgotten now, but were then highly influential—Columbus Delano, of Mt. Vernon, and William Lawrence, of Bellefontaine. Both had strong connections with nearly anyone who counted in Washington, D.C., where Delano had served twice in the Congress, later as the Internal Revenue commissioner, and finally as President Grant's secretary of the Interior. Lawrence, who led the National Committee of Wool Growers, had once been a congressman and had helped create the Justice Department and the American Red Cross. He also had been the comptroller of the Treasury Department. So the lawyers were loaded with contacts, and the three took turns as president of the Ohio Wool Growers' Association during the 1880s and 1890s.

Delano and Lawrence were big-time sheep men too, so they were interested in tariff protection, thus allying themselves with David Harpster made sense. And their political prominence could not compete with Harpster's savvy when it came to politicking. Delano, in particular, had been receiving newspaper criticism for years; in 1875, for instance, the *New York Tribune* called him "a man who from time of his entry into politics thirty years ago has been followed by constant suspicion; a man who by some sad circumstance, or else by some innate perversity of character, has always and everywhere been suspected of taking care of himself and his family and friends at the expense of the public." Of course, Delano said such attacks were inevitable with politics. But he might have been especially disliked by an Indiana judge who once struck him on the head with a walking stick over a personal dispute in Washington.

When the three wise men of Ohio went to the capital to speak with legislators about strengthening all kinds of tariffs, the opposition mocked them as "the lobbyists," "the third House," and "the wool trinity." The *Ohio Democrat* continued in 1891:

> We earnestly advise David and William and Columbus to order Congress during the last few weeks of its existence as a Republican combine to enact a law fixing fifty cents a pound as the price of domestic unwashed wool and requiring the woolen manufacturers, or somebody, it doesn't matter who, to buy at that figure all the wool that David Harpster and William Lawrence and Columbus Delano offer them.
>
> A good while ago, during the Dark Ages, an English King who wanted to help the Delanos, Lawrences and Harpsters of his day decreed that the dead should be buried only in woolen shrouds. Something of this kind might help the three Shepherd Kings of Ohio until something adequate could be provided. If they would settle their claims against the country for pensions of, say, $100,000 each annually, it would be economical to buy them off.

The story was reprinted in other papers, which started a round of new rumors. People started repeating them as if they were headlines: "Dead to be buried in wool, Harpster decrees! Wool to be used for everything, Harpster says!" It was as though David Harpster really was the king of wool.

Harpster's rise as the wool industry's national spokesman came slowly. He served as president of the Ohio Wool Growers' Association for about ten years, being reelected annually as the planner for farmers who earned their living from sheep.

Before Congress changed the wool tariff, Harpster seemed pleased with the state of the industry. But afterward, the Wool King became livid. "No portion of the people familiar with American interests asked for or desired any changes," he told members of the Ohio Wool Growers' Association in Columbus on January 24, 1888. "The Ohio senators and representatives in Congress neither asked for or desired any change in the law which secured these beneficial results. Every loyal heart was animated with just pride that our people had reason to believe that they would soon cease to be dependent on foreign capital, enterprise or skill, for any kind or amount of wool or woolen or worsted goods."

Harpster argued that what was good for American farmers and workers should be good enough for politicians. This viewpoint made him something of a populist, for he wanted Americans protected from foreign workers. But not every sheep farmer agreed with him. At a meeting of the Ohio Wool Growers' Association in Columbus on September 5, 1889, D. E. Williams of Licking County stood and opposed the group's plan to ask Congress for more tariff protection, saying the price of wool would go up if the product didn't have a tariff. It was like David standing up to Goliath and losing. Expressing such "arrogance" before the lockstep group took nerve, and it resulted in some name-calling. By then the association had become so important that the *New York Times* reported on its session. "He was opposed by many members," the newspaper said of Williams, "and the discussion grew personal. David Harpster, the wool king of Wyandot County, finally denominated Mr. Williams, who is a young wool grower and a Democrat, as a 'smart aleck.' The address was adopted with but one dissenting vote—that of Mr. Williams." The newspaper headlined the story, "A 'Calamity Howl' from Columbus."

By the time Harpster visited the White House in September 1890, he was unhappy about what he perceived as a lack of tariff support. He did not remove his hat. No one knows why, but it is likely that he just didn't believe the president took wool seriously enough. The issue became another anti-Harpster story for the newspapers; after all, civil Victorians had strict rules of etiquette about when a man should remove his hat—always inside a building, and always at the dinner table, during the singing of the national anthem, and at other times when a man should show respect. So when Harpster, an invited guest, failed to remove his hat at the White House, opponents claimed he was insulting President Benjamin Harrison as well as anyone in his presence.

During the previous presidential election, Republican Harrison had campaigned on a tariff protection platform, but after taking office he compromised on the McKinley Tariff Law of 1890 by making reciprocal trade deals with America's top trading partners. Ohioan William McKinley, then a member of the U.S. House of Representatives and a Republican expert on protective tariffs, had deliberately set certain tariff costs too high to ensure that corresponding foreign goods would not enter the country, thus protecting American workers in that field. As a result, the tariff would boost both production and consumption of those goods. So perhaps Harpster *was* sending a message to the president. "The President's assumption that the wool tariff is for the *exclusive* benefit of 'those who have sheep to sheer' is unsupported by fact or reason," he said. "In his anxiety to inaugurate a system of legislation 'necessary for the benefit of foreigners,' he may have the distinction of finding one that benefits no American system."

The Wool King asserted that a new wool tariff would benefit all workers in the long run. "All the foreign wool-growers—our rivals—our commercial enemies—desire a repeal of the tariff," he said. "They do not desire it for *our* benefit but for *theirs*. It is safe for us to ascertain what our *rivals* want, and then see that they do *not* secure it. The President consults our enemies and proposes to do what they ask. We consult our friends—the American people—and propose to do what *their* interests require."

The Democrat newspapers responded with all their firepower. In the fall of 1890, Frank G. Carpenter wrote in the *New York World*: "The question of a wool tariff has brought one of the most remarkable farmers in the United States to Washington. This is David Harpster of northern Ohio. He has thousands of sheep on the Western Reserve and is one of the millionaire sheep-raisers of the country. He has large estates scattered over other parts of the Union, but does not look as if he were worth a dollar."

When Carpenter began describing Harpster for his New York readers, several city-country stereotypes and prejudices of the era came to mind. "He is about five feet, four inches high, is as broad as he is long, and he has a round, cannon ball head, pasted down upon a pair of broad, fat shoulders," Carpenter wrote.

> His roly-poly form is clad in rough goods that might have been put together by his wife, and a big derby that comes well down towards his ears and shades his fat, florid face.
>
> Harpster is a great friend of [Ohio's U.S.] Senator John Sherman. He was sitting the other day in Senator Sherman's committee room when John B. Alley, ex-Congressman . . . came in. Alley is a millionaire. He is proud of his riches and he, I am told, is a little inclined to pose. When he entered Senator Sherman's room Mr. Sherman introduced him to Dave Harpster, saying: "Mr. Alley, I want to make you acquainted with one of our representative farmers, Mr. Harpster."

"Ah, indeed," replied Alley as he shook hands. "You are a farmer, are you? I am always glad to meet farmers for I am something of a farmer myself. I have a farm in Texas consisting of 40,000 acres."

"You have," muttered Harpster, "and where is it?"

"It is in such a county," Alley said, naming the county, "in the central part of Texas."

"Indeed," replied Mr. Harpster, "it must be good land, for I own the whole county next to it."

This surprised Alley and took the wind out of his sails, but his actions showed that his respect for David Harpster, the Ohio farmer, had perceptibly risen.

David Harpster had indeed risen, and he had the power and influence to show for it. He owned a $15,000 mansion one-half mile north of Harpster. The house was his refuge, and it represented his financial and business successes. There he hosted fancy parties, celebrations, and weddings. The townspeople called the place the House of David. In today's prices, the house would cost at least $5 or $6 million, if a contractor could even find the skilled labor to build such a place.

Meanwhile, as Little Sandusky and Harpster grew, their rivalry became a battle over two methods of transportation—Harpster's railroad and Little's old highway for stagecoaches. Little was a formidable competitor: it had a lawyer, a blacksmith, a doctor, and numerous business people, as well as a church and a school. When the automobile arrived in the early 1900s, Little also benefited: its saloons kept the town busy. Everyone knew you couldn't get a drink in Harpster because The Man discouraged drinking and attached liquor restrictions to deeds when he built and sold houses to families.

"Little Sandusky was a buzzing town with a real going church served by circuit riders," said Harpster resident Fern Erickson, who was eighty-seven when interviewed in 1995. "But the town also had seven taverns. Eventually, the place deteriorated. I believe it was because of all those bars. Because Mr. Harpster didn't appreciate liquor, our town wouldn't allow it to be sold. The town council passed a law prohibiting it. Things stayed that way here for years. Mr. Harpster eventually outsmarted Little Sandusky by giving the railroad a way through his land. He even promised to build a hotel for railroad workers to stay in. Little Sandusky wanted the railroad badly. Many people over there have hated our town ever since. Even when we tried to merge the towns' two churches a few years ago, they refused to cooperate."

The good David Harpster was, in fact, the major force in his town until his death in 1898. More than any other Ohioan in this book, he was connected to the land and to his community. The land was his livelihood; the town was his namesake. He worried about the community more than himself. But he worried most about his wool.

Today, his personal empire of wool is gone, lost in a sea of polyester and high-tech fabrics, of international trade and few American tariffs. Yet his town still exists, preserving his name and memory in a time when most people have forgotten him.

The town is all that matters now.

On the state map, a thin red line identified as State Route 294 connects a black dot marked Harpster to U.S. 23 and the world. The lines and dots have changed over the years, but Harpster's green landscape has always carried a pleasing symmetry: generation upon generation, field upon field, accented by a few white houses and brick buildings. In the middle of it all sits a grain elevator, its silos looking like five silver missiles.

By the first decade of the twenty-first century, however, Harpster had become just another small town fighting to stay alive. The echo of David Harpster's name had long faded from the marble halls of Washington, D.C., and even from the Statehouse in Columbus. From 1876 to 1985, the Harpster General Store operated on a strategic corner in the center of a cluster of buildings that made up the town's core. The finest business building in town, once owned by David Harpster himself, has housed an antiques shop and other merchants since the early 1990s.

The town still bears the Wool King's name, though these days wool is not associated with the place. Some people still call Harpster a kingmaker, and maybe he was. The town's condition reflects his standing in state history: hanging by a thread—though a woolen one, perhaps. The town was his other vision, his home, and his life. Now, it's a farming community of 204 residents who live fifty-five miles north of Columbus. It is also a village in transition. The elementary school is closed, as are most of the businesses. The village does, however, feature something unusual: the Hickory Grove Country Club and eighteen-hole golf course, set in the middle of cornfields. David Harpster would probably appreciate this bold entrepreneurial gamble, for he built what was once called the world's largest slatted corncrib, a mansion, a railroad depot, a grist mill, a bank, a store, and his own world.

Harpster is not yet a dying town, although there are warning signs. Harpster represents rural America's past, present, and future, but especially its present—drowsy, uneasy, expectant. Here, the threats of big farms and school consolidations are just beginning to affect life, and the more general issue of America's bigger-is-better mentally is not yet welcome. This attitude is not without irony, for Harpster's wealthy founder grew richer in part on the concept of the big farm. And so it goes on. Modern Harpster is a town on the verge of something, people agree, although nobody knows exactly what. Some believe the town will grow slightly; others say it will remain the same; still others predict it's headed for extinction.

On its streets, David Harpster's presence remains, a subliminal image. Some people mention Harpster so frequently that a stranger might think he only recently died. But most don't know anything about him. He is a ghost of Ohio politics and agriculture. "There isn't nearly as much talk of him as one may think, given that the town bears his name," said Roberta "Robbi" Sigler, a Wyandot County extension agent who grew up in Harpster. "There is more talk of the Sears family and J. L. Lewis, who had a later economic impact on the community. Anecdotally, I can tell you there isn't as much sheep farming in Harpster or Wyandot County as there was even twenty years ago. When I was a 4-Her, there were maybe thirty-some kids involved with the sheep program. Now [in 2013], there are only sixteen. The proliferation of sheep raising is not what it once was."

Not much is left of the town's economic structure. A bank still operates—the Commercial Savings Bank branch, and the Pitt Township Volunteer Fire Department building, and a pizza place. In September 2013, the brick building that once housed the Harpster Bank burned, killing three people who lived in apartments upstairs. County officials want to obtain a state grant to demolish what's left of the burned-out shell.

Because of big changes in farming, the people of Harpster are concerned about the future. They are right to worry, for Harpster's problems are the problems of American agriculture. All across the country, when small farmers retire or lose their land, they displace the communities around them. Economists estimate that for every farmer who goes out of business, the nearest town loses a worker and a store. Big farms get larger, small towns get smaller, and more farmers leave for city jobs.

Columbus and Franklin County are markedly different from Harpster and Wyandot County. Wyandot has fewer people than some Columbus suburbs. "In 1870," Sigler said, "there were twenty-two thousand people in our county. Today, there are twenty-two thousand people in our county. But the number is configured differently in other places." Being flat in some parts, Wyandot also looks like a small version of the Great Plains, except the soil is more fertile. In summer and autumn, when the fields around Pitt Township are full of corn, soybeans, and wheat, strong winds blow inconsistently hot and humid while big combines rummage around eighteen farms that surround the town.

Like most of rural America, Wyandot County has watched its farms decrease in number and increase in size since the Great Depression days. In 1935, the county had 2,509 farms, with an average size of 130 acres, according to the Ohio Cooperative Extension Service. In 1990, the number of farms had dropped to 770 and the average size was 296 acres. In a critical period of the mid-1990s, when small towns were dying across the country, Wyandot County agricultural extension agent Rick Grove said,

> Some people call that decline, but others call it progress. I guess it all depends on your perspective. What we're dealing with is a matter of consolidation—the free enterprise system at work. By getting bigger, farms can become more effective, presumably. If a farmer has enough money to—pardon the word—plow back into his business by buying more land, who's to say he's wrong? You could argue that his action is harmful to small towns because it takes more people out of farming. On the other hand, you could argue that some people ought not to be farming anyway. They should liquidate and get out of the business before they lose everything. It's all in the perspective. But consolidation is happening, and happening big.

The Wool King might have enjoyed this, for he was a megafarm owner before there were megafarms, and he was a certified free-market Republican. Yet he never realized that his own policies would one day affect his town.

In 2008, local freelance writer Gene Logsdon depicted life in Harpster in a novel called *The Last of the Husbandmen*. He changed the town's name to Gowler and based an important character, Emmett Gowler, on David Harpster. The village, "just a little spot in the road today, was a very thriving and very wealthy village," Logsdon told writer Celeste Baumgartner. His book shows the major changes in farming and rural life in the early twentieth century, and how the town was affected.

Even today, some things in town are the same as when the King lived here. The village's streets are Cherokee, Oneida, and Shawnee. Their names come from history: In the first half of the nineteenth century, most of Wyandot County was an Indian reservation—until 1843, when farmers wanted the land and the Native Americans were removed to Kansas. Since then, the ghost towns of Wyandot County have served as dark reminders to any community foolish enough to think it will last forever: Bowsherville, which opened saloons near the Indian reservation and grew until the Indians left; Brownstown, Pleasant Grove, Scot Town, Wyandot, and other farm towns that lost their economic and cultural bases and died slowly. All are gone now. Since the 1990s, Little Sandusky, to the east, has declined, and Harpster has sat alone. Its prospects for survival change day to day, depending on the whims of business and commerce.

Harpster's streets sparkle with neatly painted houses built a century ago. Their yards are mowed, trimmed, and planted with flowers. On the east side of town lies the Harpster United Methodist Church and the bank, once the two most important institutions in the community, and both influenced heavily by David Harpster. The bank is now a branch of a bank in Upper Sandusky.

In the 1990s, postmaster Cecil W. Dennis watched people grow up and grow old. He was accepted in the community, some people say, because he treated it as he would his own hometown, although he lived in a neighboring village and originally came from Cincinnati. When the oldest tree in Harpster blew down in a storm, he saved a piece of it to carve a clock for Fern Erickson, the town matriarch. He gladly volunteered in emergencies. And when the school board threatened to close the local school in 1989, he spoke out against the move. "Used to be," he said in 1996, "people would bring their kids to school and do their banking. Now, the school's closed and they can't even get a loan in the bank. It's just a branch. The larger percent of young people don't want to live in this town anymore. When the school board was ready to close the Harpster school, I went to the board meeting and chewed out the superintendent. I said, 'You've got a gun in your hand. Pull the trigger and you'll kill Harpster.' He pulled it anyway. Now, this town's not progressing and it's not dying. It's standing still."

Once, Harpster featured a tile factory; a carriage and wagon factory; slaughterhouses; a grocery store; stockyards; a post office; a doctor's office; and the Harpster Bank, established in 1883 by David Harpster and businessman John L. Lewis. Lewis managed the bank for years and became the second most important person in town. His son, Charles Henrickson Lewis, followed him as president. He married Francis Sears, granddaughter of David Harpster and daughter of Sarah Harpster and Cyrus Sears, who received the Medal of Honor for defending the 11th Battery of Ohio Light Artillery after nearly all the cannoneers and horses had fallen during a Civil War battle in 1862. The Wool King's other daughter, Ivy, married wealthy dry goods wholesaler William Bones, and soon they moved to his native New York City; Bones couldn't stand small-town life. Sarah remained in Harpster with her well-respected husband.

Charles Lewis was one of Harpster's important—and busy—citizens. He served on the village school board for twenty-five years and on the Wyandot County Board of Education for ten years, farmed a thousand acres, raised cattle, published the family's *Daily Union* newspaper, and obtained more than seventy patents for devices that could treat polluted water. In 1924, he was elected Ohio's lieutenant governor (in those days the governor and lieutenant governor were elected on separate tickets). He served one term of two years.

John Lewis and his wife took Fern Erickson into their home when she was orphaned in the 1920s. In the 1990s, she was the only person directly connecting the old village aristocracy—its royalty—to the town's modern residents. She lived in Charles Lewis's Victorian home, a tidy showplace, when she grew old. Her memory was sharp, and she remembered the village fondly, noting that David Harpster passed on his sense of community involvement to other important citizens who were younger. Through them, his influence remained for decades.

"John Lewis, or Mr. J.L., as I called him, was a witty, humorous, and scholarly man who graduated from Hillsdale College in Michigan in 1867," she once recalled. "Early in his career, he owned and wrote for one of the newspapers in Upper Sandusky. He was a staunch Republican, and any time he wrote about people—if they were Republicans—he'd tell a lot about them and mention their party affiliation.

If they were Democrats, though, he'd barely mention their names and never their party. . . .

"Oh, that Mr. J.L. was a character. When he wrote his column, 'Fowler Fumes,' he'd use the name Timothy Teedlepitcher or Rodney Rainbeau, just to be funny. At the breakfast table, he was always making jokes in front of his wife, whom I call Auntie Lewis. She'd finally get the point five minutes after he'd told a joke. So English, she was. Those were quite lovely times."

Erickson grew up, married, and moved to Chicago with her husband. In retirement, they moved back to Harpster to live in the old Lewis mansion, just west of town. Although she liked Chicago, Erickson knew that Harpster offered her things a big city could not—an identifiable history, a personal past, a sense of place. "That's why I stay," she went on. "The town just wrapped itself around me. I love it. There have always been so many interesting people here, so much warmth. We wanted the town's children to keep going to school here, of course, so they could set down their own roots, but the school board had other ideas. We have to live with its decision. I know some people think the town is doomed, but I don't. Families have lived here for generations. They work hard. Harpster will always be here."

The village continued to grow after the turn of the twentieth century. Farmers shipped their grain worldwide. When the hotel was torn down, new businesses popped up—a mechanic's garage, a Ford dealership, a gasoline station. Harpster even had a little park with a reflecting pool, paid for by a wealthy benefactor.

"My mother," Logsdon told the authors in a 1995 interview, "used to take me to the little Harpster Park. It was our Lake Erie beach. We couldn't afford to go to the shore, but we could always go to Harpster. July 4 was Al Brendt's night. He owned the general store, and on the Fourth he'd always have a colossal fireworks display in the park. In 1937, in the middle of agricultural country, that was a big deal. People used to jam into the park. In summer Al would also put on free outdoor movies. That was our theater. Hundreds of us kids would flock into town for the shows—my uncle Lawrence Rall hauled neighborhood kids in his pickup. The man who showed the movies had the projector set up on the back seat of a big Packard, and all he had to do was open the door and turn the thing on, aimed at the screen."

By 1995, Harpster was suffering from what Logsdon called social consent. He wrote about it in a magazine article: "The murder weapon appears to be the piston engine, which, in the form of automobiles, carries the people away to the city in search of the money they have spent there, and, in the form of tractors, which melds little farms into big ones and sends the surplus farmers away, too." He argued that Route 23 was "an accessory to the crime, taking traffic from the railroad, which was the reason Harpster existed in the first place."

Some Pitt Township schools were closed in the 1950s and 1960s and consolidated into a new high school in Upper Sandusky. That caused a fight: rural people do not give up a school easily, nor do they often vote for school levies after consolidations. Without their high schools, Harpster and Eden, towns previously recognized for their outstanding students, became isolated physically and academically. Gradually, local people say, Harpster lost its identity, as teachers persuaded its young people to think of themselves as members of the more cosmopolitan Upper Sandusky School District, not a country-town school, and to think of a city education as better than a country one.

A small town like Harpster is fortunate to have a golf course and country club; it means the place is doing more than existing. The enterprise, founded by farmer Craig Bowman and his son Kyle, gave the town psychological pride. Craig, a fourth-generation Harpster resident, grew up on local farms in the 1940s. His grandfather was Colonel Cyrus Sears, the Wool King's son-in-law. As a teenager, Bowman trained his pony to enter the general store without flinching. His friend Gene Logsdon had to go to the filling station in town to call his friends on the old crank telephone. Gene said the village operator, Fannie Day, gave callers the latest gossip. The town was busier then, Logsdon said, with people coming and going at the train depot and farmers coming into town to take their grain to the elevator.

These days, so little remains. But, at least for now, David Harpster's town still is there.

When David Harpster died of complications from a stroke at age eighty-two on October 29, 1898, the wool industry mourned the loss of its champion. His family received telegraphed condolences from President William McKinley, major business figures across the nation, and other important politicians. They took him seriously, for Harpster was a serious fellow. For a half century, he had helped shape wool-related legislation. Sheep farmers across the country looked to him for guidance and advice, so did Republicans on every level. "He made his numerous friends through his pleasant business relations," a newspaper in Upper Sandusky observed, perhaps a bit too kindly, upon his death.

The end of the Wool King's empire came just before his death. His obituary explained it best, and bitterly: "The wool tariff act of 1890 was inadequate to make wool growing in Ohio sufficiently remunerative, and the Dingley Wool Tariff of 1897, much less protective, utterly unjust and insufficient, drove him to a considerable extent to change the use of his lands." He returned to raising cattle, and he no longer made himself a public target. By this time he was simply David Harpster, frustrated Ohioan.

The newspapers, once his worst political enemies, generally wrote admiringly of him at his death. A paper in competing Upper Sandusky carried this headline: "CROSSED OVER." The long story spoke highly of the man who knew senators, farmers, and congressmen.

He was the second of the Shepherd Kings to go. Columbus Delano had died first—on October 23, 1896, in his hometown of Mount Vernon. William Lawrence would die on May 8, 1899, in Kenton. On November 3, 1898, the newspaper in Upper Sandusky noted that Harpster's funeral was "undoubtedly the largest ever held in this county. Arrangements were made with the Hocking Valley railroad, whereby their passenger trains were stopped at Harpster, thus enabling the hundreds of friends of the deceased to attend. . . . The services were of a very simple, unostentatious nature, very impressive."

David Harpster is buried in Harpster's Oak Hill Cemetery, under a large monument that still marks the grave of the Wool King and his holy cause, the controversial American tariff.

5

LUCY WEBB HAYES

The Soldiers' Friend

When Lucy Hayes became First Lady of the United States on a cold, cloudy March day in 1877, she was in the midst of a national controversy over disputed election results. Compounding the situation, she would soon be courted by groups that wanted to use her to support their agendas. Yet, she would remain faithful to her own priorities: her husband, her family, and the men of the 23d Ohio Volunteer Infantry.

Rutherford B. "Rud" Hayes had been given the rank of major in June of 1861, just a few weeks after the first shots of the Civil War were fired at Fort Sumter in Charleston, South Carolina. He was ready for war, as was his wife. "Lucy enjoys it [war news] and wishes she had been in Ft. Sumter with a garrison of women," Hayes wrote to his uncle Sardis Birchard in Fremont, Ohio. Hayes, Cincinnati's city solicitor, was thirty-eight at the time and Lucy was twenty-nine. They had been married for eight years and had three little boys. By the end of the war, Lucy was known as the Mother of the Regiment, a title she cherished for the rest of her life.

Lucy Webb Hayes seemed fulfilled by her roles as a caregiver and parent in an age when progressives and idealists wanted to mold her into their image of the "New Woman." She was the first president's wife to hold a college degree. She was a teetotaler and a strict Methodist with a social conscience; as a result, the temperance and suffrage movements both assumed she would espouse their causes once she moved into the White House, though she had other plans. That she was so well-educated and had a husband who supported her decisions might account for her polite refusal to comply with others' expectations.

Lucy Webb Hayes, circa 1866. (Courtesy Hayes Presidential Center, Fremont)

Lucy was born on August 28, 1831, in Chillicothe, Ohio's first capital. Her father, James Webb, was a physician who grew up around Lexington, Kentucky. Her mother, Maria Cook Webb, was from Chillicothe. James's family owned slaves, whom he—as heir—would one day inherit. Having grown more repulsed by slavery as he matured, James traveled back to Lexington in the summer of 1833 to sign the papers to free his slaves. Once there, he discovered the entire household suffering with cholera. He attempted to treat everyone, but unfortunately, he, his parents, and his brother all succumbed.

Left to raise little Lucy and her two older brothers, Joseph and James, Maria Webb eventually moved the family to Delaware, Ohio, so the boys could enroll at what would become Ohio Wesleyan University. The school, affiliated with the Methodist Church, had been chartered in 1842 as a boys' preparatory school, whose success led to the establishment of a college.

Lucy attended classes at the prep school, rather unusual for a girl at the time. She also earned a few credits in the college department. Just before her sixteenth birthday, she met Rud Hayes at the local hot spot: the old sulphur springs on the college campus. Hayes, almost ten years older, was in town visiting friends and family. He had grown up in Delaware; his parents—Sophia Birchard Hayes and Rutherford Hayes Jr.—were both New Englanders who settled there in 1817. The elder Hayes, a Presbyterian and an advocate for education, was a farmer and businessman who was co-owner of a distillery. He died of a fever just three months before Rud was born on October 4, 1822.

Sophia's cousin and her brother, Sardis Birchard, helped raise young Rud and his beloved sister Fanny. After attending prep schools in Norwalk, Ohio, and in Middletown, Connecticut, Hayes enrolled at Kenyon College in Gambier, Ohio. By the time he met Lucy, he had finished his law studies at Harvard University and passed the Ohio bar. He had courted two other young women before meeting Lucy, but he had been more intent on building his law career than settling down.

Lucy made a lasting impression on the young barrister. Not quite yet her adult height of five feet, four and one half inches, she was already slightly taller than average for the time. With her slender build, wide hazel eyes, and inky black hair, she was close to the physical ideal then. Only a tendency to freckle easily marred her fair complexion, Hayes wrote teasingly. Of average height for the day—five feet, eight and a half inches—he was considered handsome, with his sandy hair and blue eyes. He was also a hard worker and deep thinker who loved culture, traveling, and socializing with friends. But those were qualities Lucy would discover later.

A lifelong diarist, Hayes recorded his first impression of his future wife—a "bright sunny hearted little girl not quite old enough to fall in love with—and so I didn't." He went back to practice law in Fremont (then still called Lower Sandusky), where his uncle Sardis lived. In 1849, he moved to Cincinnati to further his career.

Meanwhile, Lucy went to Cincinnati to attend the Wesleyan Female College. Like the Delaware school, the Cincinnati college was affiliated with the Methodist Church. It was one of the first chartered colleges in the country to award degrees to women. Its classes were held in a large three-story stone building on Vine Street. Four hundred young women attended classes on the first two floors and chapel on the third floor. Lucy, along with other out-of-town students, lived in a boardinghouse next door.

Lucy was homesick at first, but she soon grew to love her fellow students, her studies, and the delicious meals at the boardinghouse. She studied geology, astronomy, rhetoric, geometry, and mental and moral science; she may have also studied trigonometry and a foreign language. The assignment Lucy dreaded the most was the fortnightly essay on some lofty topic. With themes such as "Is Emulation a Greater Promotive of Literary Excellence than Personal Necessity?" it's easy to understand why she wasn't an enthusiastic writer.

On the whole, Lucy enjoyed college. When her mother moved to Cincinnati to join her brothers there during Lucy's third and final year, the girl's family was reunited. Meanwhile, Sophia Hayes had been keeping her son informed about Lucy's life. She wrote that Maria Webb had decided to send Lucy to Cincinnati to college because she was becoming too popular in Delaware. Lucy "will do well if she can keep from being carried off by a Methodist minister till she is of age," Sophia wrote.

Hayes took notice. He began dropping by Friday evening receptions at the Female College where the students could socialize with young gentlemen under proper supervision. By the time Lucy graduated with a liberal arts degree in June 1850, he knew he was in deep waters. He had believed himself to be in love with another young woman for two years, but now he was in turmoil over that relationship, and his thoughts turned more to Lucy.

Lucy, meanwhile, was enjoying life as a young single lady in a cosmopolitan city. Free of her studies, she now had more time to enjoy all the culture Cincinnati offered: literary readings, lectures, theater, music. The college degree she earned was to improve her mind and broaden her horizons, not to prepare her for a career; the career of choice for most young women in 1850 was still wife and mother.

On his twenty-eighth birthday that October, Hays wrote of his increasing restlessness and his resolve to find a sweetheart with whom he could build a future. The sudden death of a much younger cousin that fall; the death of his beloved nephew, six-year-old Willie Platt; and the wedding of one of his best friends convinced him to stop procrastinating. On June 13, 1851, he declared his love to Lucy and asked her to be his wife. "A puzzled expression of pleasure and surprise stole over her fine features," he wrote in his diary. "She responded with a slight pressure of her hand and said, 'I must confess, I like you very well' . . . and the faith was plighted for life."

While Lucy's response seemed restrained, Hayes was euphoric. He endured their engagement impatiently, writing to her every few days. "How fast you are becoming the 'be-all and end-all' of my hopes, thoughts, affections, my existence," he wrote to her a week later, then borrowed a poetic sentiment from Milton: "If there be an Elysium of bliss It is this,— it is this!" They were married at Maria Webb's home in Cincinnati on December 30, 1852, amid a group of thirty relatives and friends.

It was the beginning of a happy marriage, which lasted thirty-six years. Lucy and Hayes were exceptionally suited to each other. Family ties were of great importance to them, they supported each other in their respective dreams and decisions, they strove never to be apart longer than absolutely necessary, and they delighted in their children. They had seven sons, three of whom died as toddlers, and one daughter. During this time, Hayes lost his older sister, Fanny Hayes Platt, who died at thirty-six on July 16, 1856, in Columbus.

After the couple married, they lived with Mrs. Webb for almost two and a half years, before moving into their own home on 6th Street in Cincinnati. They primarily spent vacations visiting relatives in the Columbus area and Fremont. Occasionally, they went back East to visit family. With the births of Birchard Austin ("Birch") in 1853, Webb Cook in 1856, and Rutherford Platt ("Ruddy") in 1858, Lucy was increasingly preoccupied with domestic life. She usually had two household servants to help her. One woman, simply known as Eliza Jane, was a free African American, whom Lucy taught to read and write. Some of the servants from their early marriage stayed with them through the White House years, including Winnie Monroe, a black woman who was the cook and a second mother to the children, and Monroe's mother, who the family simply called Aunt Clara.

The Hayeses opposed slavery, as did their families. Hayes detested the Fugitive Slave Law of 1850, which allowed slave owners and bounty hunters to track down escaped slaves anywhere in the country and return them to captivity. Only the Ohio River separated Cincinnati and the slave state of Kentucky, and the Queen City became an important entry point for those seeking freedom. As an attorney in a Cincinnati law firm, Hayes often defended escaped slaves, procuring freedom for many of them.

Lucy was keenly interested in politics and eagerly discussed the topics of the day with her husband and immediate family. The Hayeses believed, as did many people, that free and slave states could continue to coexist until slavery became too impractical to continue. They did not believe that the Union would dissolve or that war would ensue. As late as Election Day 1860, Hayes wrote in his diary that even if South Carolina and some of the other southern states seceded, the more conservative states would remain. "But at all events, I feel as if the time has come to test this question," he added. "If the threats are meant, then it is time the Union was dissolved or the traitors crushed out. I hope Lincoln goes in."

Both he and Lucy opposed Kentucky senator John J. Crittenden's compromise, which proposed that the Fugitive Slave Law be strengthened and that slavery be permitted in the District of Columbia. Even though Lucy still had cousins in Kentucky who supported states' rights over the slavery issue, she did not soften her beliefs or comments on the topic. Patriotism ran high and hot in Cincinnati. "The Northern heart is truly fired," Lucy wrote to a niece. "The enthusiasm that prevails in our city is perfectly irresistible."

After Fort Sumter, northerners like the Hayeses put aside thoughts of compromise and coexistence. In the letter to his uncle in which he mentioned Lucy's reaction to Fort Sumter, Hayes described the rest of the family's reactions: "Mother thinks we are to be punished for our sinfulness, and reads the Old Testament vigorously. Mother Webb quietly grieves over it. . . . Dr. Joe [Lucy's eldest brother] is for flames, slaughter, and a rising of the slaves. All the boys [Hayes's sons] are soldiers."

As war fever spread throughout Cincinnati, people appeared to have little realization of what civil war would mean. Everyone underestimated how long and bloody the ordeal would be. In a May 8 letter to his former college classmate Guy M. Bryan of Texas, Hayes argued that the secessionists had forced the war upon the country. "We cannot escape it," he wrote. Both Hayes and his wife had numerous college friends who hailed from the South, and that made them reluctant to vilify the new Confederates. Hayes wrote to Bryan that he hoped they would remain friends and that he believed people's better natures would be brought forth by the war. "People are more generous, more sympathetic, better, than when engaged in the more selfish pursuits of peace," he wrote. He ended the letter with regards to Bryan's wife and son, adding, "Lucy and the boys send much love." Around that same time, Lucy became pregnant with their fourth child.

Hayes, who had no military background, did not immediately join the army. He questioned whether he had any skills that would be useful, but he decided he would take action if Kentucky seceded, an event that would have increased the odds of combat in the hills and riverfronts of Cincinnati. Lucy's younger brother, Dr. James Webb, did join the effort early, hoping to contribute in a way that was not "warlike." He secured a position as an assistant surgeon of the 2d Regiment.

Hayes and fellow members of the Cincinnati Literary Club formed a volunteer company to learn how to drill. Concerned about the family's safety, Sardis Birchard invited them to come to Fremont, a prospect that the independent Lucy didn't relish. Hayes diplomatically declined, saying, "Lucy hates to leave the city in these stirring times."

By mid-May, Hayes and a close friend, Cincinnati judge Stanley Matthews, decided to join the army together. By June, they were part of the newly formed 23d Ohio Volunteer Infantry, led initially by Colonel William S. Rosecrans. Matthews was commissioned lieutenant colonel and Hayes, major. The regiment was sent to Camp Jackson, near Columbus, for six weeks of intensive training.

In the first few weeks Hayes was absent, Lucy spent a considerable amount of time organizing clothing, linens, and sundries such as sewing supplies and soap to send to him in the field. She also lobbied for her brother Joe to be assigned to the 23d so that husband and brother could watch out for each other. Webb did join Hayes later that year, which pleased her greatly. Soon her concern spread to the other men in the 23d as well.

"I can sympathize with your feelings as the men are sworn in," she wrote to Hayes on June 13, 1861. "Oh how my heart fills with joy and feelings . . . as I think of our brave men." She recounted how she was greeted in the street by a young man in uniform, then recognized him as the boy who used to serve her at the neighborhood butcher shop. "He grasped my hand warmly," she wrote, "and I felt that he was not a poor boy but one of our defenders."

Although the war certainly did not erase class distinctions, circumstances often arose that nullified them, at least for a time. Already that June, Lucy's thoughts were with the other young men of Hayes's regiment. "My greatest happiness now would be to feel that I was doing some thing for the comfort and happiness of our men," she wrote to Hayes. She would not be able to follow her impulses for a few months, but in letters to her husband she continued express her concerns for the soldiers.

Hayes, meanwhile, was totally occupied with training and earning the respect of the twenty-five hundred men under his command. He soon showed himself to be a compassionate, able leader. According to one private from Niles, he "was so generous and his relations with his men were so kind, and yet always dignified, that he won my heart almost from the start." That young man, William McKinley, went on to serve with Hayes in many campaigns and later became the twenty-fifth president of the United States.

Just eighteen at the time, McKinley later told how Hayes demonstrated his leadership one day in July 1861 when General John C. Frémont (the pioneer pathfinder and Lucy's personal political hero) was slated to review the troops at camp. The men had been issued battered, out-of-date muskets, converted from using flints to percussion caps. Many of the men scorned the weapons and refused to take them. While Stanley Matthews flatly told his men they would be shot if they didn't carry the muskets, Hayes took a more reasonable approach. He went to tents and cabins and spoke to the men about how some of the greatest battles of the American Revolution had been won with the most rudimentary firearms and weapons. He called on their commitment to the cause and told them they would get better guns later as they entered battle. According to McKinley's account, a boisterous Irish private shouted, "Bully for Hayes!" and led his companions down to the arsenal to pick up their muskets. "From that moment our confidence in our leader never wavered," McKinley wrote.

As the time approached for Hayes's regiment to be deployed, Lucy's feelings shifted from those of ardent patriot to those of anxious wife and mother. Prior to Hayes joining the war, he had written to Birchard that he had enough money to sustain his family for a year, or two, while he was in the field. But no savings account could quiet Lucy's fears. She, the children, and her mother traveled to Columbus to be near Hayes during his last few days at Camp Jackson. Lucy coaxed her husband into letting her spend the last night with him in camp. In the evening, they visited the men, who were busy preparing food for the trip ahead. The next day, as the regiment's train pulled out of the High Street station, Lucy tried to hide her tears.

She vowed to maintain a brave facade for her children and others around her. In addition to the war, Lucy had to contend with intermittent severe headaches and bouts of rheumatism, which she had experienced since she was a young woman and which pregnancy often exacerbated. There would also be other struggles during the war, which she could not anticipate.

In August, soon after she had parted with Hayes at Camp Jackson, she wrote to him about the men under him, saying, "You know my great desire is that you and Joe [Webb] will constantly feel for the soldiers—do what you can to lighten their hardships." It appears that her husband—a naturally decent man—strove to do so whenever possible.

Already filled with a keen sense of duty to his country, Hayes soon developed a strong attachment to his troops. In comparing his men's camp abilities to those of men from other states, he wrote, "They build quarters, ditches, roads, traps; dig wells, catch fish, kill squirrels, etc., etc., and it is really a new sensation, the affection and pride one feels respecting such a body of men in the aggregate."

The regiment had its first encounter with Confederate troops that September, in what would become West Virginia. Their mission was to secure the Kanawha Valley, guard the railroads, and protect Union supporters. Bordering Ohio, the area was of prime concern to the North. Rebel guerrillas roamed the region; they knew the terrain intimately, were stealthy and unstoppable warriors, and had plenty of sympathizers who sheltered them. Union troops hated and feared them.

Hayes wrote to Lucy that first blood was shed when Confederates fired upon the patrol he was leading. Over the next few weeks, the regiment continued to have intermittent encounters with the enemy. Hayes was philosophical about the dangers he and his men faced. He did not go into deep details in his letters to Lucy, but he did not pretend that there was no danger, any more than Lucy shielded him from news of their sons' various illnesses.

Hayes adapted well to military life. He was disappointed when he was removed from the regiment for several weeks to act as a judge advocate for court martial cases throughout West Virginia. Lucy worried about him traveling so much, believing he would be safer with his regiment. Anxious to be back with his men, he was allowed to return in late October 1861. He brought with him a new rank: colonel.

Back in Cincinnati, Lucy was busy nursing the boys through sickness, tending to household matters, and corresponding with Birchard and other family members about Hayes. Her letters to her husband often discussed politics. Lucy was not a strong Lincoln supporter at first, and Hayes often urged her to be patient with the president's policy, believing he was the best wartime president that the Union could have had. Lucy also worried about what Hayes might do with any escaped slaves who turned themselves in to him. "Above all things Ruddy," she wrote that October, "if a contraband is in Camp—don't let the 23rd Regiment be disgraced by returning [them to their owners] or anything of the kind—Whenever I hear of you—you are *highly* spoken of—so much liked by the men."

In the same letter, Lucy asked if his men needed clothing: "We hear sad accounts of the freezing condition of the men." Her neighbors were forming a circle to sew for troops and wanted to choose a regiment to serve. "Everybody is interested [in sewing for the soldiers]," she wrote again on October 16, "and if you only knew how it saddens us all to hear of the suffering and destitution of our brave men it would make you feel that all feeling was not lost."

Lucy was outraged by stories that some of the injured and dying soldiers in the military hospitals were receiving "unfeeling treatment," and she chafed at not being in a position to go to the hospital and help. Approaching the last few weeks of pregnancy, she was dealing with her own ailments as well as those of her sons.

The Hayes household also was beginning to feel the privations of war. In late October, she received a shipment of apples from Birchard in Fremont. Writing to thank him, she noted that apples in Cincinnati were scarce and expensive. "My three boys would (if they had all they wanted) break me up buying Apples," she wrote. Webb, then about five, was particularly thrilled about having a whole apple to himself.

Although Lucy was not able to see her husband that fall, her brother Joe came to Cincinnati in early December so he could assist when she gave birth. Joseph Thompson was born on December 23. Hayes wrote to her lovingly after learning of the boy's birth, adding, "It is best it was not a daughter. These are no times for women."

One day soon after the baby's birth, a soldier from the 23d arrived at the 6th Street home to deliver a message from Hayes, who had been promoted to lieutenant colonel. The man, who had obviously been celebrating his furlough with alcohol, pushed past the baby nurse to see Lucy personally. Knowing that the tale would get back to her husband, Lucy—whose family abstained from alcohol—asked him not to discipline the soldier because "getting home had quite overcome him." Hayes did not get a furlough to meet his new son until February 1862, when Lucy first saw him with the full beard he had grown since being away.

Her letters—many signed simply "Lu"—were written wherever she was, visiting relatives or at home with her mother and the children. Many were written hastily, with the chaos of a young family at her elbow. Knowing Hayes doted on their sons, she always gave full accounts of what they were doing: Birchie and Webb's lessons, Rud's delight in a toy, a status report on baby Joe, who suffered chronically from colic and whose needs often ended letter-writing for the day.

The letters are also full of reports on friends and neighbors who were war casualties. She visited many soldiers home on furlough, avidly discussing specific battles, rumored promotions, and politics. "You know whenever anyone from the 23rd comes I always ask them to stop with us," she wrote to her uncle on March 16, 1862. Two recent visitors had praised Hayes highly, telling her, "There is no one in the Reg that would not give his life for Col. Hayes . . . if after this length of time all love him and speak well of him—his talent for governing is fixed." Clearly, Lucy believed her husband could have any future he wanted if he survived the war.

More than once, she asked Hayes if he would intercede on behalf of a soldier, even if the man was not in the 23d. Her belief in her husband was strong and intensified as the war progressed. Sometimes she asked if he could help a man find a job or arrange to have a soldier transferred to the 23d so Hayes could look out for him or cut through red tape so that an injured or discharged soldier could get the pay he was due.

Letters to her brother Joe often reminded him of how important his role was in the war. "It is in your power to relieve the suffering of many a poor soldier," she wrote to him on July 28, 1862. "I know that you will try faithfully to do what ever you can. Speak kindly—deal gently with the sick and wounded."

Every soldier she saw on the streets of Cincinnati reminded her of her husband and two brothers in uniform. In mid-May she encountered four soldiers—two sick and two wounded—attempting to get to Chicago. When she saw them, they had gotten to the station too late to buy tickets for the evening train and were sitting dejectedly on the pavement. The doctor attending them was not familiar with Cincinnati and didn't know where he could take them for the night. Lucy invited them all to stay at her home. She helped get them on the streetcar, finished her errands, then took the streetcar home.

Lucy and the cook prepared quarters for the men in the back parlor of the house. They got up early to make sure all the men had coffee by 5:00 A.M., when they had to leave for the train station. "I thought of you in a strange country—wounded and trying to get home," she wrote to Hayes on May 19; "but if any one was kind to you—would I not feel thankful."

Repeatedly in her letters, she asked Hayes and Joe to let her know immediately if they became seriously ill or wounded. She would make arrangements for baby Joe's care and come to them immediately. The almost inevitable day came on September 18; Lucy had just finished a long letter to her husband, in which she wrote, "you do not know how changed your absence makes me feel—a sadness—and oh dearest a fear which I try to banish." There had been newspaper reports the previous week that Hayes had been wounded in battle, and now she learned his injuries were the most severe he had suffered to date.

Hayes had been wounded on September 14 at the Battle of South Mountain in Maryland. General George McClellan had ordered the Union troops to secure Turner's Gap in South Mountain, and Hayes and the 23d were chosen to lead the assault. A musket ball hit Hayes's left arm, leaving a sizable hole, fracturing the bone, and bruising his ribs. Although injured, he continued commanding as well as he could. He was eventually removed from the battle to a field hospital, where Joe Webb tended the wound. Lucy Hayes's biographer, Emily Apt Geer, wrote that "expert treatment by Dr. Webb probably prevented the amputation of the arm." An ambulance then transported him to the community of Middletown, where a local merchant took him into his home to be nursed. Hayes had a telegram sent to Lucy and two other people the next morning.

A mix-up with the telegram led Lucy to believe that her husband was in a hospital in Washington, D.C. She quickly made arrangements for the children's care, then took a stage to Columbus, where Hayes's brother-in-law, William Platt, joined her for the train trip to Washington. The obstacles she faced in locating Hayes became such a part of the family's folklore that when Hayes was in the White House family members persuaded her to have the whole story written down by a White House stenographer with one of those new typewriters.

Distraught over her husband's fate, Lucy forgot to take with her special passes that would allow her and Platt into the military area at the depot. She pretended to be with another party to slip through the restricted area. Even so, it was a week before she and Platt reached Washington. Once in the capitol, they searched numerous hospitals and a hotel where the injured were sometimes tended. No one knew anything about Hayes. At the military hospital that had been set up at the U.S. Patent Office, personnel treated her in a very "cruel and unfeeling manner." Undaunted, the duo kept searching.

Platt finally tracked down the original draft of the telegram where Washington had been substituted for Middletown. They went back to the patent office, hoping to learn more. There Lucy noticed several wounded soldiers with "23" on their hats, waiting on the office steps. When she called out to them, they immediately recognized their leader's wife and told her exactly where to find Hayes. Meanwhile, Hayes was fretting over whether his telegram had reached Lucy. "Had hoped to see her today; probably shan't," he wrote in his diary on September 20. "This hurts me worse than the bullet did."

Three days later, after a long, dusty journey, Lucy and Platt arrived in Frederick, Maryland, the closest stop to Middletown. There they met Joe, who had faithfully ridden over every evening to see if they had yet arrived. When they finally reached Hayes, he was on the mend.

After hearing their story, he joked about their visits to Washington and Baltimore. Lucy was not amused, but she was glad to see her husband.

She learned that the 23d had been the hardest hit of the Union regiments at South Mountain, sustaining 130 casualties, including 32 deaths. Hayes's commanding officer recognized him for having "gallantly and skillfully [brought] his men into action." Anxious to know how the campaign was progressing, the still bed-bound lieutenant colonel paid his host's son a dollar a day to watch for troops marching past and to report on their movements and appearance.

Lucy helped nurse Hayes and also visited wounded soldiers in field hospitals and private homes. "Lucy is here and we are pretty jolly," Hayes wrote to Birchard on September 26. "She visits the wounded and comes back in tears, then we take a little refreshment and get over it." By October 4—his fortieth birthday—Hayes was well enough to tour the battlefield where he had been wounded. Lucy and three men accompanied him. "Hunted up the graves of our gallant boys," he wrote.

The next day, Hayes was well enough to return to Ohio. Six or seven injured soldiers traveled with him and Lucy by train. At one depot where they had to change trains, there were not enough seats in the everyday coaches for the group. Lucy led them into the swankier Pullman car, occupied by wealthy passengers returning from a spa vacation in Saratoga, New York. The looks on the vacationers' faces told Lucy they did not appreciate sharing their car with a bunch of ragtag soldiers. But when a messenger entered the car, paging *Colonel* Hayes, the socialites warmed up, offering the men fresh fruit and other treats. Lucy frostily refused them; she was probably reliving the frustration of having been treated as a nobody by the Washington bureaucrats. To her, every Union soldier deserved respect, regardless of rank, and each soldier's family deserved compassion.

After seven weeks convalescing in Ohio, Hayes returned to the war, joining the 23d at winter quarters in Camp Reynolds, West Virginia. Near year's end, he wrote that many of the men were being sent home and that Lucy could expect to have several turn up for a visit, indicating that this was a typical occurrence. Hayes added that his cook, William T. Crump, would be staying with Lucy and the family for a time. "If you are curious to know how we live, put him in the kitchen a day or two," Hayes suggested. "The boys [the Hayeses' sons] will like him."

When Lucy wrote to him on their tenth anniversary that December, she commented on Hayes's previous praise of his men: "It did me so much good to hear you speak well of the boys . . . watch over them for my sake." The men of the 23d were "our boys" whether they were in the field or home on furlough. Lucy seemed to believe Hayes was her surrogate in the war, protecting the sons of other mothers who waited anxiously at home.

The time spent together during Hayes's convalescence made the subsequent separation more difficult. He and Lucy soon started making plans for her and their four sons to visit camp. While it seems odd today, spouses visiting camp during wartime was a tradition dating to when Martha Washington joined her husband in the field during the Revolution, many times acting as his secretary. Julia Grant also visited General Grant in the field during the Civil War. The Hayeses had always been a close couple; the war made them appreciate each other even more. They strove to be together whenever they could.

By January, the family had moved into one of camp's log cabins. The two-room structure consisted of a bedroom–sitting room connected to a kitchen by a covered passage—very humble surroundings compared to the family home back in Cincinnati. Still, they were happy to be together. They had a "beautiful view, and the roaring of the waters make it very delightful," Lucy wrote to Birchard on January 25, 1863.

The older boys fished, rowed boats, built dams, and enjoyed the outdoors. Still, they had to remain alert to the realities of war. One day when Lucy and her brother Joe had ridden some distance from camp, they discovered that the Union picket lines were gone—they had to make a quick retreat, with Confederate soldiers in pursuit. As spring approached, military activity increased and the family returned home.

Hayes and his command moved to Camp White, opposite Charleston, West Virginia. When Lucy learned in early April that Union forces had turned back a Rebel raid on a strategic point in the Kanawha Valley, she wrote to Hayes of her delight. She also discussed the recent election in which the local Republican ticket had won across the board. She criticized an officer who was leaving his military post to assume his new elected office, but Hayes would soon face the same scenario when friends persuaded him to run for Congress.

Lucy, her mother, and her sons came to Camp White in mid-June. Just a few days after their happy reunion with Hayes, eighteen-month-old baby Joe became very ill. On June 24, he died of dysentery—the same fate as a host of soldiers during the war. Lucy, who thought little Joe resembled Hayes so much, was devastated. "I have hardly seen him," Hayes wrote to Birchard, "and hardly had a father's feeling for him. To me, the suffering of Lucy and the still greater sorrow of his grandmother are the chief affliction." Arrangements were made to ship the body back to Cincinnati, where Lucy's other brother, James, made arrangements for burial at that city's Spring Grove Cemetery. Watching the boat bearing her youngest child sail away was the "bitterest hour" of her life.

Pregnant with the couple's fifth child, Lucy decided that the family should leave Camp White and seek the safer, healthier environment offered by relatives in Chillicothe. There, in July, she witnessed the effects of one of the war's most legendary raids as Confederate general John H. Morgan penetrated Ohio borders and surged north. Hayes commanded two regiments who were in pursuit. In Chillicothe, residents frantically tried to preserve their valuables—sending their horses off into the woods, hiding the family silver in the well.

Accustomed to the better-trained troops of the 23d, Lucy reported somewhat humorously that the "unarmed sheep"—the local militia—were so frightened that when they saw other militiamen, they mistook each other for Morgan's raiders, "and on coming to Paint Creek bridge so terrified the guard that they set the bridge on fire—in an instant the whole was in flames—while Morgan had not even a scout near," she wrote to her husband.

Once the raiders had been routed and Morgan captured, Hayes returned to Camp White. Lucy visited him for a month in the fall, then she, her mother, and the youngest sons—Ruddie and Webb—moved to camp, and Birch stayed in Fremont with Uncle Sardis Birchard. The visit lasted through the winter, with the family becoming an active part of camp life.

The term "camp follower" referred to any woman attached to a camp, whether an officer's wife, a nurse, a laundress, or a prostitute. Naturally, an officer's wife was accorded more respect than the laundress. Lucy, however, good-naturedly helped any way she could. She had her sewing machine shipped out from Cincinnati and installed in the drafty old farmhouse where the family lived in camp. She made miniature bright blue uniforms for her sons, which they proudly wore. She also tended the ill, sewed and mended for the soldiers, and talked to them and counseled the younger men. One of her favorites was Lieutenant McKinley, then about twenty. He spent so many hours tending the camp's primary fire that Lucy nicknamed him Casabianca, after a young French naval hero who refused to leave a burning ship in the late eighteenth century.

While most of the men knew of Lucy, not all recognized her on sight. A young soldier named James Parker learned firsthand of her generosity and good humor. He was perplexed one day because his blouse was badly in need of mending, and he had no idea how to sew. His friends sent him over to Hayes's tent, where, they told him, there was a seamstress who would take care of his problem. Realizing gullible Parker had been set up by his friends, Hayes quietly took the shirt and had Lucy repair it. When Parker showed the men what a good job the camp "seamstress" had done, they decided the joke was on them.

Late in April 1864, the 23d broke camp and headed southeast along the Kanawha River for what would become a memorable and bloody campaign. Lucy and some of the other officers' wives followed them down the Kanawha on a chartered boat for a few days, cheering and waving to the marching troops. The two Hayes boys marched with the troops for most of the time. As the result of the family's extended time in camp, Lucy and Hayes "gained stature in the eyes of future veterans," wrote biographer Geer, "Lucy for her interest in their personal welfare and Rutherford for his firmness and fairness as their commander." Geer also posits that young Webb's camp experience influenced him to do volunteer work with the armed services as an adult.

When the family parted with the regiment, they returned to Chillicothe, where Lucy rented two rooms in a boardinghouse so she could be near relatives in the latter half of her pregnancy. She sent Hayes a flag for his men to "let them know how near they are to me—that not a day passes that our gallant soldiers are not remembered by me." When she learned that the flag was flying in front of headquarters, she told her husband that she had meant it for the soldiers, rather than the staff. Hayes obligingly had the flag taken down and presented to the regiment at a dress parade.

Hayes was now commander of four regiments that made up the First Brigade of infantry, serving under General George Crook. During the spring and summer, Crook's Army of West Virginia, charged with disrupting communications and destroying railroads, proceeded deeper into Virginia. The battles that Hayes fought during this phase of the war would cinch his reputation as a fearless military leader and set him on the path to the White House.

During the Battle of Cloyd's Mountain in May, the 23d led the assault against southern troops. Witnesses described him as being all over the field that day, on foot, "recklessly" leading the men and inspiring them onward. When the Rebels broke and ran, Hayes gathered five hundred men from his brigade and pursued them. It was a grand victory for Crook's Army, due in large part to Hayes and the 23d. The army also sustained heavy losses: 688 casualties total, with the 23d suffering 250 of them.

In July, during the Battle of Winchester, near Kernstown, Virginia, Hayes's leadership and bravery were credited with saving Crook's army of nearly twelve thousand men during a thorough drubbing by General Jubal Early's superior forces of seventeen thousand. In his diary, Hayes wrote that "poor cavalry allowed the general [Crook] to be surprised. . . . My brigade covered the retreat." Poor scouting reports by an insufficiently trained cavalry caused problems. With two of Hayes's brigades under deadly attack by the Rebels, Hayes ordered a withdrawal. His horse was killed in the thick of the battle, and Hayes received a slight shoulder wound. He rallied his men behind a stone wall, where they stood steadfast, allowing the Union forces to retreat in orderly fashion.

That August, Hayes's friends and supporters back in Ohio nominated him as their congressional candidate for Ohio's Second District. With Lucy's encouragement, Hayes accepted but said he would not leave the field to campaign, as some other would-be politicians did. He was elected to Congress that October but did not take office until after the war ended.

While Joe Webb wrote reassuringly to his sister at the end of September 1964 that the Confederates were weary of war, Lucy worried more than ever about her husband and brother surviving. She had been concerned since the beginning of the conflict about her relatives in Kentucky, but now there was another threat, closer to Chillicothe, where she was awaiting the birth of her fifth child. Butternuts—rural Confederate sympathizers—had been threatening to burn the barns of Union loyalists. But in Virginia, Webb saw the tide beginning to turn. "Many

[Confederates] are coming in from the mountain," he wrote on September 28. "All say they are tired of this war. The people are getting tired, and many noted Rebels are willing and anxious to close this out."

The following day, the fifth Hayes child was born in Chillicothe and named George Crook, in honor of his father's general. Two weeks later, the local newspapers were reporting that Hayes had been killed during the Battle of Cedar Creek in Virginia. General Early's troops once again surprised and overwhelmed the Union forces on October 19. Hayes's horse was killed beneath him; he was thrown to the ground and briefly rendered unconscious. Some of his men erroneously reported to the press that Hayes had been killed, and the story was printed. In truth, he rallied, with what he called "only a slight shock." Although he had to elude the Rebels by escaping into a nearby wood, the battle was a Union victory. "We flogged them completely, capturing all their cannon, trains, etc., etc.," he wrote to Lucy. Fortunately, a relative had withheld the incorrect newspaper account from Lucy until the truth could be determined.

Hayes did not muster out of the army until June 1865, but Cedar Creek was his last major battle. He left service with the rank of brevet major general. That May, he and Lucy had attended elaborate army reviews in Washington, sitting in the congressional stands. "While my heart filled with joy at the thought of our mighty country—its victorious noble army—the sad thoughts of thousands who would never gladden home with their presence made the joyful scene mingled with so much sadness—that I could not shake it off," Lucy wrote after the ceremonies. Later that month, she and her husband traveled to Virginia to view the destruction of Richmond and Petersburg. As the full extent of the war's desolation struck her, she became more somber; she excused herself from the 23d's official mustering-out ceremonies in July because of the memories of all the men who had not survived.

As Hayes assumed his congressional duties, Lucy remained keenly interested in the politics and mechanics of reconstruction in the South. Remaining with the family in Cincinnati, she once again found letters an unsatisfactory way to remain close to her husband. She visited him in Washington when she could, but family responsibilities kept her at home most of the time. Little George contracted scarlet fever in the spring of 1866 and died on May 24, at the age of twenty months.

Lucy's mother and Hayes's mother both died that autumn.

Issues related to the war naturally occupied most of Hayes's term in Congress. He and Lucy had long believed that African American men should have the right to vote and that all people of every race should be educated. Hayes joined with other Republican lawmakers to pass the Civil Rights Act of 1866.

In 1867, Hayes was given the chance to run for governor of Ohio. He took it and won. Now he could both be with his family and work on important issues. During two terms as governor, his many proposals included improving conditions at state prisons and welfare institutions. Lucy frequently accompanied him on visits to prisons, hospitals for the mentally ill, and other institutions—at the time a rather unusual step for a governor's wife.

Lucy worked on one of her own pet projects as well: establishing a home for orphans of the Civil War. She was one of several people who helped procure land near Xenia for the institution. The home officially opened as a private establishment at Christmas 1869. Lucy lobbied for it to become a state institution so that more funding would be available in the future.

As governor, Hayes also oversaw the creation of a school for the deaf, a reform school for girls, and the Agricultural and Mechanical College (the nucleus of the future Ohio State University). Lucy was involved in almost every project, often working with the young people at the various institutions. In a letter to his brother-in-law, Hayes wrote that Lucy was teaching the children at the Deaf and Dumb Asylum to make wreaths for Decoration Day, helping lay wreaths on soldiers' graves and working with the boys at the Reform School at Lancaster.

While governor, Hayes also worked for greater civil rights for African Americans and saw black men vote in Ohio for the first time. Neither he nor Lucy ever publicly supported women's suffrage. Hayes held the popular belief that voting in political elections was not compatible with women's roles as mothers and homemakers, and Lucy supported his views on this, as she did regarding other issues throughout their marriage. They may have also believed the issue was too politically volatile, or they may have naively assumed that husbands in general represented their wives' political choices, as was true in their own very close marriage.

Their family continued to grow during this period. Fanny, named after Hayes's beloved deceased sister, was born on September 2, 1867.

Once again, Joe Webb assisted his sister at the birth. Fanny soon became Hayes's darling. Scott Russell was born on February 8, 1871. The couple's last child, Manning Force, was born on August 1, 1873. Lucy was critically ill after the birth, suffering convulsions so severe that she had to be treated with morphine. Although she recovered, little Manning was never a strong baby. He died on August 28, 1874—Lucy's forty-third birthday. The family was then living at Spiegel Grove, the mansion Sardis Birchard had built in Fremont with them in mind. After he died in January 1874, the Hayeses made the estate their permanent home.

They enjoyed their respite from public life for a few years, but by 1875, Hayes and Lucy both thought it was time to return. That fall, he was elected to a third gubernatorial term. Just a few months after he took office, Republican power brokers approached him about running for president. When he agreed to run, numerous veterans' organizations strongly supported him. Despite such backing, Hayes was not the favorite at first. Congressman James G. Blaine of Maine was the favored nominee at the 1876 Republican National Convention, held in Cincinnati. But a large field of candidates, including Senators Oliver P. Morton of Indiana and Roscoe Conkling of New York, split the delegates' votes. As a result, several candidates withdrew, and Hayes won the nomination on the seventh ballot. New York governor Samuel J. Tilden became the Democrat nominee.

The autumn's election was very close and ended with one of the most hotly disputed results in American history. With tallies from three southern states—where each party alleged fraud—still inconclusive, it appeared Tilden was just one electoral vote short of victory. Hayes had lost the popular vote by only 250,000 votes. For the next three months, partisan politics kept the country in an uproar. At home, Lucy followed her husband's lead, keeping quiet about the dispute and proceeding with daily life as normally as possible. As Hayes's most ardent supporter, she must have had a hard time remaining calm. Hayes had been known for his integrity and decency his entire life, and she cherished other people's good opinions of him.

As the months progressed, events took an uglier turn. Threats and warnings of danger began arriving in Hayes's mail in Columbus. As the family ate dinner one evening, a gunshot blasted through a window of their home. It was never known if this was an actual assassination attempt, but after that, Webb—about to turn twenty—insisted on accompanying his father on his nightly walks, armed with a pistol. Scott, just five years old, actively worried about the Democrats killing his father if he were elected. Lucy somehow maintained her sense of humor, at least while trying to reassure her children. In a letter to Birch, who was studying at Harvard, she wrote that she and Hayes had become "*more* and *more* attached to each other" during the election dispute.

By January, a bipartisan Electoral Commission had given power to rule on the disputed electoral votes. That group was plagued by its own set of problems and could not reach a consensus. Inauguration Day, March 4, was fast approaching without a final decision. In the end, the two sides negotiated a compromise: Hayes would be awarded the necessary electoral votes if the Republicans agreed to remove Federal troops from the South. It was supremely ironic that the man who had fought so hard for civil and voting rights—particularly for southern blacks—became the president who ended Reconstruction.

Although Hayes was not shown to be involved in any deceit, many Democrats persisted in referring to him as "His Fraudulency" or "Rutherfraud" during his term in office. Because of the controversy over the election, Hayes pledged that he would not seek another term. Once he was named president-elect, he and Lucy traveled to Washington. He was sworn in on Saturday, March 3, in part because custom did not allow for an inauguration to be held on a Sunday, and in part because the short notice would thwart any disruption by protestors. The ceremony was held in the Red Room of the White House, marking the first time a president took the oath of office there.

During the public inauguration, held March 5 on the East Portico of the Capitol building, Lucy stood at Hayes's side, wearing a simple black dress and bonnet. The details of the ceremony, including Lucy's appearance, were enthusiastically described in newspapers and periodicals across the country. This began Lucy's role as one of the most public First Ladies of that time. For the next four years, she accompanied Hayes on an unprecedented number of official occasions and trips around the country. Perhaps because they hated all the time they had spent apart during the war, the couple stayed together whenever possible. As Hayes's causes were also Lucy's, she was his counselor, encourager, and confidant. "For one who ever saw them together could never think of speaking of them apart," wrote contemporary historian John W. Burgess.

During his term, Hayes pursued issues that had long mattered to him: civil and voting rights, prison reform, improving the lives of the very poor, ending the spoils system of political patronage, and narrowing the chasm that still divided the nation a decade after the war's end—and a century after its founding. With a Democratic House of Representatives and lasting rancor over the election, Hayes was not particularly successful. But he did keep these issues in the public's consciousness and opened the door a bit wider for change in the future.

One issue that arose early in Hayes's administration wasn't on his agenda: temperance. Mention Lucy Hayes's name to anyone today, and the response—if there is one—is "Lemonade Lucy." The image is one of a pucker-faced, priggish sort of woman who tried to keep everyone else from having a good time. The media storm over the Hayeses not serving alcohol in the White House is an good illustration of how a public person's whole existence can reconfigured within the limits of one label.

Sarah Polk had not served alcohol at White House dinners during her husband's administration, and Frances Cleveland pointedly refused to have a wine glass at her place at dinners, yet Lucy is the First Lady most associated with—and ridiculed for—her stand. Hayes announced the no-alcohol policy, but Lucy was certainly involved in establishing it. She had grown up in a temperance home and belonged to a religious denomination that frowned on alcohol consumption. Her grandfather Issac Cook became a noted temperance advocate in the Chillicothe area after joining the Methodist church. According to family lore, he caught a fatal cold at age seventy-five, after riding through a winter storm to lecture on temperance.

But as Geer noted in her biography, Lucy was no fanatic. Hayes had sometimes enjoyed a beer with his friends back in Cincinnati. In camp during the war, promotions were toasted with a drink. Hayes once awarded bottles of wine to winners of a camp contest. Sardis Birchard, the revered uncle, had a respectable wine cellar, to which the Hayes family sometimes made contributions. Lucy simply believed she had the right to not drink alcohol, and other people had the right to do as they chose. But she also knew that alcoholism was a real problem, with widespread—even deadly—consequences. She may have believed she was doing her part simply by modeling a life of temperance. For years, the Women's Christian Temperance Union pressured Lucy to become their champion, even naming some of their groups for her and commissioning an expensive painting of her. But she steadfastly, politely refused their advances.

Because Lucy was college-educated, articulate, and clearly interested in contemporary issues, many female leaders assumed she would actively support their issues, whether the topic was suffrage or temperance. But she wasn't one to be manipulated or maneuvered. Her priorities remained her family, her work with Civil War veterans, and helping the needy. Many times she lent tacit support for a cause simply through her presence, rather than by speaking or lobbying. When an old college friend invited her to attend the 1878 commencement exercises at the Woman's Medical College of Philadelphia to support higher education and careers for women, she declined. However, later in the same year she made a quick visit to the school. At another time, she visited Hampton College, one of the few institutions of higher learning that admitted blacks, thus giving her quiet support.

Although advocates for women's issues were frustrated by Lucy's failure to endorse their causes, writer John B. Roberts contends she may have had more of an impact by remaining true to her principles: "Lucy's subtlety may have been a more effective tactic for changing entrenched nineteenth-century attitudes about sex roles." he wrote. They [modern biographers] miss the point that Lucy accomplished something more zealous advocates could never have achieved—she managed to be a leading role model for women's causes without simultaneously becoming a polarizing and alienating figure." He said Lucy led by example, providing her "brand of quiet social activism."

As his presidency progressed, Hayes and Lucy continued to delight in meeting with veterans. During the hot, humid summer of 1877, Lucy and the family stayed in the presidential cottage on the shady grounds of the National Soldiers' Home outside of Washington. While Hayes worked at the White House, Lucy spent her days visiting disabled men in the home or inviting friends to visit her. She frequently had fresh bouquets cut from the White House's numerous conservatories sent to hospitals around Washington. On Memorial Day that year, she and her daughter, Fanny, joined by a few friends, decorated the graves of the Civil War dead at Arlington Cemetery. At one point, mother and daughter slipped away to place flowers at the Tomb of the Unknown Soldier.

During a trip to Vermont and New Hampshire that August, Hayes and Lucy attended the centennial celebration of the Revolutionary War Battle of Bennington, Vermont. In the fall, they visited a veterans' gathering in Marietta, Ohio. Later, Lucy hosted a supper for veterans of the 23d Ohio at Spiegel Grove in Fremont.

After Christmas, the couple prepared to celebrate their twenty-fifth wedding anniversary. The minister who had married them saw them renew their vows in the Blue Room at the White House. Lucy wore her original simple, white gown—with the seams let out. A highlight of the event was when members of the 23d presented Lucy with a silver plaque that pictured the cabin at Camp Reynolds where she, Hayes, Birch, and Webb had lived for a time in 1863. The plaque was inscribed "To The Mother of Ours From the 23rd O.V.I." The verse on it read:

To thee, our "Mother," on thy silver "troth,"
We bring this token of our love, Thy "boys"
Give greeting unto thee with brimming hearts.

Kind words and gentle, when a gentle word
Was worth the surgery of an hundred schools,
To heal sick thought, and make our bruises whole.

After the family left the White House, Lucy continued to attend annual reunions of the 23d, where, Geer writes, "she reigned as a special favorite of the old comrades." She and her husband visited veterans' groups and attended ceremonies throughout Ohio and West Virginia. In 1883, she received an honorary membership in the Society of the Army of West Virginia. In 1888, the Ohio Woman's Relief Corps presented her with a gold badge in recognition of her service on behalf of Ohio soldiers and their children.

On June 22, 1889, at Spiegel Grove, Lucy suffered a stroke. She had been in her bedroom sewing, watching Fanny and Scott play tennis with their friends outside when the attack happened. Just weeks earlier, she had experienced a smaller stroke, and, as a result, had discussed her end-of-life wishes with Hayes. She died on June 25. The minister who had officiated at her wedding and at the silver anniversary vow renewal conducted her funeral. Members of the 23d marched on either side of her hearse during the drive to Fremont's Oakwood Cemetery.

The family, particularly Hayes, grieved deeply. For thirty-six years, she had been the heartbeat of the family—at the Cincinnati home on 6th Street, in cabins at Civil War camps, at the Columbus house near the state capitol, in the White House, and at Spiegel Grove. Her accomplishments, her grace and kindness, were remembered in obituaries across the country. Perhaps the most meaningful tribute was in a letter that Carl Schurz, former secretary of the Interior, wrote to Hayes: "I have known your family life, and I have never seen anything more beautiful."

Hayes continued to mourn Lucy but remained active for the remainder of his life. Now when he traveled or attended events, Fanny accompanied him. On January 14, 1893, he was at a Cleveland train station when he suffered a heart attack. He demanded to be brought back to Spiegel Grove. There, in the room he and Lucy had shared, he died on January 17. His last words were, "I know I'm going where Lucy is."

What a final reunion they must have had.

| 6 |

MOSES FLEETWOOD WALKER
Writer-Ballplayer

Like modern astronomers finally spotting some overlooked planet, historians have discovered Moses Fleetwood Walker.

Of course, Walker will always be associated with baseball because the game earned him a niche in history—in 1884 he became the first black man to break the big-league color barrier. The achievement "at least kept Walker from slipping through the cracks of time," biographer David W. Zang wrote in *Fleet Walker's Divided Heart: The Life of Baseball's First Black Major Leaguer.*

But Walker is still on the fringe of public perception, as he has been since his baseball career ended in 1889. He remains one of those murky characters who occasionally rise, larger than life, from the depths of history, only to resubmerge and leave us wondering whether they really existed. Yes, Walker did exist, and he is faintly remembered only for his achievements on the diamond. His writings for early black publications, his quest for blacks to emigrate to Africa, and his entrepreneurship during the nickelodeon days were eclipsed by a few turbulent years of his youth.

After his death in 1924, fame continued to elude him. Only seven decades later would Walker begin to receive some recognition, which came in the form of the biography, the Internet reissue of a small book on race that Walker wrote in 1908, a letter of commendation from the commissioner of Major League Baseball, newspaper and online stories, a movement to honor his birthday, a historical marker in Toledo, a marker for his grave, and even his own retro baseball card.

He earned the card for having become the first African American player to sign a contract and play regularly in the big leagues, in baseball's new

Moses Fleetwood Walker in Toledo uniform, 1884. (Authors' collection)

American Association, on May 1, 1884. Soon, at Eclipse Field on the Ohio River in Louisville, he stroked a single for the visiting Toledo Blue Stockings against the Louisville Eclipse—the first minority hit.

Nowadays, baseball historians are beginning to reexamine his career as well as the significance of the American Association, for which Walker played. "He played in forty-two games that year, hitting .263, which was respectable enough, but his defense was ragged," author Cait Murphy wrote in her baseball history *Crazy '08*. She called black ballplayers the invisible men, because they were ignored and shunned. Edward Achorn, author of *The Summer of Beer and Whiskey,* wrote, "Walker had his heart set on becoming a professional baseball player at a time when the doors that had been briefly pried open by Reconstruction were slamming shut again on blacks all over America."

For the record, another player could have been the first black man to enter the big leagues—William Edward White, who played for the Providence Grays on June 21, 1879. But he lasted only one game, and he had no contract. "This is an important distinction," said Craig Brown, a Salem, Ohio, resident and a lecturer in political science and American government at Stark State Community College and the Kent State University. In 2013, Brown learned of Walker's story, became intrigued, and began a public-awareness campaign for the player in his home state. "Like a lot of people, I couldn't believe I'd never heard of him," Brown said. "He's a tragic figure who needs to be remembered."

Because Walker played in baseball's first century, he received little appreciation. Then baseball historians discovered him, writing stories about him on the Internet. Today, all the attention goes to Jackie Robinson, the first African American in the Major Leagues of the modern era. While Robinson was integrating professional baseball in 1947 with the Brooklyn Dodgers, however, memories of the deceased Walker—and the Blue Stockings—were sliding further from the public's mind.

Walker is worth remembering simply because he was interesting. Not only was he the last black man to play for a big-league team in his era, his unwanted presence on the Blue Stockings' roster prompted the fast reestablishment of the color barrier, which would last until Robinson's arrival sixty-three years later. "He's the reason African Americans weren't allowed to play in [white] baseball leagues," said Brown. But Walker made the most of his time in the game, which at the time was the national sport. During his six years in professional baseball, he became half of the first all-black battery in organized ball, when as catcher he teamed with pitcher George Stovey, who that year won thirty-four games for Newark's minor league team. If not for antiblack feelings among so many white players, the battery could have played big-league ball in the days before the Negro leagues were popular.

But Walker was much more than a neglected and gutsy baseball player. He was an inventor, an entertainer, a saloonkeeper, a night-club and hotel owner, a weekly newspaper publisher, a theater owner-operator, and a postal worker. More dramatically, he was imprisoned for tampering with the mail while employed by the post office and tried and acquitted for the murder of a white man who assaulted and attempted to rob him on the street. But in the quicksilver world of history, Fleet Walker will forever be remembered for baseball. He got there through Oberlin College, where he played on the school's base-ball team and attracted attention for his talents.

In his era, the game was much different than in the twentieth and twenty-first centuries. Fans were insanely passionate, but they had much less perception of the "big leagues"—and the minors; the distinction between the two was a bit foggy. Teams played in three leagues—the American Association, the Union Association, and the National League. Only today do we think of the Major Leagues—the ultimate big-time. Back then, fans understood that some teams were wealthy enough to re-cruit and pay the better players; they had the best teams, but their leagues didn't necessarily promote themselves as the biggest and best. Also, fewer home runs were hit then, and the distance between mound and home plate was only fifty feet (in 1893 it was lengthened to sixty feet, six inches). In the era of the single and double, players weren't obsessed with power—at the plate or collectively. Gloves were a "luxury," and they looked more like padded winter gloves made of lambskin than today's baseball gloves. Walker occasionally used one, but he preferred to play barehanded.

Most ballplayers were hard-edged characters. Many were identi-fied by colorful nicknames, such as Lipman "Lip" Pike, a slugger who played with the Cincinnati Red Stockings in 1877 and a part of 1878. On professional teams, most players were white, but generally people of all colors played organized baseball—in minor leagues, industrial leagues, local fraternal leagues, or in pick-up games. Often Fleet was the only black player, or one of only a few, on his teams. Despite little help from trainers and physicians to cope with the physical rigors of the game, a surprising number of men played for many years. Lip Pike, for example, played for nearly a quarter of a century, for various teams. Fleet's career ended prematurely due to racism, his insistence on carrying a revolver, and the minor leagues' decision that they could do without black players. Most black players received little support from their own teammates. This is another way Walker's case differed from Jackie Robinson's: at least once Robinson had become established with the Dodgers, his teammates didn't sabotage his game. Walker had to cope with antagonistic players on his own team as well as opposing teams. Retired player Ned Williamson explained the situation in the October 24, 1891, issue of the popular *Sporting Life:*

> Ballplayers do not burn with a desire to have colored men on the team. It is in fact the deep-seated objection to Afro-Americans that gave rise to the feet-first slide. . . . They learned that trick in the East. The Buffaloes had a Negro for second base [Frank Grant]. He was a few shades blacker than a raven, but was one of the best players in the Eastern League. . . . The players of the opposing team made it a point to spike this brunet Buffalo. They would tarry at second when they might easily make third just to toy with the sensitive shins of the second baseman. The poor man played only two games out of five, the rest of the time he was on crutches. . . . The colored man seldom lasted.

One could assume that such mean-spirited play wore down Walker's spirit until he soured on America, and maybe it did; he didn't discuss it specifically with reporters. Baseball was hard, tough, and rough. So were its players; many of them had reservations about playing with blacks or even having blacks associated with the game. As Craig Brown explained: "Slavery had ended only about twenty years earlier. The mindset of white folks of that era was that African Americans were not only intellectually inferior but physically as well. Today we know this is ridiculous, but back then there were many strange theories about race. Walker was the first guy who showed that African Americans *could* compete. He was a novelty: 'Come see the great black catcher.'"

Though Walker played professionally from only 1883 to 1889, he saw a lot of action during that time. Much of it was in Ohio, where he learned the game from his father, whom black Civil War veterans had tutored in the game's rules. Despite a nomadic summer life as a ballplayer, he chose to live in Ohio.

Ohio was home.

Fleet Walker was born on October 7, 1857, in Mount Pleasant, a small town in east-central Ohio, not far from the Ohio River. His father, Moses W. Walker, was a barrel maker then, and his mother, Caroline O'Harra Walker, a midwife. Both parents were biracial.

Three years later, they moved to Steubenville so Fleet's father could practice medicine. At that time, one didn't need a medical degree to practice medicine—only an apprenticeship. The elder Moses Walker was the only black doctor in the town, which welcomed African American residents. They could attend public events and mingle freely in public. Walker and his younger brother, Weldy Wilberforce Walker, attended the integrated Steubenville High School.

The Walkers were a middle-class black family. By 1870, the family consisted of the parents and five children, who lived in an integrated neighborhood. Mr. Walker became a pastor in the Methodist Episcopal Church. In his free time, he played baseball with his sons.

In 1877, Fleet, a catcher as interested in baseball as anything else, arrived at Oberlin College in Ohio. He weighed 160 pounds and batted and threw right. He was personable and smart. He wanted to be a lawyer. Weldy, who soon joined him at Oberlin, aspired to a career in homeopathic medicine, like his father. Perhaps Oberlin's nondescriminatory admissions policy led the Walkers to believe the college was their doorway to a racially equal world. Nationally known for its early admission of black—and later female—students, Oberlin College became a major part of the Walker sons' lives. Fleet joined the school baseball team, for which he hit leadoff. Weldy later joined him on the team as an outfielder.

When he wasn't playing ball, Walker studied Greek, Latin, German, French, world history, English, rhetoric, astronomy, botany, geology, zoology, and other subjects. He later described his college experience as "excellent." For the Walkers, Oberlin must have been a citadel of justice. Only a couple of decades earlier, in 1859, a federal grand jury had indicted thirty-seven local people for violating the Fugitive Slave Law. The trouble had begun in September 1858 when an escaped slave named

John Price was found living in Oberlin. A federal marshal arrested him and jailed him in the neighboring town of Wellington. The Oberlin locals descended on the jail, liberated Price, and sent him away. Later, the Federals sued Oberlin village and Wellington for violating the Fugitive Slave Law, which had not yet been challenged. The Ohio Supreme Court ruled that the Federals could take the slave. But Oberlin received the praise of an abolitionist northern public for supporting Price, and that may have attracted the Walker brothers.

Their adjustment was undoubtedly difficult. College life was not the real world; as the *Sporting Life* put it as late as April 11, 1891: "Probably in no other business in America is the color line so finely drawn as in baseball. An African who attempts to put on a uniform and go in among a lot of white players is taking his life in his hands."

Meanwhile, that summer Walker accepted a roster spot on the Whites, the baseball team sponsored by Cleveland's White Sewing Machine Company. He met discrimination everywhere. During a trip to Louisville, he was refused service when he attempted to eat breakfast at the Saint Cloud Hotel. Then he went over to the baseball field, where some players for Louisville's Eclipse protested his presence in the Cleveland lineup. The game started with him sitting on the bench. When the Whites' catcher claimed his hands hurt, a team official asked Walker to warm up. The crowd of two thousand to three thousand spectators applauded.

A *Louisville Courier-Journal* story published the following day related that the crowd understood how the Cleveland team was at a disadvantage without its starting catcher.

> The very large crowd of people present . . . at once set up a cry in good nature for "the nigger." Vice President Carroll, of the Eclipse, walked down in the field and called on Walker to come and play.
>
> The quadroon [Walker] was disinclined to do so, after the general ill treatment he had received; but as the game seemed to be in danger of coming to an end, he consented, and started in the catcher's stand. As he passed before the grand stand, he was greeted with cheers, and from the crowd rose cries of "Walker, Walker!" He still hesitated, but finally threw off his coat and vest and stepped out to catch a ball or two and feel the bases.
>
> He made several brilliant throws and fine catches while the game waited. Then Johnnie Reccius and Fritz Pfeffer, of the Eclipse nine,

walked off the field and went to the club house, while others objected to playing that afternoon.

The crowd continued to cheer Walker and insisted that he play. "The objection of the Eclipse players, however, was too much and Walker was compelled to retire. When it was seen that he was not to play, the crowd cheered heartily and very properly hissed the Eclipse club, and jeered their misplays for several innings, while the visitors . . . obviously under disadvantages, were cheered to the echo."

In desperation, the Whites' third baseman finally had to catch. The team lost the game, 6–3.

After two years of valuable experience on the college baseball team, Moses Walker left Oberlin, without graduating, to attend the University of Michigan, where he studied law and played on the baseball team. In the summer of 1882 he returned to Ohio to marry Arabella Taylor, a biracial woman from Xenia. He didn't stay in Michigan for long, however, for he received an invitation to play for the New Castle, Pennsylvania, Neshannocks, nicknamed the Nocks. The local newspapers welcomed Walker and called him the best hitting amateur catcher in the nation. Of course, he was not using a glove most of the time—apparently he could grip the ball better when he caught it barehanded. As a result, his fingers were often swollen and bloody. But he played on and he played while hurt.

Then William Voltz, a former Cleveland sportswriter who had seen the Walkers play for Oberlin, was named manager of the Toledo Blue Stockings in the Northwestern League, a minor league. He asked Walker to be the team's catcher. Walker agreed. But during the 1883 season, a foul ball broke his thumb, which put him out of action. Nonetheless, Walker quickly became known as a hard-hitting catcher who could play good defense.

The pay was better than any salary he could earn elsewhere. The *Sporting Life* reported, "Columbus has a deaf mute and Cleveland a one-armed pitcher, Toledo a colored catcher and Providence a deaf center fielder; and yet these men can earn about $2,000 per annum apiece." That was a good salary by working-class standards. Walker earned his money that 1883 season, hitting .251 in 152 at bats, swinging four home runs, knocking in twenty-three runs, stealing forty-four bases, and scoring forty-five runs in sixty games. In this era, baseballs were not made to fly out of ballparks, and home runs were often panned by the veterans, who specialized in hitting singles and doubles. While he played in the Northwestern League's medium-sized cities such as Peoria and Springfield, Illinois; Fort Wayne, Indiana; and Grand Rapids, Michigan, Walker longed for the bigger cities and their more prominent teams.

The big-time arrived at an exhibition game in August 1883, in the form of the Chicago White Stockings and its manager, Adrian C. "Cap" Anson. Anson would become Walker's—and any dark-skinned player's—nemesis. The White Stockings, a National League team, came to Toledo to play the Blue Stockings. The Blue Stockings and its management, led by a Charlie Morton, believed the team was ready to compete in the big leagues. Their players were good enough, and the crowds were large.

But the day Anson arrived, Walker's hands were injured, so he couldn't catch and must have had a hard time gripping a bat. Anson didn't care; he wasn't accustomed to seeing African American players on the field. A few played in the minor leagues and for local city teams, but not in the big leagues. Anson demanded that Walker not play at all because he was black; he even threatened to call off the game if Walker was in the lineup. Just to irritate Anson, Morton ordered Walker to play right field. When told Chicago would forfeit the game and the gate receipts, Anson backed down. He said, "We'll play this here game, but won't play never no more with the nigger in."

Walker played the entire game in right field, making no errors. The White Stockings defeated the Blue Stockings, 7–6.

In 1884, buoyed by the Blue Stockings' strong performance against a big-league team and its continued success against its opponents in the Northwestern League, Toledo management entered the American Association. Then only two years old, the association was one of three major leagues of the time; the others were the National League and the weaker Union Association. The Blue Stockings' American Association opponents were the New York Metropolitans, Columbus Buckeyes, Louisville Eclipse, St. Louis Browns, Cincinnati Red Stockings, Baltimore Orioles, Philadelphia Athletics, Brooklyn Atlantics, Richmond Virginians, Pittsburgh Alleghenies, Indianapolis Hoosiers, and Washington Nationals. The American Association was nicknamed the "beer and whiskey league" because a number of its club owners were brewery and distillery magnates who sold beer to fans and played games on Sunday. That year, the Blue Stockings retained a few of their 1883 players, including Fleet Walker, and signed many new and more talented ones.

In the majors, the salaries were higher, the players better, and the crowds larger. The game itself was still rough, tough, and filled with boozers and brawlers. Players took the game seriously and openly disliked their opponents. Routinely, they were arrested for violating laws prohibiting baseball on Sunday. Catchers usually volunteered to be arrested in place of the managers. Moses Walker was no exception.

At home in Toledo, the fans cheered Walker. On the road, he received mixed messages—home crowds cheered and jeered when he came to the plate. Some groups of black fans traveled to games to give him confidence. But in Richmond, the manager received a letter demanding that Walker be benched during his time in town—or else. He couldn't play anyway. He was injured again.

Overall, however, the fans appreciated his prowess as a catcher. One baseball poet celebrated Walker:

There was a catcher named Walker,
Who behind the plate is a corker.
He throws to a base with ease and grace,
And steals 'round the bags like a stalker.

That year, 1884, the Blue Stockings went to play in Chicago, but this time Anson didn't have to protest Fleet Walker's presence. His hands were injured again, so the backup, Jimmy McGuire, caught. Several months prior to the game, Chicago's team management had written to the Blue Stockings and asked that any black players be benched while playing the White Stockings. The Chicago management took no responsibility, blaming the team's players.

Anson, the former star first baseman, who is now in the Baseball Hall of Fame, didn't singlehandedly chase black players out of big-league baseball, but he was influential, and he had help from owners, fans, and society. Many other white players disliked their black counterparts and sought to disrupt their play. Tony Mulane, a native of Cork, Ireland, didn't want to play with a black man, let alone pitch to one. Mulane was a star pitcher for the Blue Stockings, but a roughneck. He said Walker was the best catcher he had ever played with, but he could not bring himself to cooperate with his teammate. For example, when Walker would call for a curveball, Mulane would throw a fastball. All that season, he threw any kind of pitch he wanted to Walker, to surprise him. This had to contribute to Walker's injuries—as well as his number of passed balls.

As a batter that season, Walker also became a human target for anyone's baseballs. Struck in the abdomen, he suffered a broken rib. (He wore no chest protector, although they were in limited use by then.) Injuries hobbled other teammates as well, and the Blue Stockings needed good players so badly that they signed Weldy Walker to play outfield. Nevertheless, the team finished in eighth place, winning forty-six and losing fifty-eight. (In the 1884 season, the Metropolitans finished first and Columbus second.) Fleet Walker batted well enough, hitting .263, the second highest average on the team that season. Because of his many injuries that season and the club's financial reversal, the Blue Stockings released Walker in September, having cut Weldy in August.

The catcher was out of baseball, the game he loved.

Three months later, Fleet was hired as a postal clerk in Toledo, and Weldy returned to Steubenville to open a restaurant. The Blue Stockings, which would last only one more season, didn't want either player back because the team was nearly broke. But Fleet Walker could not walk away from baseball so easily. He found work with minor-league teams, including the Cleveland Forest Cities of the Western League in 1885, the Waterbury Brassmen of the Eastern League in 1886, and the Newark Little Giants of the International League in 1887. That year, Walker stole thirty-six bases for the Little Giants and hit .264. He also suffered additional harassment from Cap Anson, whose White Stockings arrived for an exhibition game. Probably to appease Anson, Newark benched Walker and George Stovey, the team's most important pitcher. Anson's boys won the game.

By 1888, Walker was playing with the Syracuse Stars, champions of the International Association that year. Walker hit only .170, but he stole thirty-four bases in seventy-seven games and was the team's main catcher. The *Sporting Life* reported on October 3: "The Syracuse Stars . . . returned home from Rochester Saturday night last and were given a royal reception. The team . . . were escorted to carriages amid fireworks, booming cannon and shouts of thousands of citizens. A line of marchers was then taken up through the principal streets. . . . Over 25,000 were out to see the show. . . . Catcher Moses Walker, of the Star team, returned thanks to the directors and citizens on behalf of himself and fellow players and everyone was happy."

The next year, the American Association returned to its policy of unofficially prohibiting blacks from playing on its teams. The National League had banned them starting in 1876. When the Union League went out of business, its out-of-work players provided more available white talent for teams in both leagues—blacks simply weren't needed.

By 1887, an estimated twenty black players played for minor-league teams. People came out to see them out of curiosity. "The beginning of the end for Blacks in organized ball was in 1887 when Dug Crothers was suspended for refusing to sit for a photograph because a Black was in it," Ulish Carter wrote in a 1974 story in the *Pittsburgh Courier.* "After several of the white players in the league complained, the International League, which was on a minor league level, held a meeting in mid-season and it was decided that no more Black contracts would be signed." The International had about eight black players that year; perhaps it was sensitive to criticism from the *Sporting Life,* which wondered if the League would change its name to the Colored League. "How far will this mania for engaging colored players go?" the publication asked.

By the start of the 1888 season, only three black players were in all of white baseball—minor and major leagues. By the early 1890s, Carter said, most black players had given up on playing with the white teams, so they entered the Negro Leagues. As a result, the Negro Leagues began to expand across the country, with teams popping up in Cleveland and Cincinnati.

In 1891, Walker's life changed. He had been drinking alcohol more often (a habit he picked up from other ballplayers), and his family knew it. He continued to live in Syracuse, where he had last played. Despite his drinking, he entered a more cerebral period, receiving a patent for an exploding artillery shell and other devices, while he grew more introspective about race issues. Then he was arrested for the April 9 stabbing death of a local white man. The incident occurred when Walker was searching the taverns of the Seventh Ward looking for his former Syracuse Stars manager, "Icewater" Joe Simmons. After drinking several beers, Walker began walking home. One man in a group threw a rock and hit him on the back of the head. Then the group surrounded him, making racial slurs. A convicted burglar named Patrick "Curly" Murray tried to rob him. In the struggle, Walker fatally stabbed him; he was charged with second-degree murder. District Attorney T. E. Hancock noted Walker's "peculiar disposition" and added that if he "magnifies every trivial incident into a cause for crime, then he ought not to touch [alcohol]." Nevertheless, an all-white jury acquitted him and newspapers took his side. The judge told him to stop drinking, and then shook hands with Mrs. Walker. Walker thanked each juror personally.

The bad times weren't over yet. In 1895, Arabella "Bella" Walker died of cancer, leaving him with two sons and a daughter. He wanted a distraction, so he began considering changes in his life, including his occupation and where he lived.

Three years later, he married Ednah Taylor, whom he had also met at Oberlin years earlier. By 1902, the Walkers were living in Cadiz, Ohio, and singing and giving exhibitions of Edison's kinetoscope, which played early films. He and Ednah toured Ohio, Pennsylvania, and Indiana, giving lectures and entertaining in churches, singing and acting. Walker also published a weekly black newspaper called the *Equator*. Walker, whose byline was "M.F." instead of "Moses Fleetwood," owned the paper with Weldy. Two years later, Walker and his wife assumed proprietorship of the Cadiz Opera House, where they also lived. The couple presented movies, plays, operas, and lectures and rented the place for independent presentations of vaudevillians and minstrel actors. By 1905, Walker had joined the nickelodeon craze, turning Walker's Opera House into a theater. He brought the movies to Cadiz, for citizens of all races. Meanwhile, he worked on more inventions, including several that would help make the showing of films more convenient for the projectionist.

In 1908, Weldy Walker published his brother's brief book, *Our Home Colony: A Treatise on the Past, Present, and Future of the Negro Race in America*. The forty-seven-page publication—a well-written and thoughtful treatise on racial issues—claimed that blacks and whites could never live in harmony in the United States. Some people took offense. Writer Barry Regan believes the book "caused American society in the early twentieth century to diminish his [Walker's] achievements to the point where history no longer remembers him."

What did Walker say that made him so controversial? He stated that black Americans could find "superior advantages, and better opportunities, on the shores of old Africa." But what caught more attention was his idea that "the Negro should be taught he is an alien and always will be regarded as such in this country, and that equal social, industrial, and political rights can never be given them."

Walker maintained that it wasn't necessary to remove African Americans immediately, but the time was coming when it would be beneficial to the nation to do so. Possibly foreseeing the strife of the 1960s, he wrote, "The Negro race will be a menace and the source of discontent as long as it remains in large numbers in the United States. The time is growing very near when the whites . . . must either settle this [racial divide] problem by deportation, or else be willing to accept a reign of terror such as the world has never seen in a civilized country." No one knows how long it took Walker to conclude this, but it could have been based on his time in baseball.

"The only practical and permanent solution of the present and future race troubles in the United States is entire separation by Emigration of the Negro from America," he wrote. "Even forced Emigration . . . would be better for all than the continued present relations of the races; but there would be no necessity for force if the proper measures are taken and Negroes are offered reasonable help to return to their native land."

Walker's playing days gradually faded to distant memories for most people. On August 30, 1913, the *Sporting News* remembered him with these words: "'Fleet' never wore a catcher's mitt. . . . Walker was a marvelous player, as every old-timer knows. . . . Every club Walker played with won the flag with the exception of his second season in Toledo."

Moses Fleetwood Walker died of pneumonia on May 11, 1924, not long after his wife had died and just as a new baseball season was starting. He was sixty-seven. "He died alone in Cleveland, clerking in a pool hall," Craig Brown said. "He's someone who is easy to forget, but he should not be forgotten."

Perhaps he wanted to remain unknown. Though he could have afforded a simple stone, he chose to be buried in an unmarked grave in Steubenville's Union Cemetery.

In 1990, Oberlin College's Heisman Club, an athletic support group, heard about the situation and donated time and money to research Walker's career and purchase a headstone for him. He was elected to Oberlin's Hall of Fame. The group scheduled a graveside ceremony, and then–baseball commissioner Fay Vincent sent a letter listing Walker's baseball accomplishments. School athletic director James Foels loaded the 350-pound marker into his pickup truck and took it to Walker's grave for the ceremony. The marker reads that Walker was the "first black Major League baseball player in USA." At the gravesite, his grandniece, Sara Freeman, said, "The family always knew that Moses was a ballplayer, of course, but we never really realized how important he was."

In February 2014, the state representative Steve Slesnick, a Canton Democrat, introduced House Bill 436, to designate October 7, Walker's birthday, as Moses Fleetwood Walker Day every year in Ohio. Slesnick submitted the proposal to legislators at the request of some students at the Kent State University and Stark State College who had learned about Walker from their professor, Craig Brown. As Brown told the *Toledo Blade,* "Justice is slow, but justice still happens anyhow." The students vow not to give up until Moses Fleetwood Walker Day is celebrated through Ohio.

As for Moses Walker, the score of life was finally evened in August 2014, when he achieved every modern baseball fan's dream. The Toledo Mud Hens, a minor-league team, sponsored Moses Walker Bobblehead Night.

It was an excellent likeness of him, too.

ZACHARY LANSDOWNE
Airship Commander

Lieutenant Commander Zachary Lansdowne never wanted to be an international story. He wanted any attention to go to his stately dirigibles, those behemoths that glided across America's skies in the 1920s. Unfortunately, Lansdowne would become a big story anyway, dying in what a story on the Department of the Navy Web site calls "the nation's most dramatic aviation disaster yet"—the crash of the USS *Shenandoah* on September 3, 1925, in Noble County, Ohio.

Until its crash, the *Shenandoah*, the pride of America and the first dirigible made in the United States, had been called the safest dirigible in the world, because its helium gas could not explode. The world's only known large supplies of the gas had been recently discovered in petroleum fields at Fort Worth, Texas, a fact not lost on naval leaders, who envisioned the airship as a major showpiece as well as a practical military craft.

Reputation was not the only thing big about the *Shenandoah*. The infatuated public had difficulty comprehending how anything so large could fly: forty-one tons, nearly 682 feet long, and 80 feet in diameter. The ship came with five three-hundred-horsepower, six-cylinder Packard gasoline motors, manufactured by the Hartzell Propellor Company in Piqua, Ohio. The motors could push the ship to a comfortable cruising speed of seventy miles per hour. Inside, the airship was crammed with twenty gas cells fashioned from the intestines of nine hundred thousand cattle. It was the first dirigible to use helium—2.3 million cubic feet of it. But helium was expensive—more than ten times the price of the highly flammable hydrogen, the most-used agent for ascension.

Zachary Lansdowne in civilian clothes, 1924. (Authors' collection)

As predicted, the *Shenandoah* did not blow up. Instead, wind blew it apart. The accident brought the proper and humble officer more attention than he would ever have imagined; his photograph even appeared on the cover of *Time* magazine. At the same moment, his close friend and defender, Colonel William "Billy" Mitchell, was court-martialed, and there was a federal investigation into Lansdowne's handling of America's most popular dirigible.

Today Lansdowne is a minor figure in aviation history, but in the autumn of 1925, headlines blared his name. Succeeding years of flight history have left Lansdowne in the shadows and two *Shenandoah* monuments at the main crash site. "Few people have heard of Commander Lansdowne," said Don Harless, a docent at the Garst Museum in Greenville, Lansdowne's hometown in Darke County. "But if things had gone the other way and dirigible flight had turned out to be safer, the story might be different."

Instead, *Shenandoah* crashed, a sad, costly mistake that taught all dirigible commanders a lesson: don't fly anywhere near a storm. Of course, Lansdowne already knew better; he had even warned the Navy of his airship's potential destruction by high winds. Only a year earlier he had escaped a serious situation, when a thunderstorm blew the big airship away from its mooring mast in Lakehurst, New Jersey. He later convinced officials to cancel plans for a voyage to the Artic, which President Calvin Coolidge had suggested. Later, summer storms convinced them to also cancel plans for the impending three-thousand-mile goodwill flight across the Midwest, but then the navy reversed its decision and ordered Lansdowne to procede with it on September 2, 1925. The airship was scheduled to be away for six days, flying over forty cities and being exhibited by air at state fairs.

The American public wanted a peek at any dirigible—the largest thing in the skies. It had been invented in 1900 by retired Prussian army officer Count Ferdinand Graf von Zeppelin. In the years just before the invention of the airplane, he equipped a long, rigid, cigar-shaped, gas-filled bag with a motor—and he flew it. Intrigued, he continued to perfect more lighter-than-air craft, named in his honor.

Under Zeppelin's guidance, Germany became the most successful builder of dirigibles. During World War I, these were used as a terror weapon, having become sophisticated enough to fly from Germany to

England to drop bombs on London. For a time, the zeppelin competed with fixed-wing aircraft for dominance of the skies, but airplanes were cheaper to build and less dangerous. After the war, the Germans built some of America's dirigibles, which the navy at first also called zeppelins.

By the early 1920s, the American public was entranced by the grace of any flying dirigible, but most particularly that of the *Shenandoah*. The nation's first American-made dirigible used new, high-tech parts and nonflammable helium instead of the explosive hydrogen gas originally used in the zeppelins. The navy wanted to make sure it didn't repeat the army's mistake with its dirigible *Roma,* which crashed near Hampton Roads, Virginia, in 1922, killing thirty-four men. So naval leaders were careful, at first sending the *Shenandoah* up only when the weather seemed calm.

Unlike its smaller cousin, the blimp, essentially a big balloon, the dirigible was a rigid airship with a metal frame inside its long exterior, with huge cells inside to hold the gas needed to lift it high into the sky. Any dirigible commander, pilot, or crewman would be insulted to hear someone say he was a blimp man: blimps were passive bags of air, while dirigibles were the dragons of the sky, capable of making war, flying passengers to far-flung destinations, and entertaining the public.

Unlike most other dirigible disasters, the *Shenandoah* crash did not end in fire, because no hydrogen was on board. This saved many members of the forty-two-man crew. The wind did considerable damage, however, sending debris over a twelve-mile stretch between the small towns of Ava and Caldwell, in southeast Ohio.

The *Shenandoah*'s shocking and sudden demise brought native son Lansdowne back to Ohio forever—the crash will always be Ohio's most tragic dirigible disaster. It killed Lansdowne and thirteen members of his crew. Most of the survivors were in the front and rear sections of the dirigible; both sections stayed aloft after wind tore the craft apart. Lansdowne's last words, in a radio message, were: "I'm losing my seat." He and his officers came crashing to earth in the control car, which hung from cables beneath the ship; a monument now marks the spot where the car hit the earth.

The control car landed in a cornfield owned by a farmer named T. R. Davis and rented by a tenant farmer, Andy Gamary, who woke up at 5:30 that morning when he heard the storm. Today an impressive granite marker, erected in 1976 by the Noble County Bicentennial Commission, stands near Gamary's house. Another lists the fourteen men who died in the crash. On the field, a crudely carved sandstone boulder reads: THIS IS THE SPOT WHERE LANSDOWNE DIED.

Lansdowne and his men were yanked from the sky by a squall line—a narrow weather zone inhabited by strong and abruptly shifting pressure and decreasing temperatures; squall lines occur frequently before a cold front enters. Even today, most Ohioans probably don't know the technical definition of squall, although they have seen them in action. The squall in the early hours of September 3, 1925, brought unusually strong winds, of up to seventy miles per hour, and rapidly shifting clouds followed by a storm.

A man named C. L. Arthur was looking for the airship that morning; he wanted to see what it looked like. Then he saw it—sailing through the clouds near Belle Valley, Ohio. "It was a beautiful thing as it glided through the sky and we stood there, almost overawed, by the thing as it came on through the sky and toward the spot where we were standing," he said in *National Geographic* in 1925. "Then suddenly there was a roar that resounded over the countryside and the giant bag [dirigible hull] split . . . but even after it was chopped in two, this main part of the ship did not crash to the earth; it seemed to stay up here, motionless for some time, and then gradually sink." One of the airship's three pieces remained aloft for an hour before the crew managed to release enough helium to let their section settle to the ground.

In a macabre hunt for souvenirs and information, thousands of people swarmed the crash site, like ants drawn to a picnic. Meanwhile, reporters arrived in Noble County to interview eyewitnesses. Airplanes flew over the site, with photographers capturing images of the wreck. Farmers charged sightseers a dollar a car to park in their fields, and an additional twenty-five cents to walk to the wreckage. Other entrepreneurs sold lemonade, water, food, ice cream, and hastily made postcards of the twisted remains. Like vultures, the visitors picked at the wreckage, removing anything that wasn't too heavy to carry, including hull fabric, food, and motors. Any item from the airship was a souvenir or something to recycle. Nothing was too personal; one scavenger, who saw Lansdowne's body where it lay in a cornfield, half a mile from the crash site, stole his eighteen-karat gold pocket watch, a gift from the people of Greenville.

The navy sent a team to Noble County to recover as much of the debris and personal items as possible, but much was already gone. Aghast at the looters, the *New York Times* criticized the community, in an editorial titled "Ohio Manners and Morals."

Reprimands aside, the more ambitious hunters still came with shovels, picks, and axes to help break up pieces of the *Shenandoah*. They even removed clothes and jewelry from the wreckage—and the dead bodies. Scavengers also stole Lansdowne's Naval Academy ring, and, in the frenzy to get more jewelry, they hacked up the body of one unfortunate member of his crew. (Lansdowne's ring was later found in a garden in a nearby town.)

The day after the wreck, the *Cincinnati Enquirer* told the story on page one:

Craft Caught in Ohio Gale

———

Front Cabin Is Death Trap for
Commander and 12 Others.

———

Score Ride Ten Miles on Wreckage
And Descend without Injury.

———

Third Section Alights in Grove with
Three Clinging to Torn Rigging.

———

"Line Squall" Brings End to Pride of Navy—
Greenville Officer Perishes with Crew—
Heroism of Aviators Stand Out in Accident—
Fliers Realized Predicament
And Tried to Save Ship, 'Tis Said.

But the tragedy was more than just another airship disaster. It helped discourage pubic support for further dirigible use. Later, a naval panel determined that Mother Nature had caused the crash. Strong Ohio winds had ripped apart the ship's silver-painted cotton exterior and torn the great airship in two. An obsessed and thieving public took care of the rest of it. As historian John Toland once wrote, the two parts of the *Shenandoah* "looked like skeletons picked to the bone."

The crash occurred only two years and one day after the multimillion-dollar airship's maiden voyage, on September 3, 1923, at Lakehurst, New Jersey. The ship had been barely broken in.

Dirigible expert Zachary Lansdowne was born on December 1, 1888, in his grandparents' home at 338 East 3rd Street in Greenville. He was the youngest son of James M. Lansdowne, who began his career as a cashier at the Farmers' National Bank, and Elizabeth Knox Lansdowne.

He attended the Episcopal Church and Greenville schools. His two older brothers were John, born in 1878, and Harry, born in 1880. John, a businessman, eventually moved to Cincinnati; Harry, a mining engineer, to Utah. Their mother continued to live in town after the death of her husband.

After Lansdowne graduated from high school in Greenville in 1905, Congressman Harvey Garker appointed him to the U.S. Naval Academy. The recommendation came easily, for he was a bright young man and a nephew of Admiral Harry Knox (his mother's brother) and a descendant of the Calvinist reformer John Knox. Lansdowne entered the Naval Academy that fall. Before graduating in 1909, he had read Jane's *All the World's Airships* and become fascinated by dirigibles. At that moment, he knew what he wanted to do, but his mother, to whom he was close, thought flying too risky. Out of respect for her, he left for two years as ensign aboard the battleship USS *Virginia*.

In 1913, the navy sent him back to Ohio, to become a recruiter in Cleveland. There he met and married Ellen MacKinmon, a Wisconsin native. They had a son, Falkland "Mac" Lansdowne, who was only one year old when his mother died, at just twenty-eight, in 1916. The couple had been married only three years.

Seeking a change of scenery after her death, Lansdowne asked for a transfer to the naval-aviation training program in Pensacola, Florida. Months later, he became the United States Navy's 105th trained aviator, learning to fly a Curtis flying boat. In August 1917, he left for Akron and the navy's lighter-than-air training program, which continued to fascinate him; something about the size and speed of the airships intrigued him. The rubber-manufacturing city in northeast Ohio was also a center for the navy's balloon and dirigible operations.

Recognizing his interest and ability, the navy soon sent Lansdowne to Wormwood, England, to learn more about dirigibles. By World War

I, the British were ahead of the Americans in dirigible manufacturing, knowing they had to keep up with rival Germany. "During this time he [Lansdowne] became well-acquainted with his British airship contemporaries, who recognized in him a leading expert in lighter-than-air development," wrote Nick Walmsley, editor of the British periodical *Dirigible: The Journal of the Airship and Balloon Museum.*

England, Germany, Italy, France, and other European countries were all more advanced in dirigible technology than the United States. Airplanes were not yet powerful or sophisticated enough to fly extremely long distances and carry a crew or dozens of passengers. But the dirigible could.

In 1918, when America finally entered World War I, Lansdowne was given command of the United States Naval Aviation Base at Guipavas, near Brest, France. The base initiated convoy patrols in western waters. When the base was closed in 1919, the British recognized Lansdowne's growing knowledge in lighter-than-air craft, Walmsley said, and asked him to join them in developing postwar dirigibles. That July, he became the first American—a "guest," they called him—to fly nonstop across the Atlantic in the newly built British dirigible R-34, which was 634 feet long. The voyage took 108 days and twelve hours. For his contributions to the R-34's successful mission and other acts, Lansdowne received several medals, including the Air Force Cross from the King of England and the Navy Cross from the United States.

Acknowledging his talents, the navy made him commanding officer of the naval station at Akron. Two years later, he left for a new job—White House military aide. During his time in Washington, D.C., he met Margaret "Betsy" Seldon, nineteen, who worked in the office of the new Federal Bureau of Investigation. Lansdowne asked her to lunch; she accepted. When she realized a bureau agent was observing them, she complained to director J. Edgar Hoover, who explained that a third person at the lunch, Lansdowne's high school friend Kurt Winder from Greenville, was a suspected communist sympathizer. After that, every time Hoover would see her, he would ask, "And whom are you lunching with now, my lass?"

Lansdowne and Seldon were married December 7, 1921, at the Washington Cathedral. Two months later, the couple left for Lansdowne's latest assignment—assistant naval attaché in Berlin. There, he often visited the zeppelin works to monitor construction of the new ZR-3, which Walmsley called a war prize awarded to the United States at the Treaty of Versailles. Soon this German airship would become America's second dirigible, the USS *Los Angeles,* joining the service just after the *Shenandoah.*

Meanwhile in Berlin, the Lansdownes welcomed a daughter, Peggy, born on October 7, 1922. (In 1942, she would christen the USS *Lansdowne,* a destroyer named for her late father. Ironically, it would become known as the "Lucky L," for its charmed tenure in the Atlantic, where it sank two German U-boats, and in the Pacific Theater, where it received twelve battle stars. It also received fame for taking Japanese envoys to the USS *Missouri* to sign the surrender documents that ended World War II. The *Lansdowne* featured a poignant good luck charm—Zachary Lansdowne's class ring, displayed courtesy of the family. The destroyer was scrapped in 1973, by which time Lansdowne's name had faded from the public memory.)

In 1924, at age thirty-six, Lieutenant Lansdowne took command of the new *Shenandoah,* and he guided the nation's premier airship to California and other places and through all kinds of weather. By then, he looked much older than his years. He stood just over six feet tall and had eyes that seemed to look through people. He had a thin, narrow face and receding hairline. He was stern, reserved, and quiet, and preferred to deal with his men personally. They liked him for his straightforward ways and high expectations. Toland once described the commander as "a tall, rangy, rawboned man who had a reputation as a strict disciplinarian aloft, but also as an understanding and affable officer who lent a sympathetic ear to the personal problems of the crew."

His airship was a behemoth. Even at less than capacity, the *Shenandoah* could hold more than nine thousand pounds of water and sixteen thousand pounds of gasoline. Its midsection diameter was seventy-eight feet, nine inches, and its normal cruising speed was sixty miles per hour. The crew lived in quarters in the keel corridor. Stars and Stripes were painted on the end of the vertical rudder, and a United States Navy star graced each side of the ship, whose Native American name, in Algonquian, meant Daughter of the Stars.

"This big airship," Lansdowne told *National Geographic,* "is in reality a floating laboratory, which by its construction and operation is developing not only into a new element of national defense, but is testing the efficiency and adaptability of allied industries which in time will become of extreme importance in . . . air navigation as a commercial enterprise."

Stripped of its cotton exterior, the *Shenandoah* looked like a big skeleton. Girders—made of Alcoa's special Duralumin, a new lighter-weight alloy developed by Alcoa especially for this purpose—covered every part of the framework. At the time, the navy believed airships would become a successful adjunct to airplanes. In 1919, Congress agreed, authorizing money for the first American-built dirigible. But construction had to be delayed while a huge hangar was built in Lakehurst, New Jersey. It cost $3.5 million—an expensive undertaking in those days.

America wanted to finally enter the dirigible era because other nations were continuing to use rigid airships for military and nonmilitary purposes. They were expensive, time-consuming, and labor intensive, requiring a ground crew of three hundred to four hundred men. The nation's first, the *Shenandoah,* initially called ZR-1 (Zeppelin Rigid One), was built similarly to a German zeppelin named L-49, captured in France during World War I. Many of that ship's features were copied for the ZR-1. But Lansdowne and American designers had added improvements, making their airship larger, better, and safer. It could carry more gas—the new and inflammable helium. Its motors—in part also made of Duralumin—were fitted at the navy's dirigible headquarters in Lakehurst. The ship, as tall as an eight-story building, had a cruising radius of nearly four thousand miles. Its bow was expanded to allow mooring to a mast. And the controls for its fins and rudder were redesigned to conform to wind tunnel tests.

American naval engineers changed one important feature: they used helium instead of natural gas to inflate the rigid airship. Helium could not be set on fire—under any circumstance. This was a major advancement, as earlier dirigibles were prone to catching fire and exploding. Engineers also redesigned the airship's fins and rudders and built an in-flight walkway for inspection on top of the ship. After waiting for months for Congress to approve funds to build the ship, workers finally began constructing the *Shenandoah* in 1920 at Philadelphia's large naval aircraft factory. The airship's parts were manufactured in Philadelphia and at the navy's lighter-than-air complex in Akron.

Two decades after the American wonder was built, aviation writer Lewis H. Gray explained the *Shenandoah*'s purpose: "Her official mission was to serve as a scout for the fleet, and she made several flights scouting and reporting on an imaginary enemy. But *Shenandoah* had, by the very fact that she was there, another role to fulfill: that of a national symbol. Requests literally poured into the Navy Department asking the ship to fly over this and that town, and to generally display herself as a tribute to Yankee ingenuity." He ended by saying he hoped that "this dirigible will help sustain the dream of all airshipmen, past and present, who believe in the ultimate worth of rigid airships."

Gray noted that the *Shenandoah* had many firsts during its brief career: it was the first "made-in-USA rigid," the first rigid to be inflated with helium, and the first to be moored to a floating mast—on the naval oiler USS *Patoka*. The mooring was celebrated with a feature story in the January 1925 issue of *National Geographic*. (In that story, the magazine also noted, with what would later seem irony, "Lansdowne is one of the types who foresees difficulties and does not get excited, but deftly and quick avoids them.")

The *Shenandoah*'s helium feature separated the American wonder from the many stately but dangerous European dirigibles. Out of an estimated 190 dirigibles built from the early 1900s through 1937, 110 had gone down, usually in flames. In the public's mind, the *Shenandoah* was not supposed to end in disaster. The public believed that since it could not suffer the usual flaming fate of other dirigibles, it was unbreakable. A month after the *Shenandoah* first took flight, the French dirigible *Dixmude* exploded and crashed off the coast of Sicily. Yet Americans remained confident: their dirigible would not burn.

A monument to Zachary Lansdowne stands behind the spacious Garst Museum, operated by the Darke County Historical Society at 205 North Broadway in Greenville. Indoors, curators devote a corner to him and the *Shenandoah* crash. The exhibit features newspapers that reported on the disaster; the old *National Geographic* story about a previous flight of the airship; books on the airship disaster; a letter from Lansdowne written on *Shenandoah* stationary; two china plates commemorating the fiftieth anniversary of the crash; photos of the airship and of the captain; the captain's hat and epaulettes, watch, and buttons; pieces of the airship's wood and fabric; and a part of its hull.

The display also features a black 78-rpm Victor phonograph record— "The Wreck of the *Shenandoah*" by singing star Vernon Dalhart, and the sheet music with fancy letters and photographs of the *Shenandoah* in flight and in its wrecked state. In the 1920s, nationally known accident victims whom newspapers had made unfortunately famous, often became the subjects of Dahlhart's recordings. In "The Wreck of the *Shenandoah,*" songwriter Maggie Andrew told the tragedy in rhyme:

In the little town of Greenville
a mother's watchful eye
was waiting for the airship
to see her son go by.
But alas, her boy lay sleeping
his last great flight was o'er.

A piano roll and a Victor record of the song are also on display.

Newspaper headlines inside a glass case tell the story. The *Greenville Daily News-Tribune* said residents went wild when they saw the big airship flying over the town on Saturday morning, October 25, 1924. As the ship hovered over his mother's house, Lansdowne spoke with her briefly by shortwave radio. The newspaper reported, "America's first dirigible, under the command of noted son Zach Lansdowne, arrived over Greenville this morning, just as the courthouse clock was striking ten, causing all local citizens to rejoice."

Another headline read: "Shenandoah Flies over Greenville, Zach Lansdowne Signals to Mother." He talked to her over a radio and then dropped a weighted bag bearing this message: "Hello, mother! Hello, mother! Greetings and best wishes to the old town from the Shenandoah. We are making fifty knots per hour on our trip from Fort Worth to Lakehurst and hope to maintain same speed." Commander Lansdowne "never made a trip west in the *Shenandoah* without soaring over Greenville," the local *Daily Advocate* reminded its readers, "entirely encircling the city in salute to his mother."

In these displays of civic pride, the slim, dapper officer—whom many knew as a continental man—showed he was still a Greenville boy at heart. His career may have been international, but he never forgot where he grew up.

The *Shenandoah* caught the public's attention because newspapers wrote about it and supported its use. The navy, in turn, used the *Shenandoah* to boost its reputation as an innovator. Naval leaders wanted the airship to represent a new American military pride, much as the new powerful fleet of warships did just before the Spanish-American War. But mostly, naval leaders wanted the new airship to become a scouting vessel.

On February 12, 1924, the navy turned the *Shenandoah*'s command over to Lansdowne, the most experienced and advanced officer involved with dirigibles, and the only one with real dirigible flying experience. First, he docked it at sea, and then he flew it on some goodwill trips. Then the navy planned a nine-thousand-mile trip throughout the country. In the fall of 1924, he took the ship down the east coast, across the South, over the Rockies, out to California, and then to Seattle. On that flight, Lansdowne carefully guided the airship *through* the Rocky Mountains instead of flying over them, to save helium. He worried about crashing, not about exploding.

People pointed when they saw the sleek ship gliding across the sky. On the way back, Lansdowne left Fort Worth and headed to Ohio—specifically to Greenville. Then he headed to Dayton and went off to the dirigible docking stations in Lakehurst, New Jersey. By now, people from all over the nation were clamoring for Lieutenant Commander Lansdowne to fly the *Shenandoah* over their towns. The navy realized it had a public relations gimmick like no other, albeit an expensive one.

About this time, the nation's second rigid airship, the USS *Los Angeles,* also known as the ZR-3, arrived from Germany. The navy planned to send the *Los Angeles* on trial runs, but insufficient helium supplies forced a transfer of the *Shenandoah*'s reserves to the *Los Angeles.* When the new ship had an accident and needed repairs, the navy moved the gas back into the *Shenandoah* and sent it on a six-day flight over five states. It chose September, because many midwestern state fairs would then be in progress.

The risky voyage pitted Lansdowne against two powerful forces—the weather and Curtis Dwight Wilbur, Californian secretary of the navy. Wilbur was new to the job, President Coolidge having appointed him on March 19, 1924. Coolidge still wanted the *Shenandoah* to take an arctic voyage someday, but that trip was delayed while Wilbur enticed the public with the airship showing up above their fairs. He either didn't read or ignored Lansdowne's letters about autumn bringing bad weather for flying in the Great Lakes region. Lansdowne also told his wife and his friends in the service about his concerns. He wrote a second letter about it to the navy, and then he put everything he had written in a file and gave it to her.

With trepidation, Lansdowne flew the airship out of Lakehurst at 3:00 P.M. on Wednesday, September 2. While flying over Chambersburg, Pennsylvania, crewman G. W. Armstrong wrote in the ship's log, "Below it looks like a picture under a Christmas tree, and we think of the kiddies at home and wonder if they are all asleep." Factories blew their whistles as the dirigible flew over Wheeling, West Virginia.

As Lansdowne and the airship entered Ohio about 5:00 A.M. on Thursday, September 3, the *Shenandoah* entered a storm over Noble County. Lightning flashed, and the ship suddenly rose six thousand feet, which it was not designed to do. Lansdowne tried to change course, but he could not. The squall swallowed the *Shenandoah* and tore it into three pieces. As eyewitness Eva McCoy told the Associated Press fifty years later: "It was if one of Jupiter's arrows had entered her vulnerable point and had stilled forever the beating of the great heart. In a last spasm of effort, she turned entirely over, and pointed straight downward, plunging a head weight, down down."

Greenville residents were shocked to read in the *Daily Advocate* the next day, on September 4, 1925: "Wind Crashes Shenandoah; Commander Lansdowne, 12 Men Killed; Greenville Bows with Grief for Her Noted Son; Citizens Were Shocked beyond Measure by the Terrible Tragedy That Robbed Them of Their Noted Son." After this article was printed, the death count rose by one.

Immediately after the crash, some officials started blaming Lansdowne, as he had made some changes to the airship's initial design, eliminating a sixth motor, mounted in the rear, and modifying other originally designed parts. But army air colonel William "Billy" Mitchell spoke out in defense of his friend and against the government, which brought him a court-martial on a charge of breach of discipline for public criticism of the army, navy, and the administration. Mitchell also called for a better-equipped air defense. Later, his legal troubles and exit from the army were recounted in a movie, *The Court-Martial of Billy Mitchell,* in which Lansdowne's character featured prominently.

Mitchell's risky defense of his friend helped call more attention to the *Shenandoah* safety issue, and Congress finally determined that Zachary Lansdowne did not cause the crash; rather, he did everything in his power to prevent it. The navy never got over the criticism from Mitchell and Betsy Lansdowne. Betsy, a writer who would become the first women's editor of the *Washington Star,* told her story in the January 9,

1926, issue of *Collier's*, the popular national magazine. As if losing her husband weren't enough, she had to hear him criticized by officials of his own government. "I have seen people double-cross the dead and humiliate and harass the living in order to shake off the stigma of personal criticisms for themselves," she wrote.

On the morning of the crash, at the Lansdowne home in Lakewood, New Jersey, Betsy was awakened at 5:30 A.M. by their bulldog, Barney, who was very close to Zach. The *Shenandoah* had just crashed in Ohio, although she didn't know it then. The only other time Betsy remembered the dog having barked so loudly and for so long was when the *Shenandoah* encountered serious trouble a year earlier—though then it had landed safely.

She told an Associated Press reporter on the day of the crash: "He [her husband] said to me yesterday before he left: 'I know we'll hit thunderstorms in Ohio, and I hope we'll get through all right.' He was very nervous about this trip, and has been protesting to [Navy Secretary] Wilbur since it [the flight] was ordered last June, but it was no use. They insisted he should make it for the political effect. It may sound strange but I think several of the men had a feeling of impending disaster before the trip started. . . . He said he wanted to go on this trip because he wanted to die when the ship crashed." Lansdowne told his mother that when he finished this voyage, he would be reassigned to sea duty. He also predicted to her and his wife that this would be his last flight—period. He asked his mother to raise a flag in his honor when the *Shenandoah* lifted off on its last voyage. She did so and then died only two weeks later, it is said, from the stress of her son's death.

In Greenville today, Florence Magoto recalls seeing the *Shenandoah* flying over her house. "I remember, barely, where I was standing in the yard when I saw it coming," she said. "I was only three years old, but I still have that memory of where I stood. It flew down Broadway and somebody on board took pictures of the town. I told Mom and Dad, 'It looks like a silver pickle!'"

At ninety-two and blessed with excellent recall, she strives to obtain recognition for her hometown hero. She has never forgotten the airship or its commander, and all her life she has appealed to individuals and organizations to look at his record. That has often been a difficult job: "He isn't given the credit he deserves," she said. "Here is a guy who gave his life, but he can't get mentioned."

She is often called the Lansdowne family historian, for she has collected information for four decades. "When the family moved out of his home here in Greenville, my folks bought the place. My younger sister was born there. I have been close to the family for years." She has donated Lansdowne and *Shenandoah* relics to the Garst Museum and to a museum in Noble County. She owns pieces of the airship, letters from survivors, and even a piece of rope used in the ship on its final voyage.

She has also collected information about Lansdowne from books and personal conversations. "Zach Lansdowne said on his final trip that it wasn't fit weather for flying, but the navy wanted a show and tell show," she said. "It got a lot more. When the trouble started on board the *Shenandoah*, he remained calm and he told the crew, 'We will all go through this together.' We know this because survivors have told us."

Lansdowne was "a good, kind man," she said. "He came back to Greenville often through the years. He brought his son . . . home and had their picture taken at a photography studio here in town. And after his historic nine-thousand-mile flight around the country, he came back home. The town gave him a big reception at our Memorial Hall. He stayed until the end, greeting fellow classmates and townspeople. . . . The town presented him with a watch in appreciation for his accomplishments. The town was so proud of him. Recently, the town was to celebrate the hundredth anniversary of the building, and people in town were asked to write in and give important events that occurred there over the years. I wrote in and told about Zach's reception. Later, when a history was published, he wasn't even mentioned. This is what I mean when I say he is so unfairly forgotten."

Magoto and other lighter-than-air enthusiasts nominated him for membership in the Aviation Hall of Fame, she said, "but we have never heard boo in thirty-some years. Zach was important. He designed flight suits, made improvements to the ship, and did many different things. But politics is politics. Who is left to remember him?"

She said Lansdowne always felt close to his hometown, even when he was overseas or in Washington, D.C. "Get this—he joined our American Legion!" Magoto said. "He transferred his membership from Wisconsin, where his wife was originally from, to Greenville, so he could be with his boys." She paused, thinking it over, and added, "He was always thinking of his men, you know. I can't understand why he is so ignored around here today."

The crash of the *Shenandoah* did not end the world's fascination with dirigibles. The United States began to build more airships, making them stronger, to withstand stronger winds. The USS *Akron,* built in its namesake city, was the second zeppelin the United States built. High winds caused it to crash on the New Jersey coast in 1933, killing seventy-three. Winds also crashed the USS *Macon,* another Akron product, off the California coast in 1935, killing thirty-six. Finally, in 1937 the German *Hindenburg* blew up at Lakehurst, with thirty-six dying in one of the most hideous explosions in the dirigible's fiery history.

The navy still remembered the *Shenandoah* crash, for it smashed so many hopes and came about so quickly—and with the experienced Lansdowne in command. It let everyone know that dirigible flight had major safety drawbacks.

The start of World War II effectively ended the flight of all rigid, lighter-than-air ships, and by the war's end they were gone from the world's skies. The public had turned against them, calling them "monsters of the purple twilight," "murder machines," and other such violent names. People associated them closely with the flammable hydrogen gas and massive flames and explosions. Although dirigibles were effective in surveillance and travel, they had too much baggage for the public.

The *Santa Fe New Mexican* unintentionally issued one of the dirigible's worst epitaphs when on the day of the *Shenandoah* disaster it ran a headline mislabeling the ship: "Commanding Officer Killed in Crash of Big Navy Blimp."

One can only imagine how Zachary Lansdowne would have responded.

| 8 |

BLANCHE NOYES
Champion Aviatrix

The petite brunette shielded her blue eyes with her hand and gasped in disbelief as the two jousting pilots looped and spun their WACO 9s above the busy Lincoln highway, coming within inches of colliding before darting apart. Motorists stopped abruptly, abandoning their cars to watch the aerobatics, convinced that a catastrophe was inevitable on that day in 1927.

Dewey Noyes and Merle Moltrup were airmail pilots by day but daredevils at heart. They would have cavorted in the skies regardless of the crowd, but Noyes was particularly wild that day because he was trying to impress the young woman below.

Blanche Wilcox had already made up her mind to marry Noyes—if he didn't kill himself first. They had first met in at a dinner party for Charles Lindbergh in Pittsburgh earlier in the year. The Lone Eagle was on a tour of seventy-five cities, being honored for his historic solo Atlantic crossing while he mustered support for the creation of municipal airports. Blanche, a twenty-seven-year-old stage actress from Cleveland, was in town doing a play.

Lindbergh was treated like a god wherever he went that summer, but Blanche was intrigued by the "very charming, red-headed gentleman" named Dewey, who talked nonstop about the thrill of flight. He had grown up in Vermont, where he flew gliders over the mountains at age fifteen. After a friend spun in and died in a plane crash, Dewey and his brother salvaged the wreckage and built their own plane, then taught themselves to fly it.

By the time he arrived in Cleveland in 1925, Dewey had been involved in two or three aviation businesses, as either an employee or owner. He

Blanche Noyes, November 1928. (Courtesy Cleveland State University)

had barnstormed across New England, where he had a minor following of fans. In Cleveland, Dewey joined forces with Clifford Ball, who had just secured the contract for the U.S. airmail route from Cleveland to Pittsburgh. In April 1927, Dewey became the first pilot on the route.

Early airmail pilots were sky cowboys. The job was so dangerous that these pilots were referred to as members of the "Suicide Club." Lindbergh started his flying career as a barnstormer and advanced to airmail pilot before he became an international hero. Flying the mail tested even the most experienced pilot's skill and nerve; airmail biplanes were fitted with the most rudimentary instruments, and the pilots had only railroad tracks and roads as navigational markers.

The U.S. Postal Department was determined to make the revolutionary delivery system a commercial success. To keep their contracts, businessmen like Ball had to guarantee that the mail would arrive on time, despite breakdowns, hazardous weather, and crashes. Just surviving the intense cold in open cockpits or thin-shelled, unheated cabins was an ordeal. But Dewey thrived on it, and his enthusiasm attracted Blanche.

At the Lindbergh dinner, he asked her if she would like to fly, and she immediately said yes, although she had never even seen an airplane close up before. The week after they met, Dewey drove Blanche to Bettis Field outside Pittsburgh and helped her into his WACO 9, an open-cockpit biplane built in Troy, Ohio. Once in the air, he showed Blanche his stuff, looping, spinning, and rolling the little plane.

Every time he rolled the plane, it seemed they were right over a cemetery. Blanche looked down at a gigantic monument and had visions of falling from the plane and being speared by it. Once on the ground, Dewey grinned and asked her how she felt. Blanche said she felt great. A courtship ensued, much of it spent in the air. A year from the day of her first plane ride, they married.

They set up housekeeping in Lakewood but spent most of their time in the sky or at the airfield that would become Cleveland Municipal Airport. Still a newlywed, Blanche was busy learning to cook. Dewey was late for dinner one night, and she was worried that the sausages she was frying would be ruined. He finally came home and casually asked her if she'd like to learn to fly. Distractedly, she acquiesced. The next day, Dewey came home and announced, "Honey, I've bought you an airplane." It was a WACO 10, another open-cabin biplane. Suddenly, learning to fly took priority over learning to cook. Blanche wanted to please Dewey, and if flying was something he wanted to share with her, she wanted it too.

Blanche's first lesson was with another instructor; Dewey didn't think husbands should teach wives to fly. When she went up, Dewey advised her that if she felt uncomfortable at any time during the lesson, she should drop the controls and let the instructor take over. He understood that freezing up at the controls caused too many fatal crashes. She followed his advice, a little too much for her instructor. "Your wife is never going to learn to fly," he told Dewey. "She's too timid." Word started going around the airfield that the daring mail pilot had a hesitant wife. But Dewey didn't believe it. He started teaching Blanche, pushing her beyond her fear by showing her what she could do.

He told her that once she could make three good takeoffs and three good landings, she was going to solo. She didn't sleep a wink the night before her first solo trip. All of Dewey's cronies were at the airfield that day. They'd been asking her just when she was going to solo. Her takeoff was fine. She flew for a little while, soaring over a big brick schoolhouse. Then it was time to land. By herself. She imagined the men on the ground, watching her, laughing, saying, "They'll have to get a gun to shoot her down." Then Blanche did what she would do for the rest of her flying career, she thought about what Dewey had told her. "Dewey had tried to instill in me that I wasn't just landing the plane, I was 'kissing the earth,'" she recalled fifty years later. "That was the best landing I've ever made in my whole life."

From then on, his goals for her increased exponentially. She would fly alone to Akron. "He said if I could fly from Cleveland to Akron, I could fly anywhere." Next, it was a longer flight, to Mansfield. "For a long time, I thought I was flying to please Dewey," Blanche told a reporter in 1976. Then, one day, she was hospitalized for pneumonia. She awoke one morning worrying about whether she would physically be able to fly. "From then on, I knew I was flying to please myself."

At twenty-seven, Blanche had already experienced a fair amount of the world. She started acting soon after finishing school, getting roles in local repertory productions at first. She performed often at the Gordon Square Theater on the city's west side. Several theaters developed in the district, as did Chronicle House, an acting school that drew fledgling actors from the region. Through the school, student thespians sometimes were able to act with professional actors from across the country.

Blanche was good enough that she started getting leads and playing opposite more experienced actors. She once listed Roger Pryor and George Brent as her leading men. Both men started with small, local theaters and moved up to touring stock companies, the type that frequently visited Cleveland.

Pryor made it to Broadway before the burgeoning movie industry beckoned. With his good looks and dark hair, he became known as "the poor man's Clark Gable." (Gable was from Cadiz, Ohio.) Pryor went on to romance Mae West in the racy film *Belle of the Nineties* in 1934. In real life, he married actress Ann Sothern.

George Brent was an Irishman who toured with stock theater companies for several years. By 1930, Brent was in Hollywood, appearing with one of the biggest stars of the day: Rin Tin Tin. He went on to many other films, eventually earning the unofficial title of Bette Davis's favorite leading man. He appeared with Davis in eleven films, most notably the 1939 *Dark Victory*.

Brent was also a licensed pilot who flew in some scenes of 1941's *The Great Lie*. Show business and flying were natural companions; the thrill and glamour of flying attracted actors who had the money and time to indulge themselves. There were plenty of places to fly in the wide-open spaces of the western United States, and some actors piloted their own planes to location shoots.

Famous flyers, like actors, were idolized and followed by the public. The two passions met most dynamically in one person: Howard Hughes. The young Texas tycoon began building and racing airplanes in the 1920s before turning to filmmaking. His epic *Hell's Angels* introduced Jean Harlow to audiences, but its realistic air battles (which resulted in three deaths) stole the movie.

In August 1929, anyone who was interested in aviation, from the famous to the ordinary, headed to a ten-day event that promised to be spectacular. And it was happening in Blanche's backyard, at Cleveland's sprawling, new Hopkins Municipal Airport. Cleveland businessmen Louis W. Greve and Frederick C. Crawford knew the public loved to spend Sunday afternoons at the airport, watching planes take off and land. When pilots offered paid flights or performed aerobatics, the crowds swelled appreciatively. Los Angeles had hosted a large air show already, so shouldn't the state where the first viable airplanes were invented do the same? Local government and industry and the military

backed the plan that drew hundreds of flyers and thousands of spectators to the city and to Hopkins for the Cleveland National Air Races.

Blanche and Dewey would be able to watch aerobatic competitions
featuring the top flyers, military aerobatics, parachute jumping contests,
and the Thompson Trophy Race, an exciting closed-course flying competition. Best of all, they could talk with other pilots. For Blanche, this
meant getting to know the small but highly visible band of women who
were starting to fly aircraft nationally. Most of them were young, attractive, accomplished, and just as determined as the men. Amelia Earhart was a soft-spoken social worker from Kansas. Ruth Elder was a
vivacious movie actress who hoped to be the female Charles Lindbergh.
Louise Thaden, from a small town in Arkansas, was a wife and mother.
Ruth Nichols was known as the Flying Debutante, due to her privileged
background and Ivy League education. Flying was a new and risky endeavor that had captured the country's imagination. Women in the cockpit were a novelty the press and public couldn't get enough of. Most articles about the aviatrixes commented, at least briefly, on their demeanor,
fashion, and marital status.

Aviation was not an inexpensive pursuit, so in the public's mind there
was an association between flying and wealth and status—although by
no means were people like Blanche and Dewey well off. Still, the upper
classes were being drawn to flight, and all the trappings followed. The
Women's Emergency Fund Committee of New York City put on an
aviation fashion show in 1930, showing the latest ultra-smart fashions
for flying a plane or for just traveling in one.

Publicly, most female flyers accepted the attention good-naturedly.
They sometimes used it to their benefit. Earhart, for instance, went on
speaking tours, addressing women's clubs as a way of raising funds
for future flights. But amid the general goodwill, animosity—and sometimes outright opposition—lurked in hangars and airfields across the
country. The women were determined to prove their ability and right to
fly alongside men, regardless of whether they were welcomed.

Men seemed to more easily accept many of the women who, like
Blanche, learned to fly from their husbands. At the time the first Cleveland Air Races were being planned, Blanche had only held her pilot's
license for a short time. She had become the first licensed female flyer
in Ohio in April 1929 and was the first woman to make her initial solo
flight at Hopkins. She caught the attention of the local press that spring

when she announced she was going to not only attend the air races but compete in an event.

That July, she passed the test to fly transport planes, becoming one of the first ten women in the country to do so. She and Dewey were preparing to travel to Los Angeles so they could fly a Lockheed Vega back to Cleveland, giving her more hours flying cross-country. By now, she had experienced many of the situations that either made or broke rookie pilots. A broken waterline had resulted in her first forced landing in a field, while flying to Wichita, Kansas, to pick up a new plane. Her first deadstick landing—setting the plane down safely after the motor conked out—happened in Oklahoma. Each time she faced a crisis in the air, she quickly thought back to Dewey's advice.

But nothing could prepare her completely for what she experienced that summer during the first Women's Air Derby. The event was one of several distance races included in the extravaganza; in each race, pilots began from different specific cities with Hopkins as their destination. Races were scheduled so that each event ended at Cleveland on a different day, thereby keeping up the public's interest throughout the ten days.

The women would begin their race in Santa Monica, California, and head for the finish line in Cleveland. Humorist Will Rogers, an important aviation proponent, dubbed the race the Powder Puff Derby, but it was anything but frivolous or light-hearted. The men who ran major aviation events, including the Cleveland races, did not want women to participate with the men. Many men—and Dewey was among them— were concerned about the women's safety in competing against men. The Women's Derby was the compromise: an event that would—supposedly—keep them safer, in their own sphere. Halle Brothers, a Cleveland department store, was sponsoring Blanche in a new Travel Air, which she christened *Miss Cleveland*.

There were serious problems even before the race began. Breakdowns and crackups sidelined several of the original twenty participants. As the remaining flyers were being introduced to the crowds at Santa Monica, someone shoved a microphone into Blanche's face. "Hello, Cleveland," she blurted. "Here I come!" Privately, she wondered if she'd even get off the ground.

An exchange with a ground crew member just before she took off would haunt her later. The man who packed her baggage and, according to Blanche, "had a very beautiful lady in the race," asked her if she had ever had to parachute out of a plane. She told him she had not, but would do so if she had a fire or structural failure while in the air. The man paused, wished her luck, and walked away.

Rumors of sabotage by ground crews and spectators were not uncommon during high-stake races, and such rumors persist about the first women's derby. During the race, the wings of one woman's plane were tampered with, resulting in a forced landing. Another flyer, who had to make an emergency landing when she unexpectedly ran out of gas, believed someone had partially drained her tank. Another participant returned from a race banquet to find every switch and throttle on her plane turned on. It was impossible to prove whether acts like these were deliberate sabotage, equipment malfunctions, or the interference of spectators. Regardless, the women soon began putting their planes in a wagon-train type circle at night and hired guards to watch them.

Even without sabotage, the women faced multiple obstacles. At each stop on the route, they were feted by the public and pursued by the press. The attention was more than a distraction for them; they were already exhausted by the demands of long-distance flying and a tight schedule. Now, sleep-deprived, they had difficulties dealing with bad weather conditions and the equipment problems inherent in a cross-country flight.

During a stop in El Paso, Texas, the women learned that Marvel Crosson, a young Alaskan who had set a women's altitude record that spring, was killed when, due to causes that would remain forever unknown, her plane crashed in the Gila River territory, close to Phoenix. They were stunned by her death, and an argument ensued over whether or not to postpone the remainder of the race. Ever since the women entered Texas air space, dicey weather had dogged them—first a sandstorm, then a thunderstorm. Earhart led the contingent that wanted to keep flying. Ruth Elder, who had crash-landed in the Atlantic Ocean earlier that year, argued for a postponement.

While the debate continued, another pilot was facing death at three thousand feet. About thirty miles west of Pecos, Blanche was headed for a fueling stop, when she smelled smoke. Every pilot knew crackups could be fatal, but being burnt alive in a crash was the thing that gave them nightmares.

"Her first thought was to open her parachute and let the plane crash," the Associated Press reported. But as she realized the fire was in the baggage compartment directly behind her head, she thought she could extinguish it. She tried to wrench the fire extinguisher from its bracket, but couldn't budge it.

Landing immediately was crucial, but the mesquite-covered terrain was not safe. Nevertheless, she prepared to land. "Side slipping, she drifted her plane to the ground, crashing through mesquite bushes three feet high," the story continued. Somehow, she landed safely, although her left wing was broken and a wheel was lost. On the ground, she reached into the plane's compartment, burning her hand as she removed burning debris. A cigarette butt had caught one of her flying suits on fire. Blanche didn't smoke. She suddenly had a flashback to the crewman who loaded her baggage, but she had no time to think about that. Knowing that the fire could lead to an explosion at any moment, she desperately grabbed handfuls of sand from the ground, throwing them onto the flames until they died.

A few locals who had seen the plane in peril arrived to investigate. Blanche ignored the serious burns on her face and hands and set about stitching up the broken wing with pieces of linen and a surgeon's needle. A local blacksmith welded the landing gear together. Blanche was ready for takeoff, even as an area official urged her to abandon the plane. Nothing that the blacksmith welded had ever held, he told her, but she didn't hesitate. She had begun this leg of the race in first place. Now, she knew she had probably fallen to last. If she didn't at least finish, Halle Brothers stood to lose a $10,000 investment in her and the plane. Even worse, Dewey would be ashamed. She had never hand-cranked a plane before, but she mustered all the strength in her eighty-one-pound frame and cranked it now. The first miracle of the day had been landing safely in the mesquite. The second was being able to gain enough speed on that terrain to get back into the air. To the end of her career, Blanche couldn't explain how she could do it.

At the Pecos airport, Louise Thaden saw *Miss Cleveland* circling the field in a plane that "looked like a wounded duck with a broken wing and badly crippled legs," she recalled in a memoir. Certain that Blanche would crash, Thaden called for fire extinguishers and an ambulance. Amazingly, Blanche precisely landed the plane. It ground looped but remained intact. Shaking, she emerged to tell her story and arrange for further repairs of her plane. The race continued.

Blanche resumed flying and finished in fourth place with a "tremendous ovation from her Cleveland home folk," Thaden wrote. Blanche did not investigate the cause of the fire, knowing it would be impossible to prove whether the burning cigarette had been intentional. Thaden won that first women's derby in the heavier plane division, garnering a cash prize and a gigantic wreath of roses. Gladys O'Donnell, a Californian who ran a flying school with her husband, came in second; Earhart was third; and Ruth Elder, fifth. The race brought them unprecedented public acclaim. In the years to follow, these would be the female pilots to watch. Perhaps more important to the women themselves, the derby was the start of lifelong friendships.

Aviation was progressing at a tremendous rate. There were fortunes to be made and flying records to be set, and dozens of talented, daring people were eager to do both. On the day that Blanche's accident was reported, page one of the *St. Petersburg Times* gave a glimpse of how consumed the world was with flight: it contained nine items related to aviation. Several stories were from abroad. The Hearst Graf zeppelin was in Japan, waiting to take off for Los Angeles as part of a round-the-world flight. In France, bad weather forced a well-known flyer who hoped to set some sort of international record to abandon his latest attempt. A Spanish designer was building a new type of autogyro in England. The Russians had sent off a new plane to attempt a Moscow to New York flight, just one week after their initial plane crashed.

In U.S. news, in addition to three stories about the air derby, the Department of Commerce announced new regulations that would allow transport pilots to only carry passengers in aircraft for which they had passed specific examinations. A pilot who was accustomed to flying only single-engine, open cockpit planes would not automatically be qualified to pilot a much larger tri-motored cabin craft, said Clarence M. Young, a company official. An emotional brief, reflecting flying's attraction, noted that a dozen little blind girls had "got the thrill of their lives" when they took their first airplane ride in New York.

With America posed at the brink of the Great Depression, international economic woes straining stability, and China and Russia on the verge of war, aviation appeared a possible savior. It would provide jobs through manufacturing, transport, and leisure travel. The famous flyers of the day—and there seemed to be more of them all the time—were role models for the youth and a source of optimism and excitement for the general public. Although aircraft had been used extensively in the world war, aviation was not promoted widely for military use. It was seen as a dynamic, benevolent force that would improve people's lives in innumerable ways. Female fliers intended to be part of that future.

A few months after the women's derby, Blanche became a founding member of the Ninety-Nines, an organization of female fliers named for the original number of members, which included Earhart, Thaden, Phoebie Omlie, and all the leading female pilots of the day. Over the years, the Ninety-Nines has become an international fellowship of women who fly, both in the sky and in space.

While Blanche was becoming more involved in the national aviation scene, Dewey's career also progressed. He became the chief pilot for the Standard Oil Company of Ohio when the company bought its first plane. During a 1930 visit at his home in New York State, the Noyeses convinced oil magnate John D. Rockefeller to take a flight. Rockefeller, a Cleveland native, was in his early nineties at the time. Blanche flew that day. It was Rockefeller's first plane ride, and, although he said he thoroughly enjoyed it, it was his only flight. Blanche took a great deal of teasing from her fellow pilots.

In 1931, Blanche was working for the Great Lakes Aircraft Corporation, demonstrating planes. The Cleveland company manufactured navy dive-bombers, torpedo planes, and commercial light aircraft, including the Great Lakes Sport Trainer biplane. Impressed with her ability to fly varied craft for Great Lakes, in 1933 Standard Oil asked her to demonstrate the new Pitcairn model of the autogyro, the forerunner of the modern helicopter. The craft was still in the experimental stage, and Blanche was one of the first to pilot one; it was a measure of her ability that she was entrusted with demonstrating them.

Also in 1933, the Noyeses left Cleveland. Dewey, who had started flying for the fledgling American Airlines in 1932, accepted a job with the Ethyl Company, a New Jersey firm that made fuel and lubricant additives.

As Dewey's career soared, so did Blanche's. Blanche made the news again in 1934 when she won the Leeds Race Trophy, for a race leading up to the National Air Races. She worked constantly on her flying skills. Her flying time now equaled that of her good friend Amelia Earhart, a much more experienced flyer. And Dewey was teaching Blanche instrument flying, in which one navigates and flies by cockpit instruments rather than visually, by the environment. Few women were learning this difficult technique, but Blanche mastered it, becoming one of the first instrument-rated pilots in the country. She and Dewey told friends they planned to fly around the world. With her husband as her copilot, she would take off from Newfoundland and head for Alaska, the same route Wiley Post had attempted on his fatal 1935 flight.

But that dream ended when Dewey was killed in a plane crash on December 11, 1935, in New York State. Dewey was working for Ethyl Gas, flying a company official, Elwood M. Walter, to a business meeting that afternoon. Dense fog and a snowstorm caused the four-passenger cabin plane to crash into a clump of trees near the community of Nunda, fifty miles southwest of Rochester. Newspapers reported that Dewey and Walter were apparently killed instantly, their bodies thrown clear of the demolished plane. Blanche was devastated. Throughout the ordeal and funeral, her friends in the Ninety-Nines stood by her.

Dewey's service was held in the Ninety-Nines' hangar on Long Island. Earhart took a special interest in Blanche, inviting her to join her and her husband, G. P. Putnam, at their California home. Blanche also found solace in work. The Ninety-Nines asked her to visit major cities in Ohio and Michigan to drum up interest in an all-women's derby as part of the National Air Races of 1936.

The following year, Blanche became involved in an aviation venture that gave her a new purpose in life. At the time, pilots were still relying primarily on compasses and roadmaps to navigate. Though major cities and airports were obvious and relatively easy to find in good weather, most of the country was still composed of small cities and smaller towns. Landing fields, often only known to local pilots, outnumbered full-fledged municipal or county airports. Flyers needed more visual ground guides—visible from ten thousand feet. Pilot Phoebe Omlie, who was working with the National Advisory Committee for Aeronautics, came up with a plan. She had a wealth of practical experience: One of the early female pilots, she started flying in the South and Midwest in 1921. She was the nation's first licensed transport pilot and one of the first female flight instructors. She was an excellent flier, setting many records and winning numerous air races.

Her plan was simple in design and ambitious in scope. She proposed a system of air markers be established across the country. These were to be painted on tops of large roofs in highly visible colors of black and orange or black and chrome yellow. In wide-open spaces where rooftops were nonexistent for hundreds of miles, markers would be made from white-painted rocks or compositions of bricks and concrete cobbled together. In towns with airports, the marker gave the town name, an airport symbol, an arrow with the number of miles next to it—pointing toward the airport, and a meridian (north) indicator. For towns without airports, the markers gave the name of the nearest town and of the town with the nearest airport, with directional arrows, a meridian marker, and an indication of the best route to follow in case of inclement weather.

The project started with a goal of sixteen thousand air markers, to be established at the cost of $1 million through the Works Progress Administration. Out-of-work men were hired to do the actual painting and constructing of markers. Three members of the Ninety-Nines, marshaled by Omlie, scouted site selections, oversaw installations, and made aerial checks of completed markers. The Bureau of Air Commerce in Washington was in charge of the project. In May 1936, Earhart wrote a letter to bureau director Gene Vidal asking if he could use another pilot. She told him about Dewey and Blanche. "She is pretty well shot to pieces losing Dewey, and it would be a godsend to her to have a job in the Department," Earhart wrote. "She is a good flyer . . . has her own monocoupe, and is really serious about aviation." Earhart vouched for Blanche's integrity and offered to secretly pay her fare to Washington if Vidal decided to interview her.

Vidal hired Blanche soon after. By August, she was working with Louise Thaden in Texas when Olive Ann Beech of the Beechcraft airplane company offered to sponsor Thaden in that fall's Bendix Transcontinental Race. Thaden immediately asked Blanche to be her navigator and copilot. Blanche had already turned down a copilot position from Earhart, but now she agreed to fly with Thaden.

The Bendix was one of the era's most prestigious air races, won by superior fliers, including Roscoe Turner and Jimmy Doolittle. It did not welcome women. Industry leaders believed highly publicized crashes such as Marvel Crosson's and that of a young female pilot in a Chicago race would lessen the public's support of aviation. As a result, women were excluded from major races, including the Bendix and the National Air Races' mens' events. The women still wanted to race with the men, however, and in 1936 public sentiment dictated they be allowed to participate.

Beechcraft modified a plane for Thaden by removing the rear seat to make room for an extra fifty-six-gallon gas tank. An extra twelve-gallon oil tank was added, as was a pump fitted between the pilots' seats for sending oil directly into the main oil tank. Space was so tight that seat-pack parachutes were removed; the women would still wear their personal parachutes. Thaden joked that if she weighed a half-pound more she couldn't have fit into the plane.

Nonetheless, Thaden was thrilled with the G17R Staggerwing, which she described as "a trim blue princess of the air . . . as sleek and fast as a greyhound." She and Blanche had no expectation of winning the race. As beautiful as the Beechcraft was, it wasn't a racer, and the women didn't have the competition experience that most of the men did. Thaden thought the race would be a pleasant distraction for the still-grieving widow. Blanche thought it would be "a swell way to get to the [national] races."

Thaden was trying to keep her involvement low-key, but the fact was, she was a superb pilot. Before winning the 1929 Women's Derby, she had set altitude and endurance records for female flyers. Unlike several pilots of her generation, Thaden didn't have a history of crackups and forced landings. She was skilled, confident, and she loved being in the cockpit. Blanche couldn't have chosen a better partner.

The night before the Bendix, the women discussed who would bail out first if they were in danger of crashing. Blanche insisted that Thaden would jump first, since she had two children. Sleep was elusive. Around 3:00 A.M. on September 5, they headed for Floyd Bennett Field in New York, the race's starting point. Thaden was wearing a white suit with a blue blouse. Blanche was dressed more casually, in blue-green culottes and a green flannel shirt. Just before they took off, Thaden's husband—also a pilot—remarked that they had a chance of placing in the race, if they didn't get lost.

Weather became an issue almost immediately. Thick ground fog—potentially lethal to any pilot—obscured their course. Extreme static rendered their radio useless. Ninety minutes into the race, the best they could estimate was that they were somewhere over Ohio. Suddenly, Blanche spotted an air marker outside Circleville, one she and Thaden had installed weeks earlier, and it allowed them to get back on course.

As the Beechcraft sped across the heartland, thunderstorms and a strong cross headwind presented more challenges. But the radio was working again, and they made it to their scheduled refueling stop in Wichita, Kansas, in good shape. Within eight minutes, ground crews had replenished gasoline and oil and the pilots had studied weather reports. The women each drank a glass of water and were given soft drinks and sandwiches to sustain them on the rest of the flight. At no time did they leave their craft.

Walter Beech, head of Beechcraft, leaned in to give Blanche and Thaden some spirited advice in his distinctive high-pitched voice: "What the hell do you think you're in, a potato race? Open this damn thing up!" Although the women promised Beech and his wife, Olive Ann, their best, they were determined to fly a safe race. But they almost didn't make it off of the Wichita airfield. As they started to roll down the field, an Army Air Corps plane approached about a hundred feet to their left, preparing to land. Determined not to lose time, Thaden brazenly held to her course, rather than yield to the landing plane as she should have. The army pilot also held to his course, bringing the two craft perilously close together until Thaden took a sharp left turn, rising in the air and missing the other plane by just a few feet.

A head wind blowing at 60 miles per hour forced the Beechcraft to slow down over the desert. Although they had averaged 211 miles per hour hour on the first leg of the race, they had now decreased to 153 miles per hour. They worried about not being able to reach the Bendix's conclusion at Los Angeles's Mines Field by the 6:00 P.M. deadline, an embarrassment they were determined to avoid.

Skill and decent weather were with them the rest of the way, however; as they neared LA, Blanche searched for the oil derricks that in 1936 were close to the airport. As they increased air speed to 230 miles per hour, visibility worsened. Before they could slow down, they were upon the airport, and then they overshot it. Blanche directed Thaden back to the finish line near the grandstands. It was 5:10 P.M. They crossed the finish line from the wrong direction, but they had made it. They had finished the race in a stock plane, flying mostly at cruising speed, in fourteen hours, fifty-five minutes, and forty-six seconds, a record time for women flying cross-country.

Still thinking they were in the rear, Thaden taxied toward a line of parked planes far down the field, avoiding the grandstand where the winners would be greeted. Suddenly, Blanche noticed men running beside the Beechcraft, gesturing and shouting something she couldn't quite hear. She asked Thaden to stop the plane. One of the men who had been running alongside the plane yanked the door open and ordered the women out. "We think you won the Bendix!" he said, to their shock. Thaden wrote in her autobiography that the male organizers of the race seemed a little disappointed she and Blanche had won. But that didn't concern the women. An emotional Olive Ann Beech hugged Thaden, and then Thaden and Blanche were dragged to the grandstand, where sixty thousand spectators waited to see the women who had done the impossible.

The first place prize money totaled $7,000. Never dreaming that a woman could win, the organizers had come up with a consolation prize of $2,500 for the first woman across the finish line. Thaden and Blanche took both awards. Second place also went to a woman, Laura Ingalls, a socially prominent New Yorker who had excelled in many areas, ranging from ballet to nursing, before becoming a pilot. Lack of luck on the part of some other fliers played a part in the race. Well-known pilot Benny Howard, who had won the previous year, crashed during the race, as did another top male contender. Earhart and her copilot, Helen Richey, lost time while struggling to secure an emergency escape hatch that had opened in air. They finished fifth.

Luck had certainly been with the Beechcraft that day, but Thaden's fearless flying and Blanche's keen navigation were the primary factors in the win. Spotting the Circleville air marker may have decided the race. The hoopla over their win continued for months; Thaden and Blanche had earned a permanent spot in aviation history. At the same time, another female flier was also making history. Beryl Markham, a thirty-one-year-old English society beauty and mother, had just become the first woman to fly solo over the Atlantic. To further her glory, Markham had flown what pilots considered the more hazardous route: east to west, from England to New York.

Courageous, talented, dazzling, these women seemed capable of anything. Many could be found on the society pages as well as the news pages. Some parlayed their flying skills into other careers, such as writing and film. Blanche "buckled down to serious work," she wrote two years later, finding her calling with air marking. It wasn't glamorous, but her position was fairly high profile for a female aviator. She was named head of the air-marking division of the Bureau of Air Commerce, part of the U.S. Department of Commerce in 1937. For six years she worked out of Washington, D.C., supervising the installation of thousands of markers across the country. Air safety became her passion, no doubt fueled by the memory of Dewey's fatal crash and the deaths of many friends over the years. During this time, she was said to be the only female pilot in America authorized to fly a military plane.

Then, Pearl Harbor changed everything. On that bright Sunday afternoon of December 7, 1941, Blanche was just completing talks with aviation officials about adding more safety markers across the wide open spaces of Texas. Now the vulnerability of America's air space had been severely compromised. The Civil Aeronautics Administration (CAA) soon decided the air markers would be too helpful to the enemy and that they must be obscured or obliterated. All Blanche's work would be gone.

"The war has changed the situation so completely that I don't really mind it at all," she told a *New York Times* reporter while discussing the situation in August 1942. Within twenty-six days, almost a thousand markers along the West Coast were removed. Blanche's job was to locate all markers within a sixty-square-mile region and then contact the regional CAA officials, who removed the markers. Flying in a Cessna, Blanche retraced her course over each region, making sure that no markers remained.

"Once in a while I get a little jittery wondering if some particularly zealous airplane spotter might mistake me for an enemy ship and shoot me down and ask questions later," Blanche told a *New York Times* reporter in August 1942, "for, of course, I'm flying constantly over restricted areas."

After the war, Blanche continued to work for the CAA, making sure the thirteen thousand air markers that had been removed were now put back. More markers were added, with members of the Ninety-Nines volunteering to do the work. When federal funding for the program ended, Blanche became a fundraiser, seeking donations from local communities to keep markers current and in good shape.

Air safety was her mission, and she wrote numerous newspaper and magazine articles on the subject. She collected and shared accounts of pilots and passengers whose lives had been saved by air markers. One story she gave to the Associated Press after the war concerned navy commander John S. Hill, flying a jet fighter across Ohio when he ran into trouble. Hill was headed for Columbus when he realized he didn't have enough fuel to get there. He saw the Greenville marker in Darke County and followed its arrow to the local airport. He crash-landed the jet but walked away with minor injuries, praising the air marker with saving his life.

Although she lived in Washington, Blanche's Ohio connections remained strong. She came back to visit periodically and was always delighted to interact with any Ohioan interested in flying. In 1948, she wrote to Mrs. Elden Bayley of Springfield to pass along an article about air marking and to compliment her on her daughter Caro's win in an aerobatics contest. "She flew beautifully, and her takeoffs and landings were as pretty as any I have ever seen," Blanche wrote. "I know how proud you must be of her."

Three years later, in the United States, Caro Bayley became the Women's International Aerobatics champion. In France, Bayley was awarded the coveted Bleriot Medal for her flying from the Federation Aeronautique Internationale of France. Blanche undoubtedly knew of Bayley's honors and cheered them. Encouraging female flyers—and especially girls—continued to be one of her passions. For years, she spoke to students whenever possible, even participating as a judge in a NASA–*Plain Dealer* Science Fair in Cleveland in 1962. She served as international president of the Ninety-Nines from 1948 through 1950 and attended regional meetings in Ohio whenever she could.

Blanche received so many accolades for her contributions to aviation over the years that she had to start keeping a list of them. The governments of France, Cuba, and Brazil each honored her. In 1963, she met President John F. Kennedy—twice. That January, she was one of six women presented with the Federal Woman's Award for achievement in their field. That July, the Ninety-Nines chose her to fly a commemorative stamp honoring her old friend, Amelia Earhart, from Kansas to Washington, where she presented the first-day covers to Kennedy.

As much as Blanche enjoyed and appreciated all the honors, her real reward was simply getting to do what she loved every day. "I don't think I would want to live if I couldn't fly," Blanche told a reporter in 1956 after becoming the first woman to receive a gold medal from the Department of Commerce for her work. She was still traveling around the country, checking air markings, sometimes climbing up on rooftops to check the work up close. By then, she had logged 11,075 solo flying hours doing air marking. "I'm pretty near to making my office in the air. I never seem to have time for a vacation," she said happily.

Blanche was inducted into the Aviation Hall of Fame in 1970. She continued working until she retired in 1972, at the age of seventy-one. But she never really stopped doing what she loved. While the sky had once been the limit for women, now all of space beckoned. Blanche served actively on the Women's Advisory Committee on Aeronautics and continued to lecture and freelance as an aviation consultant.

Although she lived in the Watergate Apartment Building in Washington, she also maintained an apartment in Euclid. She came back to Ohio periodically to rest and recharge, sometimes attending meetings of the local Ninety-Nines. She never remarried.

"The Ninety-Nines tried to get her to write her memoirs," said Helen Sammon, a flyer and trustee of the International Women's Air and Space Museum (IWASM) in Cleveland. But Blanche couldn't be persuaded. "She didn't like to be in the limelight. She was just a modest person," Sammon said.

When Blanche died in 1981, at age eighty-one, a brief notice in *Time* magazine noted the Bendix triumph and her friendships with Earhart and Rockefeller. But her real legacy is much deeper. Her work in air safety benefited the safety of many generations of flyers. Establishing a visible career in aviation made her a role model and inspiration for other female pilots.

Women of Blanche's generation and the one before her were "a special breed," said writer and historian Sarah Byrn Rickman of Kettering in 2013. They were, in many ways, bigger risk takers than the men, she added. They faced the same dangers in the sky, struggled with equipment and weather, and had to find the money to maintain their craft and travel. All fliers had to prove themselves, but the women especially.

They began flying under the public's assumption that they innately weren't as capable of performing as well as men. They had to be a novelty before they could just be pilots and, later, astronauts. "Blanche was a natural," Rickman said. "She was solid, steady, and she stuck with it. She was working in aviation as a career when not many women were."

Throughout her career, Blanche loved flying solo. As she told Dewey shortly after she started flying in 1929, she never felt alone in the air. Dewey's voice was always in her mind, advising her, encouraging her. And, like many pilots, she felt close to God while flying. When she had her first forced landing in 1929, she found herself alone in a little hotel in the Midwest, thinking of Dewey at home at four o'clock in the morning.

She pulled out a Bible and started reading, then picked up a pen to write to Dewey. In what became known as the "Pilot's Psalm," she paraphrased Psalm 23 for flyers. "Thou preparest an airport before me in the homeland of eternity," she wrote. "My plane flies gracefully, surely sunlight and starlight shall favor me on that last flight I take, and I'll abide in the presence of God forever and ever."

What better epitaph for the girl flyer from Cleveland.

CLAYTON BRUKNER

Aviation Tycoon

Clayton Brukner—whose name is one of the more obscure in Ohio commerce—was responsible for one of most admired small aircraft in the world: WACO planes. His company built close to five thousand aircraft between the 1920s and the early 1950s, all in the small city of Troy in Miami County. Brukner built aircraft for barnstormers, airmail pilots, bootleggers, foreign dictators, American millionaires, the United States Army, and scores of ordinary pilots.

"Ask Any Pilot" became the WACO Company's slogan in the 1930s, and, indeed, it seemed everyone who flew knew of the planes and their reputation for being reliable, fast, and affordable. The personality of the man behind the planes was as multifaceted as his clientele. Over the years, he was described as fun-loving and somber, tight-fisted and generous, aloof and just one of the men on the factory floor.

Brukner's one constant was that he loved to build airplanes that the public loved to buy. Collectors across the country still refurbish and fly the sturdy, brightly-colored original WACOs. The aircraft's allure is so strong that a company in Michigan builds replicas of the original planes to sell to wealthy pilots.

"Brukner was a genius," said Don Willis, a retired aeronautical engineer who volunteers at the WACO Historical Society's (WHS) museum in Troy. "He was eccentric but a genius." Like many of America's self-made millionaires of the early twentieth century, Brukner started out with very little. He was born in 1896 in rural Nebraska, where his father operated a general store and brickyard. As the new century began, his family moved East, looking for opportunities in more populated areas. After World War I, Brukner ended up in Ohio, drawn by the possibility

Clayton Brukner in the 1940s. (Courtesy WACO Historical Society, Troy)

of a life in aviation in a state that would forever be linked to civilization's mastery of the skies.

But Brukner didn't just want to fly planes; he wanted to build them. He wanted his planes to be the most efficient, fastest, most reliable, most coveted aircraft on the planet. He and his best friend, Elwood "Sam" Junkin, were going to build the planes together. "Sam and Clayt's relationship reminds me of Orville and Wilbur Wright. Sam designed the planes, and Clayt built them," said Valentine Dahlem, a retired aeronautical engineer for the United States Air Force and a WHS archivist, in a 2013 interview.

The pair met before the Great War in a schoolhouse in Battle Creek, Michigan. Sam Junkin, a confident teenager with big plans and a weak heart, at first thought classmate Clayt Brukner was a "conceited ass," Junkin's wife once wrote. But once Junkin overlooked Brukner's perfect marcel hairstyle, he discovered they shared a strong interest in flying. The young men became friends, and after graduating from high school in 1915, they pursued their passion together.

"Sam's father had taken him to see an air show in Chicago, and the bug bit him," Brukner once told WACO historian Raymond H. Brandley. "We both were interested in learning to fly, so we pooled our money so one of us could take a four-hour flying course." The course cost $400; the two made about a total of $28 a week at their factory jobs. They tossed a coin to see who would take the class. Junkin won.

Brukner had no hard feelings, however. When Junkin became dangerously ill in 1917 due to his heart problems, Brukner cared for him around the clock until he recovered. During the war, Brukner served as an infantryman in the army. Junkin, exempt from military service due to his health, inspected aircraft for an East Coast manufacturer.

After the war, the pals reconnected in Buffalo, where they began trying to build an aquaplane, using surplus parts from aircraft used in the war. There they met up with two acquaintances: Charlie Meyers, an American who had served with the Royal Air Force during the war, and his brother-in-law George "Buck" Weaver. Before the war, Weaver had flown in exhibition shows with some of the great early pilots, including Mattie Laird and Katherine Stinson. When the United States joined the war, Weaver joined the army and became a flying instructor, serving first at McCook Field in Dayton and later at Richfield Aviation Field in Waco, Texas.

The four men began discussing how to join forces to build aircraft. At the time, Meyers, Weaver, and Weaver's wife—Hattie Meyers Weaver—were living and working in Lorain. Brukner and Junkin joined them in Ohio in 1919, along with Harold C. Deuther, a friend from back East. The three newcomers formed the DBJ Aeroplane Company that fall and began trying to build a plane. After just a few months, however, Deuther decided to move back to New York.

Meyers and Weaver began to work more closely with Brukner and Junkin. It was the beginning of a tangle of business and personal relationships that over the next five years would take as many dips and turns as the most reckless barnstormer. During that period, the group's relations foreshadowed those of many rock and roll bands of the 1960s. They changed their group's name frequently. Individuals intermittently drifted off for solo gigs, then returned to the fold. Egos clashed: credit was claimed and blame assigned by conflicting camps. Hangers-on came and went. There were tragic accidents, forbidden love, and death.

By 1920, Buck and Hattie Weaver and their young son, Buck Jr., were renting a summer cottage and landing field from farmer Harry Woodruff outside Lorain. There the four men began working on a plane that would carry passengers more safely during barnstorming exhibitions. Similar endeavors were taking place in new hangars, old sheds, and frame barns throughout the country. In the 1920s, aviation was a homegrown enterprise. If the Wright Brothers could conceive the first successful airplane in a Dayton bicycle shop, couldn't anyone become the next giant of flight?

Due to his barnstorming fame, Weaver had the best chance of attracting investors. When the partners incorporated the business in 1920, it was named the Weaver Aircraft Company. Their plane would be called a WACO, an acronym of the company and a nod to Weaver's days at the Texas airfield. While some entrepreneurs had wealthy backers, these four men had only each other and an assortment of relatives who occasionally appeared to help them. They were so poor that it was a struggle to keep themselves fed. When they swept up their shop at night, they carefully collected cigarette butts to cull tobacco to roll the next day's smokes. At one point, Brukner and Junkin bunked in an old barn loft, where rats scrambled over them as they tried to sleep.

Their first prototype, developed primarily by Weaver and Junkin, was nicknamed "the Cootie." The single-seat monoplane was built with a lightweight wooden frame, covered by mahogany plywood, and powered by a two-cylinder engine. Some of the parts were surplus, some were new, and some were constructed in the shop. The Cootie was insubstantial and unstable, but it was a learning tool. Self-taught engineers could only learn what worked, and what didn't, from their most recent designs. Only in real time could one see how the plane handled on takeoff, in the air, and during landing. No one expected the process to be easy, or safe. Crashes were inevitable. Weaver, the group's test pilot, had to make a forced landing while testing a plane. Although he survived, his injuries were severe. After a prolonged convalescence, he continued working on the WACO, but he was never really well again.

The WACO 4 became the partners' first full-size biplane. Like the Cootie, it was built of naturally finished mahogany plywood. Its fabric wings were coated in a weatherproof dope, then varnished; there was no hint of the colorful paints and stains that later became WACO hallmarks. The focus was on safety and efficiency and room for passengers: folks who would pay for the thrill of riding along with a daredevil pilot. The Model 4 featured a rear cockpit for the pilot and a front cockpit with three passenger seats, in a clover-leaf design. The company took this model to the public to raise money. Weaver flew, and Brukner was the wing-walker.

While Meyers and the Weavers went off again to earn living expenses, Brukner and Junkin found a better factory space in Medina. They gained the support of A. I. Root, the man who founded the Root Bee Supply Company, and his son-in-law, Howard Calvert. The business moved to Medina in the summer of 1921, at which point work began on the WACO 5. The planes were exhibited at the first Detroit Aviation Exposition in April 1922 and received some notice there.

Tragically, Calvert and his wife, Elvira, died in the 1923 crash of their WACO 5 at Stow Field near Kent. But accidents, setbacks, and fatalities were all part of the process. They were obstacles to overcome, and the men were committed to success. Already, the fledgling company was beginning practices that would make it an industry leader. It designed for a specific need (enabling passengers to ride with barnstormers), and it publicized its planes wisely (exhibiting in Detroit).

Bruckner provided much of the momentum. Weaver, still unwell after the 1920 forced landing, left the team numerous times over the next two years to find work to support Hattie and little Buck. Meyers felt increasingly edged out by the others. Junkin continued to work closely on new WACOs, but he had distractions: he had become smitten with the vivacious Hattie Weaver, and his growing attraction to her was an unwelcome complication. Now, even when the men were in the same town, they no longer lived under the same roof.

The straight arrow of the group, Brukner began taking more responsibility for day-to-day operations. He didn't smoke, chew, drink, or step out with the ladies. WACO planes were his life. Weaver taught him how to fly in the summer of 1922. He learned fast and soloed by fall.

Brukner was in Troy in the spring of 1923 to check out a manufacturing site when he met Alden Sampson II, a young man who had just come into trust-fund money and was looking for a business venture. Troy, a town of about seventy-five hundred souls, had some industry but was trying to attract more. A city councilman who was working with the Troy Business Men's Association (TBMA) reported to council that the association was lukewarm to downright apathetic about the issue. The TBMA was looking for financial support from the council to help it formulate a plan.

Given that aviation companies were the time's most promising businesses and that Troy was a mere fifteen miles away from the United States Army Air Corps' Wright Field, it seems officials would be actively searching for such a firm. Anything that concerned flight and airplanes regularly made front-page news across America. The *Troy Daily News* was keeping citizens updated, prominently publishing photographs and stories related to flight. Just that spring, Trojans learned that Italian premier Benito Mussolini was taking off from Milan in his private plane for a secret mission. He was rather ominously reported to be "greatly interested in aviation and watches eagerly the progress being made in the air."

The *Daily News* carried many national stories of aviation as well. Up on Fox Island in a still-frozen Lake Michigan, pilots were making risky deliveries of food to ten marooned woodcutters who were said to be near starvation before a brave flyer discovered them. Down in Alabama, Troy native Wallace Pearson was recuperating from two broken legs as a result of a crash landing. His plane had been caught up in the wake of a cyclone, and he had narrowly managed to land it before it was drawn into the woods. Pearson's three passengers also survived as a result of his skillful handling of the plane. On a much, much lighter note, one story included a photo of the Gingham Girls of Miami, Florida, performing a dance routine on the wing of a seaplane.

Airplanes were powerful; they were heroic; they were entertainment, and they hinted at national power. Airplanes were even getting top billing down at Troy's Jewel Theater, where Tom Mix's new movie, *Do and Dare,* was showing for ticket prices of 17 and 28 cents. The movie advertisement shows Mix hanging onto the lower wing of a biplane, apparently having just leapt off his horse to go airborne in pursuit of the bad guys. It was an apt metaphor for the public's consciousness. Perhaps it was inevitable then that Alden Sampson's mother and the trust-fund attorneys agreed to invest $20,000 in the company's move to town.

Trojans first heard of the move in a brief March 28 front-page item. "Rumors are flying thick and fast that Troy has been selected as the home of the Advance Aircraft Company," a *Daily News* writer reported. Bruckner and Junkin had bought out Buck Weaver's share of the company for $1,000 and taken his name out of the business. The new name recognized the partners' fathers: Brukner's had been associated with the Advance Thrasher Company in Nebraska, where Clayt had been born, and Junkin's had worked for the Advance-Rumley Company in Battle Creek.

The new name seemed appropriate for practical reasons as well, since aircraft were the future. The new facilities were where the Pioneer Pole and Shaft Company had made parts for horse-drawn carriages—the future was supplanting the past with a vengeance. Hattie wrote in her memoir that Brukner became the "bookkeeper, champion welder, jack of all trades," and test pilot. Weaver and Brukner flew out to an air race in St. Louis in October 1923, where Weaver, now an employee, demonstrated the plane, to favorable reactions.

But no great venture proceeds without setbacks. Weaver died in July 1924 in Illinois, where he had gone for a job. Hattie was convinced that his death was related to lingering complications of the 1920 accident. Sampson, who had pledged to work at the airplane factory, soon lost interest and dropped out, along with his financial backers. Brukner and Junkin bought Sampson's shares. They were on their own again, but in a better position than before.

As Junkin and Brukner continued to make improved designs at their small factory, townspeople in Troy began to see more and more planes taking off and landing, literally in the streets at times, particularly on

Walker Street. Sometimes, farmers agreed to let the planes use their fields. One—with whom whom Brukner soon parted ways—charged $2 per takeoff.

Folks were fascinated by the planes. The concept of municipal airports was just catching on, so most of the action took place in fields, which meant rural and small-town people were as apt as their city counterparts to take a ride in the skies. Dale Francis, a onetime editor of the *Troy Daily News,* remembered moving to town as a boy in 1926 and being electrified by the regular sight of planes flying. Until then, he had only seen one aircraft in person. "It was hardly more than a speck in the sky that we watched until it disappeared," Francis wrote in 1978. "In Troy, you could not only see planes every day but see them going through intricate maneuvers, looping the loop, falling like a leaf in the wind, diving, ascending."

After a long week of working in the factory and test-flying, Junkin and Brukner spent Sundays taking locals for short rides in their two-seater biplane, for a fee of $2 per passenger, which was important in keeping the company going. Brukner and Junkin shared lodgings in town and took many of their meals at the Dog House Restaurant on Market Street.

After Weaver's death, Junkin stayed in touch with Hattie, who was living with relatives. In 1925, they married, and she and Buck Jr. moved back to Troy. Hattie soon became pregnant. Brukner's elderly father came for a visit, staying with the Junkin family. The Advance Aircraft Company was still a family affair but the dynamics had changed.

Most important to Brukner, the WACOs were beginning to be noticed—and to sell. The WACO 7 and WACO 8 were shown at the Dayton Air Races in the fall of 1924, but didn't race. Brukner was already concentrating on setting up a sales network and lining up distributors. In 1925, the WACO 9 competed in the first Ford Reliability Good Will Tour. This was the period's premier air show, started by Henry Ford, who was expanding his empire from automobiles to aircraft.

Air tours were intended to familiarize the public with flying and to foster the development of faster, better planes. Races, precision flying events, and barnstorming shows were part of the fun. The tours boosted reputations and attracted business for manufacturers such as Advance Aircraft. The WACO 9 achieved a perfect score in its class at the 1925 show, an honor shared by another popular plane, Walter Beech's Travel Air.

That year, Advance sold forty-seven WACOs. It was more than a modest success. With only a few hundred planes flying North American skies, Advance was getting into position to become an aviation leader. Production was in full swing at the plant in Troy, but tragedy loomed.

In the fall of 1926, Bruckner's father, still living in Troy, died unexpectedly and Junkin, who had suffered from a weak heart since childhood, became ill. Brukner took time from production to drive a very pregnant Hattie to visit Junkin in a Dayton hospital, where he died just ten days after Brukner's father. Brukner was devastated. Without his old pal by his side, he couldn't imagine continuing the business. But Meyers and another employee, Ed Green, urged him to keep going. Meyers jumped on the chance to be more involved in aircraft design; he and Green began to work on the design for a Model 10.

Soon after Junkin's death, Hattie had their baby, whom she named Janet. Brukner bought the remainder of Hattie's interest in the business for a generous price. She hung on in Troy for a while, but she felt like she was no longer needed or wanted. Eventually, she moved on. "The company had gone ahead by leaps and bounds," Hattie wrote in her memoir. "The WACO 9s had propelled the company to a place in the industry that made the orders for the new WACO 10 so enormous they were having difficulty filling them." Advance sold a staggering 164 aircraft in 1926, and the most popular WACO of all time had yet to be designed.

Because of Brukner's stubbornness, that plane almost didn't see creation. Sam Junkin had been Clayt's best friend and the only person who he really collaborated with well. After his death, Charlie Meyers—then WACO's test pilot and demonstrator—proposed a new plane, which Brukner absolutely did not want to build.

He wanted to build airplanes for Everyman: ordinary pilots who would fly for their own pleasure on personal trips, businessmen who would use the WACOs to transport mail, cargo, and passengers. "He wanted to make WACO's reputation as a builder of safe, reliable planes that were affordable," Dahlem said. "Charlie wanted to build high-performance racers." Meyers, who had come up through the barnstorming circuit, knew the pull of speed. With numerous aircraft manufacturers opening across the country, there would be more competition for planes that could fly farther and faster and perform more precisely.

"Movie stars and journalists were beginning to buy planes, and they wanted something fast and powerful," Dahlem said. Meyers came up with the WACO Taperwing, basically a WACO 10 with a few important modifications. The wings were tapered, similar to those on new fighter planes then being built for the army and navy. But what made the Taperwing a standout was its powerful engine: a 220 horsepower Wright Whirlwind radial engine. "When they put that engine in the Taperwing, they couldn't hold that plane down," Dahlem said. "Brukner went into production kicking and screaming, but that plane built WACO's reputation for high-performance planes. It carried the company through the Depression."

The Taperwing had a top speed of 135 miles per hour, which made it in demand for aerobatic exhibitions, closed-course air races, and cross-country air derbies. That's where the money was in the late 1920s, and competitive flyers began turning to WACOs. Meyers, however, was so disgusted with Brukner's lack of trust and enthusiasm that he broke with him for good, leaving Troy to work for Great Lakes Aircraft in Chicago. Brukner, who was uncomfortable with customers and loathed selling, knew he had to come up with a test pilot who was outgoing, well-known, and convincing.

He chose well. Freddie Lund—"Fearless Freddie" as he was known on the air show circuit—was one of the most daring and popular stunt pilots of the day. Lund, a dazzling aerialist with the long-running Ivan Gates Flying Circus, had flown planes in several movies. As Lund began promoting WACOs, his wife, Betty, also a pilot, set up housekeeping in Troy.

With business booming, Brukner either had to build new facilities in Troy or move elsewhere. Civic leaders put together almost $19,000 to entice him to stay in town. He bought 120 acres on the southwest side of town and started work on a $150,000 factory and airfield in 1928. When the company incorporated that year, its minority stockholders included a number of aviation luminaries, including Captain Eddie Rickenbacker, the World War I ace. Brukner retained 50 percent of the stock.

As president, Brukner devoted his life to WACO. Invention was a passion, not just a business for him. He never married. He had few close friends. "The hours he put in at the factory were amazing," Don Willis said. Charles Moffitt, a service manager at WACO for many years, described Brukner as a "gadgeteer," in a 1979 interview he had with Dick Fraiser, the first WHS president. "At WACO, his main interest was the plant. He didn't care about guys like me. The office was nothing. He considered the office overhead," Moffitt said. "He liked the men in the plant and he liked to work out in the plant. He'd go out there anytime . . . welding, [operating] a lathe, or running a drill press, or fixing the wiring, working on the plumbing. It was his life."

The designers would tell Brukner what sort of a part they needed and what the part had to do. He would think of the best solution, then build the prototype. The piece next went to a draftsman, who'd make a drawing of the part so it could be produced. There seemed no end to Brukner's ability to tinker and create.

By 1929, WACO was the "undisputed leader in its field," wrote aviation historian Walter J. Bayne. The Troy factory had built more than nineteen hundred planes by that time. Brukner formally changed the company's name to WACO Aircraft in 1929 to help solidify the brand. The planes became known for performance and reliability, but they had something more: a flash of sporty glamour that made them look as though they'd be *fun* to fly. When the company introduced its first cabin cruiser, it was not the only such biplane on the market, but "none were as pretty" as the WACO, Bayne wrote.

Enthusiasts often compare planes to racehorses, and the descriptions of the classic WACOs fit that analogy perfectly. With glossy, saturated bright blues, chrome yellow, scarlets, and blacks, a flight line of WACOs easily conjures up visions of horses and jockeys sporting their colors at a big race. It was another marketing strategy that paid off, and it also helped to make WACOs one of the most collectible aircraft ever.

"Unlike most of the aircraft of the time, the WACO was dressed up at the factory with things that normally cost extra," Bayne wrote of one model that is on display at the Smithsonian, "including such eye catchers as wheel pants or the sexy close-fitting cowl, which had sporty, stream-lined bumps over the rocker arm fittings." Brukner wanted to prove to customers that not only did nothing fly like a WACO, but nothing on the market looked exactly like it either.

Another of Brukner's strategies was selling his planes in other countries, particularly to foreign governments. Amazingly, in 1929, China became one of the first governments to purchase WACOs; the government of the Canton Province purchased five three-passenger biplanes in late March or early April, and the planes were scheduled to be delivered by late May. A few other provinces also bought U.S. planes from other companies, including Ryan-Mahoney that year, primarily for airmail and passenger services.

Several planes, fitted for machine guns, were sold to various military figures in Central and South America during the turbulent 1920s and 1930s, when coups and counter-coups were almost the order of the day. WACO built more than forty planes for the Brazilian government. In 1932, rebel forces targeted for destruction a shipment of five WACOs en route from Rio de Janeiro to the northeastern front lines.

The rebels were attempting to bring down the ruling dictatorship in favor of a constitutional government. The government planned to use the WACOs to keep the constitutionalists under control. A freight train was tranporting the planes to the front. Twenty sticks of dynamite, allegedly planted by the rebels, were found tied to a piece of timber, connected to the rails under a culvert. According to an Associated Press report, the device was set to explode at the instant the train passed over the spot. An unnamed railway employee spotted the explosives and alerted his boss, who reported the plot to the government officials, who came in and neutralized the device several hours before the train was scheduled to pass. The story indicated the chaotic nature of Brazilian affairs, noting that the WACOs, although delivered intact, would not increase the government's strength. Just as the Ohio-built planes were being delivered, a group of government fliers had deserted to the rebel forces, taking six other airplanes with them.

Whatever side was planning to use the planes, Brukner would have been ready to supply them. He had been quick to see the possibilities of international sales, although some of the credit for that push belongs to Lee Brutus, WACO's vice president, who became the company's public face. An engineer himself, Brutus was as outgoing as Brukner was reserved. He excelled at working with distributors and private clients. By 1931, Brukner had also hired Francis Arcier, an Englishman known for his outstanding aircraft designs. As chief engineer, Arcier hired several other engineers, who together designed many of the most popular WACOs in the company's history.

While some WACOs were being sent abroad, others had owners waiting anxiously for them in Troy. Pilots eager to get their new planes checked into the Hotel Lollis to await delivery. Customers received their planes in the order in which they had registered at the hotel; according to Brukner, some pilots paid as much as $900 to jump line.

Perhaps the most glamorous flier who came to Troy to pick up a plane was Lady Grace Drummond-Hay, who rolled into town in 1933, accompanied by her very proper male secretary. Drummond-Hay was one of those beautiful, bright, slightly scandalous "foreigners" that the American public adored. In 1920, at twenty-five, she married Lord Robert Drummond-Hay, fifty years her senior. When he died six years into the marriage, Lady Grace became a journalist.

She first wrote for the British press, primarily about aviation and specifically about zeppelins. In 1929, she become an international celebrity as the only female passenger aboard the Graf zeppelin as it made its way around the world—the first global flight. The Hearst newspaper syndicate, which sponsored the Graf's journey, hired Drummond-Hay to report on the flight from aboard the craft. The thought of a woman undertaking such a dangerous trip shocked and thrilled the public.

Her presence on the Graf was a novelty, and her reports of the flight centered on the frivolous: reporting on the comfortable quarters in the huge airship and the luxurious meals featuring green turtle soup, squabs, and strawberries and cream. When she returned to New York City intact, having filed reports all along the way, she was welcomed as if she were the biggest film star in the world. But as Drummond-Hay continued to travel the world, she began to cover major news stories in a more professional manner. While she often traveled with another married Hearst journalist, Karl Henry von Wiegand, who was her occasional lover, she also pursued serious interests. She became interested in aviation as a flier, and she earned her license.

In March 1933, Drummond-Hay was in Berlin to conduct a one-on-one interview with Herman Goering, the "most feared man in Germany today," she wrote. Goering had only recently been named head of Hitler's secret police, but he was already vowing to "exterminate this pest [Communists], root and branch, ruthlessly." He also made it clear in the interview that he had no use for Jews, whom he said could never be trusted to become German nationalists.

Troy must have been a pleasant respite for her after Germany's ominous atmosphere. She spent several days at the factory watching her WACO being built, while the secretaries and factory workers eagerly watched the celebrity client whenever they had the chance. A catastrophe threatened one day, however, when Lady Grace errantly walked into the men's restroom at the plant. A gaggle of nearby secretaries—mortified by the impropriety of the situation and awed by her ladyship—feared to enter the restroom to correct her mistake. Instead, they maintained watch outside until the lady exited, apparently unfazed by whatever accommodations she had found. When her cabin-model WACO was completed, she jumped into it and flew to New York City. There the plane was placed on the deck of a steamship to travel to England. Drummond-Hay also made news in 1933 by being the only female passenger on the triumphant maiden voyage of another new zeppelin: the *Hindenberg*.

No record has been found of Brukner's reaction to Drummond-Hay's visit. If he did speak with her it was probably about the construction and features of her new plane. For him, life was more about the building of the WACOs, rather than the clients that bought them.

Charlie Moffitt, however, vividly remembered certain customers.

Prior to 1933, many bootleggers chose WACO open cockpit models to transport hooch. "Used to take them up in Michigan and along the Canadian border to fly liquor," Moffitt said. "Those fellows had money. They'd come in for service and they always paid in cash. They'd have a wad of bills and peel it out to you." The WACO employees didn't know at first what they were doing with the planes, he said, but when the WACOs returned for service, they noticed their serial numbers had been sawed off, and they drew their own conclusions.

Another set of clients Moffitt remembered were all members of one family: the Du Ponts, one of the most prominent and richest dynasties in America. The patriarch was a French American chemist who in the early 1800s began manufacturing gun powder in Delaware. The business branched out into dynamite and, later, chemicals of all sorts. WACO, according to Moffitt, sold planes to multiple branches of the family.

"They were people who thought nothing about buying $5,000 of radio equipment, but they'd argue with me for fifteen minutes about the price of a door latch," he said. One day, Felix du Pont, great-great-grandson of the company's founder, was in Troy to get his plane serviced. He noticed that an improved door latch had been built since one of his relatives had purchased his plane. He inquired about buying one for his relative but really had to mull it over when he learned the new latch cost fifty-five cents. Felix—who later became cofounder of the predecessor of U.S. Airways—finally decided to let the other fellow buy the piece himself. "That's the way they were," Moffitt said. "Beautiful people. But thrifty, you know?"

Brukner also believed in thrift. Maybe it was the memory of bunking in a rat-plagued hayloft, or maybe just a sense of personal responsibility, but he was generally careful with money. At the end of the workday, he'd walk around the shop floor, collecting stray nuts and bolts in a battered keg to take back to the farm for his own inventions. He insisted that any supplies he took home be charged to his account, Moffitt recalled.

By 1934, WACO employed more than 175 people full-time. Brukner had been prudent in purchasing enough land to house his whole operation together. Factories and shops, hangars, landing fields, and an administration building were in one complex. Workers made about forty-five cents an hour, or about $18 for a five-day workweek.

Factory employees were required to ride in a WACO at least once a year. "They told us, "You build 'em, you fly 'em," former employee Willard Kingham said in an article published shortly after Brukner's death in 1977. "He knew the first name of everyone in the shop," said Harry Reck, another retiree.

Stories about Brukner abound in Troy, a city he endowed with good things for fifty years. Troy's cooperation with Brukner paid off for the city, as well. A hospital wing, scholarships, charitable donations, parks, and a highly regarded nature center are a few of his legacies. He never forgot the community's help in getting the business firmly planted, and he looked for ways to repay the debt. Civic responsibility was practically a religion to him. The locals lionized him, during his life and afterward.

All of this makes conflicting stories about his personality more tantalizing. Don Willis shared a tale passed on by a prominent Troy citizen who, as a boy, had done some work for Brukner. The boy had been hired to mow the magnate's large lawn for two dollars. After completing the long, hot job, he waited for Brukner to return home to be paid. But Brukner wasn't satisfied with the cutting job, and he declined to pay until the job was done properly. The boy returned the next day to improve his work and receive his pay. Once again, Brukner wasn't satisfied. After trying again and being rebuffed, the boy gave up.

Gretchen Hawk of the WACO museum shared another story, told by a museum visitor one day in 2013. The man said that his grandfather had worked at WACO and had an interesting encounter with the boss soon after starting work there. He was walking to work in the rain one day when a gentleman in a fine car stopped and offered him a ride. He asked the man where he could drop him. Upon learning that the man worked at WACO, the gentleman asked him how he liked it there.

"Oh, it's all right," the worker said, "but they sure could pay a little more." He thanked the gentleman for the ride, and went in to work. The next day, he and the other factory workers learned that a government inspection was scheduled. When he saw the inspector accompanied by the gentleman who had given him a ride, he had a sinking feeling. A coworker quickly confirmed that the gentleman was indeed Brukner. He braced himself for a reprimand—or worse—over his impudence of the previous day. But nothing happened that day. In fact, nothing happened until he received his next paycheck, when he saw with surprise that he—and presumably the other workers—had received a raise.

As for the boss, he didn't overspend on personal habits. Fine cars seemed to have been Brukner's one gift to himself. Early on, when WACO was becoming successful, he bought a robin's-egg blue Cord, which he later replaced with a roomy Chrysler Airflow. In 1929, he purchased an old family farm about one mile south of the WACO complex. His bachelor brother Clem managed the farm, where he raised dogs and Arabian horses. Brukner's other large land purchase was 146 acres of woodland five miles west of town, in 1934. The land was his personal sanctuary. He didn't hunt or fish; he just walked and observed, enjoying the beauty of nature.

Whether at the farm or the plant, Brukner was always busy: planning, tinkering, inventing. This usually took place behind the scenes. He didn't interact much with routine customers. But one day he was called into service to take a prospective customer out for a test flight. Freddie Lund was long gone by this time—killed in a fiery crash while racing a Taperwing in a closed-course race in Lexington, Kentucky, in the fall of 1931. On this particular day when a test pilot was needed, no other demonstration pilots were available. The customers, two brothers from Cleveland, were getting impatient, so Moffitt went to Brukner's office to ask what to do.

"I'll do it. It's my airplane," Brukner said, abruptly rising from his chair to walk to the landing field. Moffitt was stunned that the boss was going to deal with customers. He also had to be concerned that Brukner was going up in the company's new WACO Model N. It was no secret that engineering and construction fascinated Brukner much more than actual flying. He seldom flew. According to research by Fred O. Kobernuss, another WACO historian, between 1929 and 1933

Brukner averaged about only two and a half hours in the sky monthly. After that, he flew even more infrequently, although he maintained a pilot's license until the 1950s.

Moffitt watched anxiously as Brukner silently climbed into the cockpit with one of the brothers. Takeoff was good. The flight, although brief, went smoothly. Then Brukner came in to land. Moffitt's eyes popped when he realized that the boss had forgotten to set down the landing flaps, which essentially function as brakes.

"He brought that thing in and hit the ground. . . . He must have been going one hundred miles per hour," Moffitt said. Normally, the plane could land "on a postage stamp," but without the flaps down, the sales manager wondered if the Model N was ever going to stop. "[Brukner] was clear out at the back fence before he got that thing turned around. He got out of the airplane, never said a word, and took off for the office."

"'Hey,' asked the passenger, emerging from the N, 'did he need that much room to get that thing in there?'" Without revealing to the brothers who their test pilot was, Moffitt convinced them that the plane could be landed in a normal space, at a reduced speed. He made the sale, and he and Brukner never discussed the incident.

Another group that made Brukner uncomfortable was beauracrats. "There was always a tension between him and the government types," Willis said. "Clayt was never philosophically in tune with them." The tension was largely because he had trouble acquiescing to anyone else's demands when it came to building *his* aircraft. He didn't have a university degree, didn't hobnob with politicians in Washington or party with the millionaires who bought his planes. But he knew about airplane construction, and he knew that when a WACO left the factory in Troy, it had been built correctly. If a postproduction problem was discovered, he made it right. For example, when a problem was discovered with the 1935 Custom Model WACO after the craft had been delivered to distributors, WACO sent workers all over the country to fix it.

Obviously, Brukner had experience working with foreign governments: various Central and South American governments had bought numerous aircraft from him. In 1935, a WACO named *Friend of Iran* flew off to the Mideast to be used in locating ruins of ancient Persian cities. In the 1930s, the United States Army and Navy had both ordered WACOs to be used as trainers. Brukner and his crew could build a plane with any required specifications, and do it to the buyer's satisfaction, but

Brukner didn't want to have to justify how the planes were built—he didn't want a lot of red tape from bureaucrats whose sole construction experience was assembling a bike for their kid on Christmas morning.

So when World War II came along, it offered WACO its greatest potential commercial success, but it also presented Brukner with his greatest challenge. Germany and the Axis powers had increased the use of transport gliders to move troops and cargo. The Allies saw a similar need for gliders to make deliveries in occupied Europe. Congress authorized United States Army Air Corps commanding general Henry "Hap" Arnold—whom the Wright brothers had reportedly instructed in flying—to begin a transport glider program.

WACO was already heavily involved in wartime production, as were most aviation industries. The Troy factory was building training planes for student use in the Civilian Pilot Training Program. With most of the nation's commercial pilots pressed into military service, private pilots and nonflyers had to be trained to take over the country's day-to-day flight needs.

By September 1940, WACO was operating seven days a week to turn out three aircraft a day. Management was hustling to find and train new employees. By the end of 1942, the need for trainers abated. But then WACO announced the glider program; the company had produced a few hundred small gliders in the 1930s, but the transport gliders were a whole different species. Depending on the model, the gliders would need to transport thirteen soldiers and all their equipment; a quarter-ton Jeep; a 75 mm Howitzer cannon; or any other combination of weaponry, food, and medical supplies.

Vice President Brutus had left WACO at the beginning of the war to become head of Luscombe Aircraft Company, a bigger operation. But Arcier was still on board as chief engineer. He and his fellow designers came up with a glider that they thoroughly tested at Wright Field before General Arnold accepted it. WACO soon began building the gilders, as did fifteen other companies, who all used WACO's design.

The war drastically changed the atmosphere at the company. Up through the 1930s, WACO had never employed more than two hundred workers, and that was only during peak times. The small-town, family feeling that characterized the early days with Buck and Hattie Weaver, Sam Junkin, and Charlie Meyers had remained even as the company grew. Dale Francis remembered endless hours of just hanging around the plant after school and during the summer in the late 1920s and early 1930s, watching planes being made, two or three at a time. Industrial espionage and grueling assembly lines weren't concerns in Troy. "You could sit quietly to one side and watch, and no one minded," Francis wrote. Occasionally, one of the workmen would throw a scrap of fuselage wood to a youngster as a souvenir.

With the new glider program, however, quiet days turned into around-the-clock shifts of intensive labor. Almost two thousand employees were soon at work. That brought something that Brukner had deliberately avoided his entire professional life: a unionized shop. WACO had the reputation of being a pretty good place to work—as long as you didn't openly defy the boss. Charlie Moffitt recalled how in aviation's honeymoon phase of the 1920s, men had actually volunteered to work at the factory for free, just to be a part of the new industry. Brukner never allowed that, but he did appreciate how dedicated his employees were, and he came to expect it.

"There was never a problem about people working overtime or helping out," Moffitt said. "They were so engrossed in what they were doing that it was a pleasure for them." But with a huge government contract and a record number of employees, unionization became a fact. "Clayt hated the union," Dahlem said. "He felt that everyone who worked there was like him: they were there because they loved the work. That company was like his wife. Suddenly, he was forced to sit in the corner and watch some shop steward take over? Who the hell was that? He went crazy."

But no matter how he detested the union, he had to put up with it. The business was too important to the company, and the gliders proved vital to the Allies winning in Europe. An estimated 19,903 gliders were produced during the war, all of WACO design, and 999 of them built at the Troy shop. In addition to the United States Army Air Corps and United States Navy, the gliders were used by the Royal Air Force and Royal Canadian Air Force. One of the most evocative images of the D-Day invasion is of the huge gliders carrying troops, supplies, and medical personal into enemy territory.

Regardless of the WACO glider's use in the war effort, Brukner's attitude toward the union remained the same. When the contract finally expired in 1946, WACO maintained that the majority of its employees did not want union representation. With the war won, the government contract finished, and the number of employees greatly reduced, the union push lost steam. "Clayt said that he would rather close the plant than put up with the union, and he would have done it," Dahlem said.

WACO suddenly had much greater postwar problems than just the labor union threat. Trainers, gliders, and spare parts for both had kept business humming during the war, but those needs were gone. WACO's net sales for 1944 and 1945 were greater than $25.3 million, according to Dahlem's research. That level of sales would not be reached again. Brukner and his top officers decided to concentrate their efforts on developing and building a new type of plane. Where the majority of WACOs were constructed of wood, the new Aristocraft four-passenger, cabin model would have metal wings and a steel fuselage. The plane's landing gear and locations of the engine and drive shaft were considered unconventional.

After a great deal of time and work, the Aristocraft was deemed a bust, one no one wanted to take credit for. The fiasco seemed to sour Brukner on aircraft construction. WACO continued to build replacement parts for its earlier models, and some new planes were built, but the days of producing legendary aircraft were done. During the Korean War, the company manufactured bomb dollies, but by 1959, all production had ceased.

Brukner, meanwhile, was becoming more involved in some of his other inventions, which he had been working on for years. He had always invented and built, even when not in the plant. In the 1920s, he built his own car to drive between work and his farm. An automated log splitter was one of his proudest—and best-selling—inventions. A therapeutic sunlamp that he designed was patented in Canada.

Brukner had to be working with his hands to be happy. Even as a member of the local Stouder Memorial Hospital board, he was happier with his sleeves rolled up and a wrench in his hand than in a boardroom. When the hospital boiler broke down one day, Brukner simply went down into the basement and fixed the problem himself rather than having a plumber called in, recalled Don Willis. Brukner was in his seventies when work started on the Brukner Nature Center, but he still climbed on a bulldozer and cleared part of the land he had purchased back in 1934. The marcel waves were long gone, but his desire to create was just as strong.

Brukner's brother, Clem, died in 1976. Brukner continued living at the farm, where a housekeeper kept life running smoothly. While most people considered him a rather dour, aloof man, the housekeeper's daughter remembered him making little gadgets for her and telling her jokes, Dahlem said.

Brukner died on December 26, 1977, just one week after his eighty-first birthday, in a hospital room in Kettering, surrounded by blueprints for yet more inventions. In the *Troy Daily News*, Dale Francis eulogized him as one of the community's most benevolent citizens.

Troy had has several other important industries over the years, he wrote, but "Waco was our connection with the world. It brought fabulous people to Troy. . . . But most of all it brought pride to the community." As Willis said, "Everyone in aviation who knew Clayton Brukner respected what he did with WACO."

Just ask any WACO pilot.

| 10 |

MILDRED GILLARS
Traitor and Teacher

Like Greta Garbo, once Mildred Gillars became famous, her greatest wish was to be left alone. But while Garbo only acted out dramatic scenes of deception on screen, during World War II the former Ohio Wesleyan coed lived a life of treason as a radio voice of Nazi Germany.

Gillars spent her youth and old age in Ohio, but it was her role as Axis Sally in Berlin and subsequent treason conviction that put her in the history books as a woman gone wrong, one who was surprisingly unrepentant about betraying her country.

It's tempting to say that the seeds of Gillars's downfall were sewn in her childhood. She was born to Vincent and Mae Sisk in Portland, Maine, in 1900. The new century would witness numerous changes for women, many the result of the two world wars in America's first half century. But when Mildred Elizabeth Sisk was born, women did not yet have the right to vote. Divorce was still exceptionally rare, as was higher education for women.

Mae Sisk, Mildred's mother, soon regretted her marriage. Vincent drank heavily, smoked opium, and beat her regularly. It's not known whether he ever beat his pretty dark-haired, brown-eyed daughter, but it's fairly certain he didn't lavish much fatherly love upon her. After seven years of abuse, Mae divorced Vincent. From then on, he was dead to Mildred and Mae.

One year after the divorce, Mae married Robert Gillars, a dentist. The new family moved from town to town in eastern Canada and the United States as Gillars tended to working-class patients. By 1914, the family, which now included Edna Mae—Mildred's half-sister—was in Bellevue,

Mildred Gillars, late 1940s. (Authors' collection)

Ohio. They moved to Conneaut in 1916, where Robert established a successful practice.

Mildred took Gillars as her surname, although her stepfather never adopted her. She did not warm to Robert or Edna Mae, remaining a detached yet obedient child, according to biographer Richard Lucas. A reporter who interviewed Gillars during her treason trial suggested that Robert might have been abusive, but she never publicly spoke of any mistreatment. Her one strong bond was to her mother.

Once she entered high school in Conneaut she developed another love: theater. She enrolled at Ohio Wesleyan in Delaware because of the reputation of its theater department and of Professor Charles M. Newcomb. Newcomb would be the first of "a series of intellectual older men whose influence shaped her fate," Lucas wrote in his 2010 biography. Like many young women who grow up without a positive father figure, Mildred kept searching for a strong man who would take an interest in her. Once she found that man, she would do anything for him.

At college, Mildred became known for her stylish clothes and vampish ways. She was said to be the first coed there to wear knickers, a slightly scandalous new fashion. She idolized movie actresses, like the exotic Theda Bara, and drew her share of male admirers. She became engaged to a student with whom she spent much of her time. Ignoring her studies, she began failing or receiving incompletes in many classes. Newcomb convinced her to drop out of college to pursue stage acting.

Mae was shocked. Her second marriage was in tatters. Robert, like her first husband, had become an alcoholic, and they separated. In 1919, he left Conneaut to set up a practice in Elyria and by 1922 was working and living in Piqua. Mae hoped Mildred could avoid similar marital disasters by becoming a well-educated, independent woman. She wanted her daughter to never be dependent on men who were dangerously undependable.

But Mildred, drawn by the applause and accolades she had received in college productions, was determined to become an actress. Newcomb recommended she enroll in Chronicle House, a Cleveland drama school whose students had the opportunity to act with visiting well-known professional actors. Coincidentally, Newcomb was also leaving Delaware for Cleveland. About the same time, Mildred broke off her engagement.

In Cleveland, Mildred found a tiny room in a boardinghouse. Newcomb arranged for her to get a sales position at the Halle Brothers Department Store downtown, where she earned $15 a week, plus commission, at the jewelry counter. Once she paid her tuition and rent, she had little left for necessities. She often survived on nothing but crackers and apples; in fact, during rehearsal one evening, she fainted from hunger. When the school's director learned of her circumstances, her tuition was reduced.

After a year in Cleveland, Mildred Gillars decided she was ready for Broadway. She moved to Greenwich Village and worked a succession of menial jobs while taking acting lessons and auditioning. She toured with acting companies, but while she had a lovely voice and acceptable skill, she didn't stand out in any way. She had a good figure, long black hair, and pretty eyes. She wasn't conventionally pretty, though, and that may have prevented her from starring in the vaudeville shows she worked.

She wanted to be more than just another girl in a chorus line. She wanted fame. She sought it in Europe: in 1929, she went to Paris, where she worked as an artist's model; a nude photograph of her as a photographer's model in the Library of Congress archives suggests the type of work she was doing. Although her occupation wasn't unusual for a woman trying to work as an actress, the folks back in Delaware certainly would have been scandalized.

She showed up in North Africa in 1933. By 1934, she was in Dresden, Germany, supposedly to study music. After further travel, she was back living in Germany by the late 1930s.

Mae traveled to Europe in the summer of 1939, hoping to persuade her elder daughter to return to the States. The two enjoyed their visit, and Mae thought Mildred seemed happy. She refused, however, to consider moving home. Meanwhile, opportunities for Americans to leave Germany were diminishing rapidly. Hitler was already in power, and expatriates could not evade the gathering turmoil. Mildred's connection to Germany grew more personal when she became engaged to Paul Karlson, a German citizen.

But life had never gone smoothly for Mildred, and her contentment didn't last long this time, either. Karlson was sent to fight on the eastern front, where he was killed. With Germany already at war, it would have been difficult—though not impossible—for her to leave. But she didn't even try. After Pearl Harbor, she signed a loyalty oath to the Third Reich.

Gillars also began a relationship with Max Otto Koischwitz, a German citizen who came to the United States in the mid-1920s to become a college professor. He taught in New York, first German at Columbia

University and then German literature at Hunter College. As the 1930s progressed, Koischwitz became outspoken in his support of Hitler. Hunter officials put him on a leave of absence in 1939, and he returned to Germany early in 1940.

By spring, he was program director of the USA Zone of the German state radio company, the Reichs-Rundfunk-Gesellschaft (RRG) in Berlin. Koischwitz began looking around for American expats to broadcast on behalf of the Nazi regime. He found Mildred, alone and jobless at age forty in a foreign country. Although Koischwitz was married and had children, he and Mildred soon began an affair.

From then on, being with Koischwitz was her primary aim; after the war, Gillars referred to him as "my destiny." "A Nazi Svengali" is how defense attorney James Laughlin would refer to him years later during her treason trial. After they became lovers, she never thought of leaving Germany. Under Koischwitz's direction, Mildred attained the fame she had long dreamed of, along with the infamy that followed her to an unmarked grave in Ohio decades later.

Radio was the most far-reaching propaganda tool for both the Allies and the Axis during the war. It was the most accessible media for soldiers, and the one that American GIs were most comfortable with—by 1940, almost 90 percent of American homes had at least one radio. People listened to news, entertainment, advertising, opinions, and music on air. Over the radio waves, celebrities, presidents, and prime ministers could speak directly to listeners in their homes.

Americans were primed to believe what they heard on the radio. In 1939, when a public opinion institute asked them which source they would believe in the case of conflicting news reports, 40 percent of respondents said they would trust the radio report. Only 26 percent said they would trust the newspaper account, and a mere 13 percent would believe an official. The Nazis and the Japanese used that trust to try to demoralize Allied troops.

Gillars's most popular program was the *Home Sweet Home Hour.* As a producer, Koischwitz knew what American GIs wanted to hear: swing music, "good, combat jive," as military correspondent Edward Van Dyne called it in a 1944 magazine column. Gillars's broadcasts were programmed to pull the men in with popular music—Bing Crosby was a favorite—then assail them with innuendos about what their wives and sweethearts were up to on the home front, as well as dire predictions of their own deaths in combat.

She called herself Midge at the Mike, but the GIs gradually started to call her Sally, because she once described herself as a real Irish type. Gillars had a voice that "oozes honey" and was meant to demoralize the soldiers, Van Dyne wrote. However, the enlisted men saw through her flimflam and got "an enormous bang out of her."

Sixty-nine years later, a World War II vet in New Mexico gave the same assessment of her effectiveness. In an interview on his ninetieth birthday, Walter Dorman remembered Gillars's broadcasts as a rare light spot in the midst of horrors. "We'd listen to Axis Sally every night until midnight," he said. "She'd be telling us to give up, and that we couldn't win, but she played some good music. We just laughed about it."

But as the war intensified and more American troops were dying in combat or languishing in POW camps, Axis Sally's broadcasts became more vitriolic. She chided home-front listeners with accusations that their sons had become cold-blooded killers of innocent German children and women. She ridiculed American troops for fighting England's war and kept up a stream of anti-Semitic rhetoric.

"This is a Jewish war, and good, honest-to-God American blood is being shed for it," she said in one broadcast, reminding listeners how often President Franklin Roosevelt had promised that no American boys would be sent to fight on foreign soil. To prove that the Germans were ferreting out accurate intelligence, she revealed planned movements of American troops and read the names of captured and hospitalized soldiers.

As the situation in the war worsened, so did Gillars's personal life. Koischwitz, who suffered from tuberculosis, became a wanted fugitive in 1943, when the U.S. Justice Department indicted him and seven expatriates for treason. Despite having promised to marry Gillars, he was still living with his wife and three children, with a fourth on the way. She learned of the pregnancy just before the baby's birth and was devastated.

She tried to commit suicide by turning on the gas in her small apartment; however, a friend who knew of her distress arrived at the apartment to thwart the plan. But more sadness followed; Koischwitz's infant died soon after birth. A few days later, Koischwitz's wife, recuperating at a Berlin hospital, was killed in an Allied bombing raid. Gillars and Koischwitz's relationship continued as before, but a darkness hung over them, exacerbated by the war.

That same year, an Allied air attack heavily damaged Gillars's apartment. On another occasion, she was on air when the building across the street from the radio studio was hit and burned; she watched the devastation while continuing the broadcast without a word of what she was witnessing.

Late in 1943, Gillars and Koischwitz began interviewing American POWs in France, Belgium, Holland, and Germany. They feigned concern for the prisoners' welfare and enticed them to talk about their feelings about the war. Gillars sometimes handed out cigarettes and liquor to convince the soldiers she was on their side. At least once, she posed as a Red Cross representative. Often, she told the prisoners she wanted to interview them, to record messages for their relatives waiting at home. Later, these pieces were edited for propaganda purposes—to convince American listeners that the Nazis were treating their captured loved ones well and that the POWs were ready to denounce the war.

Getting the type of interviews that Koischwitz wanted was not easy. The Americans were wary of the producer and the long-legged woman who attempted to use her feminine charms to get them talking. At Stalag IIB—one of the most brutal POW camps—the ranking American officer flatly refused to let any of the prisoners be interviewed. Guards escorted Koischwitz and Gillars out of a large barracks, where hundreds of POWs hurled curses and insults at them.

Koischwitz next turned to playwriting to try to further the Nazi cause. In his *Vision of Invasion,* Gillars played an Ohio mother who has a nightmare about her son dying horribly in an attempted invasion of Occupied Europe. The play was broadcast just a few weeks before the actual D-Day.

As the Third Reich began to implode, so did Gillars's life. In late summer 1944, Koischwitz died while she was on assignment in France. She was lost. He had become her whole world: colleague, lover, protector. Without him, she had no one. Her zeal for propaganda was gone, but she continued broadcasting, largely because she had no other way to survive. When the Russian Army entered Berlin in spring 1945, she barely made it out of the broadcast studio. At that point, her fear of the Russians was even greater than her fear of the Americans. The conquering Russians were known for their brutal treatment and rape of survivors. She went to the home of Koischwitz's oldest child, Stella, for help, but she was turned out. So, with hundreds of others, she hid in the underbelly of the city, often surrounded by corpses. She traded her few personal possessions on the black market for food. Once the arrival of other Allied forces stabilized the situation in Berlin, she found lodging in a rented room in the British sector of the city.

Meanwhile the United States Army's Counter-Intelligence Corps (CIC) was hunting for her. Under the CIC's orders, the Federal Communications Commission (FCC) had been monitoring and recording all Axis broadcasts for months. The FCC worked from a listening post in Silver Hill, Maryland, supplying the CIC with recordings and detailed records.

After the fall of Germany, CIC officers maintained a round-the-clock surveillance on Axis Sally's known associates and the places she had lived or frequented. On March 15, 1946, she entered the house where she was staying, only to find an American soldier pointing a revolver at her and a CIC agent placing her under arrest. Knowing that this day was inevitable and exhausted by the previous few years, Gillars went along quietly to jail. She asked only to take with her a photograph of Koischwitz. It disappeared during her first night in jail.

Gillars's arrest resulted in a flood of stories in Allied newspapers—many of which were lurid and personal. After years of war, neither the press nor the public felt compelled to be objective before she was convicted. Adding to the public disdain for an accused traitor was Gillars's free admission that she had made the broadcasts and her lack of regret for them.

Judy Barden, a journalist with the North American Newspaper Alliance, was one of the first reporters to interview Gillars, who was still under house arrest in a middle-class neighborhood on the outskirts of Berlin. Gillars wisecracked with journalists as she was interviewed. Asked if she thought she was providing a good service to Americans by her broadcasts, she replied, "Surely. I'm told they all got a good laugh. That's good for soldiers, isn't it?"

Much was made—good and bad—of Gillars's appearance. She was often accused of posing for the press, and photographs support that allegation. While one unnamed Associated Press reporter called her "tall and lissome," Barden was more critical. Axis Sally must have been beautiful once, she wrote, but she had "gone to seed." Gillars wore her hair—now gray—in a velvet and net snood, in the French style of the day. Her nails—fingers and toes—were painted bright red. "She appeared very proud of her well-shaped legs, which she crossed and uncrossed continually while cameramen flashed bulbs all around," Barden wrote.

She noted that although Gillars received the same meager rations as the German citizens, there were luxuries including chocolate bars and high-priced makeup in her room. Barden left it up to the readers to determine how Axis Sally rated those perks. Gillars's most revealing statement in Barden's article, however, was that she didn't care about what happened to her in the future: "I've lost everything." That lack of concern—which various sources depicted either as despondent or cavalier—was a theme of her pretrial life. She seemed oblivious that she faced the death penalty.

England quickly tried and executed two expatriates who broadcasted for the Nazis. William Joyce, known as Lord Haw Haw, was executed in early 1946. John Amery, who attempted to convince Allied troops to join the Nazis to defeat the Russians, was executed in 1945. But the U.S. Justice Department proceeded more cautiously, closely looking at what constituted treason. Under debate was whether words—no matter how treasonous or inflammatory—were enough for a conviction. When there were no actions to accompany the words, did treason exist? The attorney general's office studied cases from the American Civil War while debating the issue. Another problem was gathering enough evidence against some of the accused to mount a successful case.

Of the seven expats indicted along with Koischwitz in 1943, only two had been convicted of treason by the time of Gillars's trial. Robert Best and Douglas Chandler were both sentenced to life imprisonment. Best died in prison in 1952, and President John F. Kennedy commuted Chandler's sentence in 1963.

Fred J. Kaltenbach, a German American who grew up in Iowa and worked closely with Koischwitz on a program for the RRG, died before he could be tried. The Russians captured him after the fall of Berlin and refused to hand him over to the Americans; Kaltenbach is thought to have died in a Russian detention camp in 1945. Charges against four other people, including Koischwitz, were dropped for lack of evidence. Charges against poet Ezra Pound were dropped because he was found incompetent to stand trial.

As Gillars awaited her future, she was treated at a military hospital for conditions related to malnutrition and exhaustion. She was also held in a psychiatric ward for a time; though she was released in late 1946, she chose to remain in military custody. With no money and no friends, she had nowhere to go. Gillars had not had contact with her mother,

Mae, or her half-sister, Edna Mae, since the war started. The women learned of her arrest in the newspapers.

At the time, Mae was living in Toronto, Canada, where she ran a boardinghouse. When she heard the accusations against her first-born daughter, she steadfastly maintained her faith in her innocence and worried about her safety. Mae died in March 1947 without ever being in touch with her again. Edna Mae was married and living in Ashtabula, Ohio, where she taught at a dance school.

The Justice Department determined there was sufficient evidence to try Mildred. She was rearrested in early 1947 and charged with multiple counts of treason. Death was the ultimate penalty, and the minimum sentence was five years in prison and a $10,000 fine. Despite the seriousness of her situation, Gillars seemed able to rationalize her way out of any responsibility. "My conscience is clear," she told an AP reporter shortly after her capture. "I have nothing to hide." She said that if her marriage to a German citizen had happened as was planned, she would have had to be loyal to Germany at any rate. As she awaited trial in the United States in 1948, her attitude never changed. Once her trial began in Washington, D.C., in early 1949, she still claimed innocence. She painted herself as a victim of circumstance: once the war began, she claimed, German authorities took away her visa. She said she was threatened with imprisonment in a concentration camp if she did not broadcast for the Nazis.

At times, when the prosecution played parts of FCC recordings of her broadcasts, she said she could not be sure it was her voice. There was, in fact, another Axis Sally making radio broadcasts at the same time as Gillars. Rita Zucca was an Italian American whose family still had considerable property and many relatives in Italy. She moved there in 1938 and began broadcasting for Radio Roma in 1943. She was called "Sally" on the air, and her programs were similar to the ones Gillars was making in Berlin.

During her trial, Mildred claimed she had demanded that Zucca not use the name Sally, because she did not want to be confused with her. Zucca was giving out military information and trying to confuse GIs, Mildred said, while she was merely trying to stay in touch with America and help troops in any small way that she could.

But the prosecution, led by John M. Kelley Jr., presented a different story. Kelley introduced numerous excerpts from Mildred's broadcasts in which she chastised and taunted GIs, made virulent anti-Semitic statements, and criticized Roosevelt's handling of the war. Wounded veterans were questioned about listening to her on the radio or being interviewed by her while in POW camps. Germans who had worked with Gillars in Berlin were brought into court to testify about her activities. One German broadcaster said Axis Sally was the second highest paid employee at the station: while he made 1,000 marks a month, she was paid between 2,000 and 3,000.

The one thing Kelley, Gillars, and Gillars's attorney all agreed on was that Max Koischwitz—not ideology—was her primary motivation for staying in Germany and broadcasting for the RRG. "I believe that a man generally means more to a woman than anything else," Gillars said under Kelley's questioning. "I would have died for him." The prosecutor hit the romantic angle hard, condemning her for an affair with a married man and stating that she had had many other lovers as well.

Gillars was by turns defiant, evasive, combative, and tearful. She continued to maintain that she had done what she had to do to survive in Germany and that her real aim was to help U.S. troops and their families. Kelley's summation for the prosecution was brutally direct. "Lock, stock, and barrel, she sold herself to the Nazis for 3,000 marks a month," he said. "She thought she was on the winning side, and the only thing she cared about was her own selfish fame."

Edna Mae Herrick, then thirty-nine, came from Ashtabula to attend much of the trial. A photograph of her, tearful and well dressed, was distributed to the wire press services, giving her a dubious claim to fame. And certainly Edna Mae had reason to cry. After nearly two days of deliberation, on March 10, 1949, the jury found Axis Sally guilty of only one of the eight treason charges for which she was prosecuted. She was convicted of treason in acting out the role of the grieving Ohio mother in Koischwitz's *Vision of Invasion.*

Gillars turned ashen at the verdict but remained silent while Edna Mae left the courtroom in tears. At her sentencing a few days later, Gillars attempted to question the judge about why she had been convicted, but he quickly silenced her. He compared her crime to those of Robert Best and Douglas Chandler. But because there was no evidence that Mildred had conferred with high-ranking Nazis to actually formulate policy, the judge showed her some mercy, sentencing her to ten to thirty years in federal prison and fining her $10,000.

At her sentencing hearing, Gillars continued to proclaim her innocence and attempted to argue with the judge over the verdict. How could she be guilty of treason for acting in *Vision of Invasion,* as charges against Koischwitz—who had written the play—had long ago been dropped? She would continue to affirm her innocence for the rest of her life.

While Gillars shakily faced prison, her sister returned home to Ashtabula "to face years of both open discrimination and quiet disdain," biographer Lucas wrote. He added that some residents of her former hometown believed Mildred deserved to be shot.

Although she had escaped the harshest punishments, the adjustment to life at the Federal Reformatory for Women in Alderson, West Virginia, was difficult for Gillars, then forty-eight. Physical ailments, fainting fits, and the continuing belief that she hadn't received a fair trial plagued her. Her attorney's failure to secure her a new trial brought further depression. Prison officials described her as moody, arrogant, and hard to get along with. She frequently refused Edna Mae's visits and letters. Some officials worried about her worsening psychological state, but that was an issue not often addressed in the 1950s penal system.

Assigned to a craft room at the prison, Mildred found tasks she was good at and enjoyed: She knitted clothing that was sold to visitors and sewed garments worn by inmates. Eventually, she was assigned to manage the ceramics kiln. She made blue Bavarian beer steins with the motto "Accept your fate, for it is sealed" etched in them in German.

Although she had been raised Episcopalian, in prison she also began to attend Roman Catholic mass, an activity that would lead to a more contented future. She found solace in directing both the Protestant and Catholic choirs at the prison.

In the 1950s, as Americans began to distance themselves from the war, life improved for another resident of the Alderson prison. Iva Toguri D'Aquina, who had become known as Toyko Rose while broadcasting for the Japanese during the war, was paroled in 1955. A first-generation Japanese American, D'Aquina had been visiting an ailing aunt in Japan at the time of Pearl Harbor. She stayed in Japan, married a Filipino man, and began broadcasting what she later called satire. After her parole, the U.S. Justice Department wanted to deport her to Japan.

According to Lucas, there was also talk of sending Gillars back to Germany when she became eligible for parole. That may be the reason she waived her option to apply for parole in 1959. She did apply in 1960 but was turned down because she did not have a job waiting for her.

That same year, Father Thomas Kerrigan, the prison's Catholic chaplain, became her champion. He arranged for her baptism and confirmation when she converted to the Catholic faith, and he began looking for someone to employ her.

He found someone later that year. Our Lady of Bethlehem Convent in Worthington agreed to hire Gillars to teach German, English, and speech to high school girls at the convent school, in exchange for room and board plus $30 a month. The Order of the Poor Child Jesus, which operated the convent, stipulated that no media be allowed on convent grounds when she arrived for her new life.

Gillars's parole was approved in January 1961. That July, she was released to live with Edna Mae and her second husband, Edwin Niemenen, in Ashtabula until school resumed after Labor Day. Twenty reporters waited in the rain for nearly a half an hour on a July morning for Gillars to emerge from the prison and into Edna Mae's waiting arms. She appeared to enjoy the photographers' attention and became more animated when she noticed the tape recorder one radio journalist carried, but her comments were few and mundane.

Now sixty, she looked it: her hair was entirely white, and her face showed her years. She dressed plainly, in a beige suit and dark jacket and hat. But there was still something of the actress about her, wrote Jack Davis, Associated Press bureau chief. Gillars "swirled a blue shawl around her throat several times . . . and seemed to enjoy the center stage immensely," he wrote.

She maintained a low profile during those few weeks in Ashtabula. Edna Mae introduced her to a Catholic family who took her to Mass with them and invited her home to dinner. Shortly before she was to move to the content, Gillars donated some expensive black lace lingerie to the local Catholic clothing drive. It was a practical decision but also symbolic of leaving her old life behind for a quite different one.

When Mary McGarey of the *Columbus Dispatch* interviewed her at the convent in August 1961, she noted Gillars's "dark eyes sad and wary of questions, her responses slow and often unwilling." After years of fame as a broadcaster and then infamy as a convict, she only wanted to be left alone to teach. The desire to totally break with her old life included eliminating Edna Mae from it; the half-sister who stood by Gillars during the agonizing trial and sheltered her during her first weeks out of prison never saw her again.

As Lucas researched his biography, he interviewed friends and colleagues from Gillars's post-prison life. The resulting image is of a woman who never discussed her past unless others pressed her. Those who discovered her story did so accidentally. Despite all the evidence to the contrary, she continued to maintain that her broadcasts were aimed at helping American soldiers and their families.

On the rare occasion when the Holocaust was mentioned, she stiffly stated that she had been unaware of what was happening to Jews. It wasn't a very believable claim, but no one seemed to want to challenge such a benign and private elderly woman. Though President Gerald Ford pardoned Tokyo Rose in 1977, Mildred never applied for a pardon because she never believed she had committed a crime, Lucas wrote.

After her release, she was bitter about what she considered an unjust conviction. But as time passed, her life slowly improved. Acquaintances described her as kind, generous, intelligent, and refined. In addition to teaching at the convent, she also tutored other children. She periodically took some of the convent students to classical music programs at Ohio Wesleyan, her old college. On weekends, she gave piano lessons to inner-city children. In her spare time, she performed in a local drama group. It was, in many ways, the most stable, contented period of her life.

In 1973, she achieved a goal that showed her resolve. By taking classes at various local colleges, she completed the coursework needed for her long-abandoned bachelor's degree in speech. On June 10, she received her degree at Ohio Wesleyan's graduation ceremony. Those in the audience likely remarked on the fact that a smiling, white-haired septuagenarian was graduating, but they probably didn't realize who she was. When the wire services broke the story, though, the secret was out. The Delaware paper ran a photo of her taken just after receiving the degree and said that aside from a "few discreet whispers," no one seemed to notice or know who she was.

By the time her probation ended in 1979, Gillars was to all appearances just another little white-haired old lady. She lived out the next few years quietly in a Columbus apartment. In June 1988, she died of colon cancer. Her death certificate listed her occupation as teacher; her estate was valued at just a little over $3,000. A few friends attended a simple funeral at St. Joseph's Cemetery in Lockbourne, in Franklin County, Ohio.

Gillars was finally at peace.

With best wishes from
Cowboy Copas

11

LLOYD COPAS
Cowboy Singer

Lloyd Estel Copas called himself a cowboy, and the world believed him. As a Grand Ole Opry star in the time of western swing and hillbilly music, he wore a white Stetson and fancy green boots. The huge hat overpowered his head but not his image; surely this man *was* the Oklahoma Singing Cowboy. But in the hollows near the tiny town of Blue Creek, in southern Ohio's Adams County, old friends and neighbors knew the truth. They smiled and welcomed him home each Christmas. They never called him anything but "Cope," for they remembered him as the quiet son of Elvin and Lola Copas, hill farmers who entertained at local Saturday-night barn dances. Friends and neighbors faithfully kept the singer's cowboy secret, for he was one of their own, even after he had left for fame in Nashville.

His music was a little bit of Ohio and a lot of everywhere else. Through the years, while performing across the nation, he heard different types of roots music—bluegrass, gospel, western swing, honky-tonk, and uptempo hillbilly—and incorporated elements of these into his own style. He began composing songs about the people, places, and situations he encountered while performing. He became an excellent songwriter, rhythm guitarist, and musical storyteller whose recordings dotted the national country music charts.

Yet most of his fans never knew the truth about his Ohio roots. Many music histories claim Lloyd Copas was born July 15, 1913, in Muskogee, Oklahoma; even Joel Whitburn's well-respected *Top Country Singles* listed Copas's birthplace as Oklahoma. The vocalist spread the misinformation all his adult life, saying he grew up on a ranch near Muskogee.

Lloyd "Cowboy" Copas, circa 1949. (Authors' collection)

A western past, he hoped, would make him more accepted by fans of the "hillbilly" music popular among America's rural people, especially Appalachians. The genre had not yet received enough respect to earn the name "country and western," but this came in time, after smooth-sounding stars like Copas gave it the style and attention it deserved.

Copas was, in fact, born on July 15, 1913, on Moon Hollow Road in Adams County's Jefferson Township, on the edge of Appalachia. He was closer to the Cincinnati Sound than the Nashville Sound.

In the early 1940s, Nashville was not yet called Music City, but since the mid-1920s it had been the home of an important hillbilly radio show: the *Grand Ole Opry,* broadcast on radio station WSM. The show assured the city of plenty of good musicians, who during the week usually performed in clubs or held regular jobs. Though at the time Cincinnati was turning out more hillbilly hits than Nashville, the Opry held a mystique that was known as far as WSM's fifty-thousand-watt signal could reach—from the Gulf Coast to the Ohio River and beyond.

Anyone who sang on the Opry stage was considered musical royalty. The show helped the Lloyd Copas story end up as a fairy tale—almost. With the Opry's pedigree behind him and a feel for what rural people wanted to hear, Copas helped mold the disorganized hillbilly style into what it has become today—an amalgamation of popular sounds known simply as "country." He also influenced many other singers of his era and helped establish the modern country sound. In Copas's day, anyone who knew anything about hillbilly music knew the country crooner's name.

Yet these days, sadly, the name "Cowboy Copas" evokes more curiosity than recognition. The first singer to record the hit "Tennessee Waltz" has become an anachronism in ¾ time. When he is remembered, he is perceived as the quintessential rhinestone troubadour, whose stage name elicits a hearty chuckle in the slick country music world. Now, nicknames and hillbilly music are out; flashing lights and big beats are in. Memories of Cowboy Copas; his first label, King Records; and the 1940s are far from the minds of fans who walk down Nashville's Music Row.

Only his melodies remain. Only cracked publicity photographs tell his tragic story.

As a boy, Lloyd Copas sat for hours on a wooden fence and strummed an old guitar. His father gently reminded him of the merits of farm work, but the boy said he intended to work hard to become a famous hillbilly singer like Vernon Dalhart. Copas knew he could never be happy working on a farm or in a mill, not even if he could play the barn dances every Saturday night as his musician parents did. He knew that the farm and Adams County offered only physical labor. So, he strummed on and longed for recognition.

In 1927, when he was only fourteen, he dropped out of school and convinced a local musician named Fred Evans to let him join the locally popular Hencacklers String Band. Evans was leery of hiring a boy, but the kid possessed a sweet tenor voice and quick fingers. That was enough. That summer, the group set out in a big Buick to perform at county fairs. They also played during intermissions at the old Palace Theater in the village of Peebles. In that theater in 1928, young Lloyd first lost his heart to the western movie.

By his sixteenth birthday, Copas realized he could never become famous by singing at the Palace. He needed a larger audience and a recording contract. But securing a record was not easy for hillbilly singers; the major labels were preoccupied with Bing Crosby and other white pop stars. So Copas kept dreaming. Then, in his late teens, he saw a performance by another local musician, Vernon Storer, who went by the name "Natchee the Indian." Storer claimed he was three-quarters Shawnee, but a family member once maintained that the fiddler was no more than one-sixteenth Native American of some kind. Instinctively knowing the power of marketing, Storer developed his Indian persona as a child when he parted his hair in the middle and wore a headband. His mother helped him create the "Natchee" name and encouraged his fiddle playing. He became known as "the Arizona Indian"—he was as much Arizona Indian as Copas was Oklahoma cowboy. As he danced, Storer was quite a sight, whirling with a fiddle and wearing a white Indian costume that accentuated his dark hair.

Natchee and Cowboy had three things in common—their Adams County home, hillbilly music, and the strong desire to play it. By the late 1920s, Natchee was playing the fiddle and Lloyd the flat top guitar all over the region. Lloyd had an unusual way of picking—moving his fingers the reverse of what most guitar players did. Using a thumb pick, he'd strum the bass strings while he picked the others with his fingers. As the boys played in talent contests in dusty small towns, Storer's brother, John Earl Storer, joined them on upright bass. They got a few radio gigs, but none that paid much.

They become known wherever they performed. Natchee is said to have won nine national fiddling contests. Unlike his partner, he was flamboyant on stage. He might have been responsible for Copas taking the Cowboy name; no one knows for sure—only stories remain. According to one, Natchee dared Copas to enter an amateur musical contest in Cincinnati. Copas agreed. The organizer saw him waiting to take his turn on the stage and said, "All right, cowboy, let's see what you can do." Copas liked that word, "cowboy." He thought it seemed appropriate and had a certain ring to it: "Cowboy Copas." "I'd rather be an Oklahoma cowboy than an Ohio ridge runner any day," he said with a laugh. A few years later, a local manager named Larry Sunbrock heard Copas telling this story, and he started promoting his client as "Cowboy Copas, Oklahoma Singing Cowboy."

Regardless of how the name came to be, it stuck. Copas's association with Natchee did not. The two continued to perform, but separately. Lloyd went home to Blue Creek and formed the Gold Star Rangers with his brother, Marion Andrew Copas, and some other local men. They performed on WCHS Radio in Charleston, West Virginia, and in the bars of the hill country. But not even his own town and band could hold Copas, for he had ambition.

One day in the mid-1930s, he convinced his brother to accompany him to Nashville to seek work on the *Grand Ole Opry*. Lloyd was confident. Broadcast every Saturday night, the *Opry* was the nation's most popular barn dance show, and a country performer's lifeline to the people. Copas knew that singing on that show was a ticket to success. Marion just smiled shyly and tried to explain that a man just can't walk into the Ryman and announce his availability, but Lloyd would not understand reality. On the drive south, somewhere between Lexington, Kentucky, and Nashville, Tennessee, Marion turned to Lloyd and said, "I ain't cut out for this kind of life. I'm goin' home." Lloyd didn't flinch. He kept his eyes on the road and his mind on his dream. "Do what you gotta do," he said, "but I'm going to Nashville."

In a few months, the city turned cold and Lloyd returned to Ohio, rejected and dejected. He missed his mother, who would die in late 1936 at age fifty after undergoing an operation in Portsmouth, Ohio. He wondered if his career would ever make him financially stable. If he couldn't sing on the radio in Nashville, he vowed, he would sing in Cincinnati. Soon, the *Boone County Jamboree,* a popular program broadcast on

WLW Radio, was featuring Cowboy Copas. He continued to sing on the show for several years. He married Lucille Markins of Peebles on its stage with a borrowed ring in 1934, when she was only a high school senior. But he wasn't contented professionally. He needed a band—one that made records. That dream was difficult to attain in the 1930s, when the larger record labels released a sparse number of hillbilly records. Yet Copas persisted.

Years passed. In 1940, after he began singing on a Knoxville radio station, he met accordionist Pee Wee King and his Golden West Cowboys. King had introduced big band music to the Opry in 1937, the year another cowboy singer, Leonard Slye—who grew up about twenty miles east of Blue Creek, in Scioto County—became Roy Rogers for Republic Pictures. After Eddy Arnold left the band, King was searching for a new lead vocalist. He immediately liked Copas and his straightforward, emotional delivery, and he asked him to become the Cowboys' new singer. Copas slipped on the Cowboys' colorful western suit and didn't look back toward Ohio—at least not for a few years. He did not disown his past, he just decided not to mention it to the publicity agents who represented Pee Wee King and his band. Copas wanted them to think of him as a ranch hand who simply eased on out of the West and into the recording studio. "Some people change their names to get ahead in life," said his sister, Mildred Rothwell, of Blue Creek, in a conversation with the authors. "Well, our Lloyd changed his name *and* his life."

By 1944, however, Copas knew he was going to need more than a cowboy name to become famous on his own. King informed him late that year that the Golden West Cowboys would move their base from Nashville to Louisville, King's hometown. Copas wanted to stay in Nashville, thinking his chances of getting work there were better, so in January 1945 he told King he planned to leave the band. In those days, Nashville wasn't the big recording center that it is today. Cincinnati had more recording opportunities, but the Opry gave Nashville the wider radio following. By leaving the band, Copas was taking a big risk; most singers would have done anything to sing with Pee Wee King's group. But Copas still sought fame and financial stability. Besides, he just enjoyed picking, even after giving a performance. He loved jamming with musicians. Later in the year, his gamble began to pay off. He received offers to sing, and the next year, the *Opry* invited him to return as a solo act. Of course, he accepted. That year he also received an offer from a new record label specializing in hillbilly music. It also would sign Pee Wee King briefly, as well as many other hillbilly stars and wannabe stars as possible. Copas thought he was in good company.

The new label, King Records, operated in an old factory in Cincinnati, about sixty-five miles west of Adams County. By 1946, his Saturday night performances on the *Opry*—and its far-ranging radio signal—helped promote his new record, "Filipino Baby," to number four on the *Billboard* folk chart, a forerunner of the magazine's country one. The record began a hit streak for him personally and became the first big hit for King Records, which had been searching for a singer to make it popular.

In the late 1940s, Copas signed an ambitious ten-year contract with King. It seems unlikely that an Opry star would sign with an upstart independent instead of a major label, but in those days the majors signed only a limited number of hillbilly acts. The rest were left to scramble for record deals. Knowing this, Sydney Nathan, owner of a Cincinnati record store, had decided to start his own label to take advantage of the excess of unsigned talent in hillbilly music and, later, rhythm and blues.

King's national ascent coincided with the rise of Cowboy Copas. King opened in Cincinnati in 1943 when Nathan, a Jewish music entrepreneur, received financial backing from a few friends and family members. At the time, King was about as unlikely a hit-making machine as any label could be. Operating capital was hard to find, but dreams were not. Nathan turned his marketing genius to hillbilly music, and he campaigned to rename it "country." He bought record presses, opened his factory, and started doing everything under one roof. He thought the word "hillbilly" was derogatory, and, being Jewish, he had some experience with pejorative names and prejudice. After hearing Copas sing on WLW Radio, Nathan asked Alton Delmore, of WLW's Delmore Brothers duo, to inquire about signing him, as Copas was a friend of the Delmores. Nathan had already signed the Delmores, and he offered Copas a contract too. Over the next few years, the short, heavy, and bespectacled Nathan would record several big hillbilly hits for Copas, including "The Kentucky Waltz," "Rose of Oklahoma," and "Hangman's Boogie." By 1950, the hits had made Copas so popular that he toured with Hank Williams—as the main act, or at the least the equal act. By then, Williams had already had several hits.

King recorded Copas singing both hillbilly and gospel music. He felt comfortable with both styles because he had grown up with them.

In the 1950s, when the long-playing albums became popular, King released *The Country Gentleman of Song, Tragic Tales of Love and Life, Tragic Romance, Hymns and Sacred Songs by Cowboy Copas,* and others. Cowboy arrived in vinyl.

According to a 1948 King Records publication, in just over a decade Copas had appeared on 204 radio stations in the United States, Canada, and Mexico and on the *Opry* in Nashville. His records were available throughout the country, and millions of people heard him sing in concert, including three hundred thousand in 1947 alone. At one concert in Indiana, about twenty-five thousand people showed up. Copas was named Top Western Artist of 1948. That year he went to Chatsworth, California, to appear in the movie *Square Dance Jubilee,* filmed on a ranch with Don "Red" Barry, Mary Beth Hughes, Spade Cooley, and Max Terhune. When the film was released the next year, it enhanced his reputation as a singing cowboy. He won Top Western Artist again in 1951.

In his 1977 autobiography *The Truth Is Stranger Than Publicity,* Alton Delmore remembered performing for the first time with the Cowboy at a fiddling contest. He said Copas, Rusty Gabbard, and Natchee traveled with promoter Larry Sunbrock, playing all the contests with him. "Those three fellows could put on a good enough show for anyone who was in the crowd. They could sing, play, and tell jokes, and among them, they could just about play any instrument that it took to please the most particular music lover."

Copas seemed most happy when he was performing. In publicity photographs taken throughout his career, he appeared relaxed and satisfied. He had hazel eyes and dark hair. He was tall and slender, with an engaging smile. On stage, he wore a powder-blue suit, green boots, and a white cowboy hat. As he grew older, he looked more distinguished in his fancy outfit, every bit the country gentleman.

The popularity of his 78-rpm records had helped established King Records as one of the top independents in the nation and made Lloyd Copas one of America's most popular country singers of the immediate postwar years. Now the new vinyl album and single were carrying his songs too. He planned to keep on singing as long as the public would pay to hear him.

A subplot of the Cowboy Copas story is the King Records tale. After King opened a recording studio at its factory in 1947, Copas most often recorded there, using talented musicians from all over the country. Copas was considered an expert hillbilly guitarist, and company producers asked him to play on other recording sessions when he was in town to record his own material.

Nathan hired the nation's top hillbilly musicians to back up his singers. He sent them plane tickets and flew them into town for recording sessions with Copas and other King hillbilly stars. Copas would wait outside the metal studio entrance door until other acts finished their work. Sometimes they were black blues singers, sometimes black or white gospel singers, and often hillbilly singers, such as Clyde Moody; the Delmores; Wayne Raney; and Hawkshaw Hawkins—another King star, who joined the label a few years after Copas arrived. With so many different kinds of people of different races making music at King, the recording environment was a roots-music party. As Nathan's label grew, it added more singers, and Nathan campaigned to change the genre's name to "country music."

Nathan and Copas made a good team. They wrote songs together occasionally and worked toward a common goal—making money. In a way, both of them were outsiders. Nathan was the Jewish guy who failed at nearly every job he had taken, until he found his niche by opening a record company. He knew what it was like to be looked down on. Copas, from the hills, likely felt that same exclusion when he visited the city. He recorded music that was not yet accepted by a mass American audience. Their pioneering work, largely ignored by Cincinnati's music establishment, was done inside an old factory at 1540 Brewster Avenue in the rundown Evanston neighborhood. The city people who mattered loved the symphony and the opera; they had no interest in a cowboy singer or an upstart label owned by a grumpy businessman who recorded mainly poor Appalachians and blacks. Consequently, the city paid little attention to what was happening inside the brick walls on Brewster, even when the national charts rang with hit after hit from King Records. Unfortunately, these were not the right kind of hits. And even less attention was paid to the artists who made the music, such as Lloyd Copas and Hawkshaw Hawkins.

When Nathan first recorded Copas in 1945, King was turning out only two hundred shellac 78-rpm discs a day and King had only a few vocalists under contract. Howard Kessel, an original King investor and the head of the company's pressing plant, said Copas was the first singer to have his 78-rpm records pressed in King's new factory, instead of some independent plant in another city. But as Copas's hits started coming and other artists were signed, King's sales increased and times got better for the investors and the stars. By 1948, jukebox operators voted King Records the sixth most active record label, thanks in part to Copas and his fellow hillbilly stars. The following year, King was selling 6 million records a year, including hits such as Copas's "As Advertised" and "Signed, Sealed, and Delivered." Nathan shared writing credit with Copas on both songs.

Nathan knew the record business from top to bottom. He sold records through nontraditional outlets, such as general stores, so often King's sales weren't fully reflected by the national sales charts. Nathan and Copas were opposites. The businessman was boisterous, profane, and city bred. He couldn't stop cursing. The Cowboy was more relaxed, refined, and bred in the country, which influenced the way he talked to people.

Nathan commanded his stars' recording sessions like a general directing his troops. He shouted orders. He ranted. He dominated. As he said, "It's my money we're spending." But he usually got along with the mild-mannered Copas, who knew that Nathan had a knack for picking songs and marketing them to mom-and-pop stores across the country. Once, after Copas returned from Nashville with some new songs, Nathan met with him in his office. The story is legend, perhaps, but it has been told many times. Copas played his new material for Nathan, including "The Tennessee Waltz," written by Pee Wee King and his composing partner, the pianist Redd Stewart. Copas had reportedly purchased the song from them for $50, but more likely he paid them for first recording rights. He made the record, which, as King record 696-A, stayed on the *Billboard* charts for thirteen weeks, peaking at number three on May 1, 1948. On the record, Copas was granted cowriting credit with King and Stewart, but this was most likely limited to only the Copas recording, as a part of the deal he had with the two writers. They wanted him to record it because he could turn it into a hit. Meanwhile, Copas recorded more hits. They jumped onto *Billboard*'s Most Played Juke Box Folk Records list and later its Best Selling Retail Folk [country and western] Records list. By 1950, people were beginning to call the music "country and western" instead of "hillbilly."

The name change did not affect Copas's record sales. But time did. In 1952, his radio success began to fade. He couldn't duplicate the sales of "Strange Little Girl," his 1951 top ten hit. It wasn't for lack of trying:

he continued to tour and promote his records at radio stations, and King kept releasing new ones. For some reason, though, the disc jockeys didn't play them. Copas descended the charts as quickly as he had risen. Neither Nathan and his marketing savvy nor his staff of songwriters and producers could improve things for Copas, although he did remain in demand at concerts. So he continued to travel around the country, singing as though he had the current number-one record. He attributed his radio popularity problem to a general slump in country music brought on by changing tastes. By the mid-1950s, there was another problem: the rise of rock and roll. Copas stopped performing for several years, to regroup.

By 1955, Nathan had tired of releasing unsuccessful country records by older acts, so he let Copas out of his recording contract three years early. King began recording rockabilly hits such as "Daddy-O" by Cincinnati radio personality Bonnie Lou and "Seventeen" by Boyd Bennett and His Rockets. The next year, desperate for another hit, Copas turned to a new music, countrified rock and roll, usually called "rockabilly," and a new record label, Dot Records. At a recording session in Nashville, he recorded "Circle Rock" with Hargus "Pig" Robbins and a group of hot rhythm players. Copas was hopeful about a comeback. As Cincinnati music historian and record label owner Darren Blasé explained: "Like many country artists who had been shown the door by rock-and-roll, Copas felt pressure to give in." Blasé said Robbins's "adrenalin-fueled piano break" made the pianist "the aural equivalent of a barroom brawl. Regardless, the record sunk." Copas felt disillusioned. He had tried a modern sound, when he preferred to remain in country music. His heart was there, and he did not feel like a rocker. He was always a crooner. He didn't understand the beat. For him to record more rockabilly would be like asking Bing Crosby to cut rock and roll. So at forty-three years old, Cowboy Copas went back to recording country. He was a waltz man at heart. He couldn't bring himself to wiggle like Elvis Presley.

As the 1950s wore on, Copas nearly dropped from the horizon of country music. Rock and roll struck it like a tidal wave, but country survived by being itself and adding a new pop element to its sound. Copas suffered some personal heartbreak too. His brother Forrest, only forty-two years old, was killed in an automobile accident in late 1957, near his home in Howe, Indiana. Only two years earlier, Forrest's wife, Lula, had died.

Then as the decade ended, so did Cowboy Copas's long streak of bad luck. The transformation came quickly: Starday Records, a Nashville company that had success in country, promoted his new single, "Alabam," all the way to number one on July 4, 1960. Copas had written the song, restoring himself to major-star status and reminding the world that he could write good tunes. The single stayed at number one for an amazing twelve-week run and clung to the country charts for thirty-four weeks. It also spilled over onto the pop charts. Cowboy Copas had now been a popular recording artist in parts of three decades.

Though he was busy writing and touring, Copas never forgot his home. He, Lucille, and their three children frequently returned to the hills of Adams County to visit relatives and friends. Local historian Stephen Kelley wrote, "The couple would try to come home each year during the Christmas season and attend services at Lucille's family church, Evergreen Baptist Church on Steam Furnace Road. It became a tradition during those services for the parishioners to urge Cowboy Copas to sing some of the many spiritual songs he had recorded. His last Christmas performance there was in December 1962."

When he returned to Adams County that Christmas, he must have been proud. Although he hadn't had a hit in well over a year, he continued to make new records. He sang well for old friends at a benefit concert that day, and he talked about another new record, "Goodbye Kisses," which was ready for release. By April 27, 1963, his last big hit would peak at number twelve.

On Sunday, March 3, 1963, Copas appeared at a benefit for the family of "Cactus" Jack Call, a supportive Kansas City disc jockey who had died in an automobile accident. Copas was joined by Patsy Cline, thirty years old and a rising country star, and country veteran Hawkshaw Hawkins, who at forty-one was ready to have his first number-one hit, "Lonesome 7-7203." None of them wanted to make the grueling trip, but they felt obligated to help the family of a man who had helped their careers. They intended to perform at the benefit and in Kansas City and to leave for Nashville on Monday morning. But when the weather turned foul on Monday, their flight was delayed. On Tuesday, March 5, the singers finally left on a Piper Comanche, a small private plane piloted by Randy Hughes, Cline's manager and Cowboy's son-in-law—married to Copas's daughter, Kathy, with whom Copas had performed and recorded when she was a girl. Bad weather forced the plane to land in Dyersberg, Tennessee, where they refueled and waited for a break in the storm. There Copas, forty-nine, called his wife for the last time. When the storm cleared, they resumed their flight. As Hughes struggled to see in another thunderstorm, the plane crashed into a mountainside near Camden, Tennessee, eighty-five miles west of Nashville. All four died. Cowboy's funeral procession in Nashville was five miles long.

As radio stations played Copas's new "Goodbye Kisses," the nation mourned the deaths of three great country music singers. In the months following the crash, the careers of Copas, Hawkins, and Cline were resurrected. At King Records, Sydney Nathan dug into his studio vault and found masters by all three singers. Nathan had previously acquired some Cline masters, and he owned many of Hawkins, a former King label mate of Copas in the late 1940s and early '50s. Nathan released new Cowboy Copas albums, which today are still being reissued on compact discs. Other companies rushed to release more recordings from the trio. One album was called *Gone but Not Forgotten.*

Unfortunately, people remember Cowboy Copas today not for his hits and popularity but for his death. His name is now reduced to a footnote: he died in the plane crash that killed Patsy Cline. Copas is buried near Hawkins and Hughes in Forest Lawn Memorial Park, north of Nashville. They rest there in semi-obscurity and in Cline's musical shadow. Even Cline's husband, Nashville music operative Charlie Dick, knows this. "When that plane went down, Copas was the biggest star on board," Dick told a reporter on the eve of the crash's fiftieth anniversary, in 2013. "Usually, today, Patsy seems to get top billing. But Patsy was a big fan of Copas and Hawk, and they were stars. Everybody on that plane was important to the music business." Dick wasn't merely being respectful to the Cowboy's memory: Copas was indeed that popular in the late 1940s and early '50s. Cline enjoyed his music, Dick said, and respected his ability. Her stardom came a decade after his, starting with "Walking after Midnight" in 1957, and she had eight country hits before she died, two of which were number-one records—"I Fall to Pieces" and "She's Got You." A few weeks after her death, her prophetically titled "Sweet Dreams (of You)" reached number five on the *Billboard* chart.

In Adams County today, people are beginning to appreciate the con-tributions of their native son again. In 2004, Lloyd Estel "Cowboy" Copas was officially honored with a historical marker before a large group of fans and family members on the lawn of the Adams County Courthouse. Kelley, a leader of the county's historical society, told the crowd, "Cowboy Copas was one serious young man who knew what he wanted to do with his life." Kelley was perhaps the first person to discover and write about the singer's Ohio roots. "He represented his home county well," Kelley said. The Copas family was represented by the singer's daughter, Kathy Copas Hughes, who recorded duets with her father when she was only fourteen years old, in 1950. "I worked with the road show for about six years," she told the group. "I stopped when I was expecting my first child. When I started my family, it was time to move on." She and her father recorded "I Love You, My Darling, I Love You," "Copy Cat," and other songs for King.

In the decade since the marker was erected, Cowboy Copas's early recordings have been reevaluated and appreciated again by music scholars and the public. They carry a certain innocence, and a sincerity and realism, that many of today's recordings lack. Ronnie Pugh, head reference librarian at the Country Music Hall of Fame in Nashville, said Cowboy Copas was a seminal performer and a favorite on the Opry for twenty-two years. "He did some marvelous songs, but he was never elected to the Hall, for some reason," Pugh said. "It just never happened." But he was important nonetheless, Pugh said, setting the tone for early country music's journey that soon would be followed by Hank Williams and other stars. In this way, Lloyd Copas was a pioneer.

Perhaps no finer tribute can be given any singer—not even to an *Ohio* cowboy.

12

SYDNEY NATHAN
Music Man

Sydney Nathan never intended to become a champion of race relations in Cincinnati. He only wanted to hire the best employees for positions in his new company, King Records, when it began operating in the mid-1940s. He was desperate to create a steady job for himself and for others crazy enough to follow him down an employment road lined with shellac: these included poor Appalachians and blacks and other minorities for whom good jobs were hard to find. To them, Nathan was the Chief, the guy who signed the paychecks and made their dreams real. On the creative side, he also turned minority performers into stars in a time when white big-band musicians dominated the record business. He saw a niche and he filled it with the most suited, and in a way the most unlikely, people.

First, Nathan hired black trumpeter Henry Glover as one of King's top producers and chief of the firm's Artists and Repertoire (A&R) department. Nathan also hired blacks and other minorities to work in his factory and offices.

By the late 1940s, his King Records, Inc. had become a significant force in the U.S. record industry, in both sales and enlightenment. The man who helped forge the sound of a modern country music also discovered many early giants of rhythm and blues, including James Brown and Hank Ballard. Yet Nathan and his gritty old factory remained unfamiliar to most Cincinnatians; the place was a secret to all but the city's hipsters and true music lovers.

Cincinnati was Nathan's hometown and he loved it, despite its general lack of understanding of his musical mission. He was born there on April 27, 1904, of middle-class parents, and later in life he would refer to himself as a Dutchman, a Cincinnati German. He fit into local society

Sydney Nathan, circa 1965. (Authors' collection)

by appearing, at least to acquaintances, to be a family man who enjoyed watching local television stars and lived in an early city suburb named Bond Hill. When he came home from work, he'd tinker on the piano and sometimes swim in the family pool. Personally, he preferred business-friendly Republican James Rhodes for governor in the 1960s and middle-of-the-road pop music. But he knew how to sell so-called hillbilly and race records like commodities.

What outsiders did not see was the *other* Sydney Nathan, the one with unending drive and a keen business sense. He was a big turning wheel that never shut down. He couldn't help himself, for he was born with a give-it-to-me-straight attitude that sometimes offended his performers and business associates. "Everybody had a Syd story," recalled Rusty York, a King rockabilly singer who hurriedly covered "Peggy Sue" when Nathan decided to jump into rock and roll in 1957. "But he was always nice to me."

Legendary recording engineer E. T. "Bucky" Herzog, whose downtown studio attracted Nathan in the late 1940s, remembered Syd as a gruff autocrat who cursed and pressured musicians when they fouled up a song. "Finally, I had to ask him to leave and not return," Herzog once said. "So he went out and built his own studio." A close associate, the promotion man Jim Wilson, recalled Syd's hidden sensitivity: Nathan once ordered him to stop the car so he could rescue a turtle they saw crawling across a country road. Then there's the Reverend Bobby Grove, who began as a struggling King country singer. Being poor in the '50s, he didn't have enough money to press an experimental gospel album. So the accounting department rejected his plea for credit. Then Nathan intervened and told his managers to press the record anyway. Syd told Grove he believed in his talent and his decision to move toward religious songs. That album launched a new career in Grove's ministry, which helped countless homeless people. Another King artist, the famous Grandpa Jones, was Nathan's earliest. Jones claimed that Syd was so cheap then, in 1944, that he paid him a royalty of only five-eighths of a cent a record side—"about a cent and a half a record," Jones explained years ago, still pained by the experience. "I sold so many records that my check for three months was over one thousand dollars. So Syd made all the money, and I didn't. But he didn't cheat me out of the publicity I got."

Today, the world is interested in Syd Nathan's dream. Music lovers everywhere discuss records he cut in his own King Recording Studio in Cincinnati's ragged Evanston neighborhood. They may speak different languages, but they know good American roots music. Syd turned out hundreds of hits, big and small. In the 1990s, an East Coast book publisher devoted two large hardbound books to the entire King discography. Nathan's world—an old office, factory, and studio at 1540 Brewster Avenue—is not just rooms of brick and metal, but a historic place, designated as such by a marker from the Rock and Roll Hall of Fame and Museum in Cleveland, which has enshrined Nathan for his pioneering work. He is also a member of the Bluegrass Hall of Fame.

Yet in his day, the local music people who mattered loved the symphony and the opera. They could not see the importance of an upstart label owned by a brash, loud, and boisterous Jewish businessman who recorded mainly Appalachians and black people singing and playing all types of roots music—bluegrass, country, polka, jazz, rockabilly, rhythm and blues, the blues, and anything else Nathan could find. Consequently, what was going on inside the brick factory received little attention, even when the national charts rang with hit after hit from his studio. Even less attention was paid to the young men and women whose dreams Nathan captured on old ribbon microphones and issued on shellac 78-rpm records with attractive maroon and blue paper labels.

In time, however, the whole wonder vanished as though it had been just a dream. King, the dream machine, is gone too from the Queen City. Today, 1540 Brewster is the home of several small businesses, and less recently it was a dairy company warehouse. The building is painted an ugly brown and looks old—very old. No music is made there anymore except for the constant humming of tires on Interstate 71 nearby, or the clanging of metal crates on the concrete floor of the plant.

The King is dead in the Queen City, but its spirit lives on in its songs.

By 1971, when King Records moved to Nashville to merge with Starday Records, Cincinnati had already been eclipsed by the Music City as an important regional music center, and Sydney Nathan was dead. But in the late 1940s and early 1950s, Cincinnati turned out more hit records than Nashville and country musicians flocked to the Ohio River city to perform and record, mostly because of King and Syd Nathan. Nathan was not exactly born to lead a record company, but once he got the chance, he led indeed.

At an early age, Nathan wanted to perform. For a time he played drums in a dance band, but poor eyesight—cataracts would later rob him of much of his vision—and asthma forced him to leave school in the ninth grade and to surrender his dream. He tried all kinds of jobs—he worked in a pawn shop, started a shooting gallery, promoted wrestling matches, and ran amusement-park concessions. None of them led to anything permanent. He ended up working in a radio store, where he met people who worked in the record business.

They knew him as a fierce bargainer. "He'd go into a pawn shop and pretend interest in some item," dance-band leader Forest Bradford once recalled to a reporter. "He had no intention of buying it. He just wanted to pit his skill against that of the pawnbroker to see how good a price he could get." Nathan would need this skill in King's early, lean years.

He still dreamed of some sort of career in music. Eventually he decided that if he couldn't play music, he'd sell it in his own record store. By the late 1930s, he had Syd's Record Shop on West 5th Street. Business was good. The city was finally poking its head out of the Great Depression.

Then one night Nathan stopped at the Beverly Hills Supper Club in northern Kentucky for a little entertainment, and the course of his life—and the nation's record industry—was changed. On the dance floor he encountered a jukebox outlet owner who owed him six dollars for some new records. Nathan told a reporter in 1949,

Six bucks meant more to me in 1938 than $1,600 now. I saw the fellow with a gorgeous blonde. I figured he would be in the next day with my six bucks. He didn't show. For three weeks in a row I saw him at Beverly with the same babe. Finally on the dance floor I grabbed his shoulder and told him, "If you can afford Beverly, you can afford to pay me." He turned red, blue, and green. He said he didn't have it. The next day he came into the shop and offered me 300 hillbilly, western, and "race" records from his jukeboxes at two cents a platter. He figured I could sell each of them for ten cents and get back my six bucks. I took him up [on it]. The first afternoon I made $18.

Selling records one at a time, however, did not satisfy Nathan. He sold the shop to his sister and brother-in-law and moved to Miami, to be near his brother, a physician, and to start a photo-finishing business. But a freak cold snap hit the Sunshine State in the winter of 1939, forcing Nathan to return to familiar ground in Cincinnati. He had $900 in his pocket when he arrived. A few weeks later, he woke up in the Hotel Gibson with only $3 left. "I decided it was time to go back into the [record] business," he recalled, "or go to work for somebody. I decided for business."

He contacted his former suppliers in the jukebox business and arranged to buy their used records. Then he opened a store at 1351 Central Avenue and stocked it with jukebox cast-offs. He had anticipated the worst—World War II. When the federal government imposed restrictions on record-pressing a few years later to save shellac and other raw materials, Nathan still had plenty of used records to sell. He stayed in business.

He still wanted to write songs and make records, however, even if they were for other artists. Friends warned that he might lose everything, but he knew what he wanted. His view was simple—the big record companies were recording only a few stars and promising singers in race, hillbilly, and western music, as the trade magazines called them. A niche could be filled, Nathan believed, if someone aggressively marketed the "music of the little people"—urban Appalachians and African Americans.

In 1943, at the height of the war, he got several friends and family members to invest and launched King Records, then he signed Grandpa Jones and some other hillbilly singers who performed on WLW Radio. In November 1944 he moved his new company into rented quarters on Brewster, where the firm remained until it was sold in 1971. Before long, he had his own recording studio and hard-to-find record-pressing equipment. Eventually, he acquired everything he needed to produce, distribute, and sell his own records. It was an unusual arrangement; as he liked to brag, a singer could walk into King in the morning and leave that night with a new record in his or her hands.

In time, Nathan built a growing business with his main label and subsidiary ones—King, Queen, Federal, DeLuxe. "Syd always had regal ideas," said his sister, Dorothy Halper, one of the company's original investors.

By 1945, King was turning out two hundred shellac 78-rpm discs a day. Nathan told friends he and the partners earned only $12.50 a week that first year, and $25 a week the next year. But King's sales increased as Nathan astutely signed long-term contracts with hillbilly stars and potential ones: Cowboy Copas, Hawkshaw Hawkins, Wayne Raney, Moon Mullican, Hank Penny, the Stanley Brothers, and many more.

Nathan put the company's slogan, "The King of Them All," above the crown logo on the early maroon labels. After all, he was the king of his personal musical kingdom, and his word was the law. He deserved to call it King. He became the consummate record-maker. When the little

45-rpm vinyl disc was introduced in 1948, Nathan was one of the first to see its potential and was one of the first to recycle surplus vinyl. By 1949, King was selling 6 million records a year, including the number-one *Billboard* hit "Why Don't You Haul Off and Love Me" by Wayne Raney. Nathan was a success. He joked, "The 'y' in Sydney is because my parents knew I was going to make money." His largest profits, though, came not from King Records but his music publishing companies, including Lois, Arnel, Blue Ridge, Blue Ribbon, and others. He owned the rights to such hits as "The Twist," which Hank Ballard originally recorded in Cincinnati, and "Fever," done by Little Willie John. Through the years, Nathan earned a lot of money on the cover versions. Using the pen name Lois Mann, he collaborated on numerous hit songs, including the hillbilly classics "As Advertised" and "Signed, Sealed, and Delivered" by Cowboy Copas. No one knows how much he actually collaborated, if he did so at all, but performers recall Syd telling them about ideas for songs and hook lines that he made up while driving to work. Whatever the fine print said on any individual record label, insiders knew Sydney Nathan was the king of King and its jack of all jobs.

In 1957, Nathan hired a young Ray Pennington as a stock clerk. One day, Pennington was walking down a hall when someone called him into the recording studio to help with a technical problem. "I don't know what's wrong with this console," the engineer moaned. Pennington studied the mass of electrical cords and inputs leading to the unit. He knew something about the equipment because he was a performer at night, using all manner of guitar amplifiers and things electric for his country and rockabilly band, the Western Rhythm Boys.

Like many King country artists, he had come to Cincinnati from Kentucky with his family so his father could get a job in a factory. Pennington naturally gravitated to King, the hit-maker. He wanted to be a star like everyone else, and a record producer, too. So Nathan recorded him—as Ray Starr for rockabilly and Ray Pennington for country—and gave him a day job in the stockroom.

On his knees, Pennington patched some wires together and pronounced the engineer's problem solved. The session resumed. Syd Nathan, watching all of this from the back of the room, was uncharacteristically silent. Suddenly, he appeared at Pennington's side and said, matter-of-factly, "Your desk is gonna be moved tomorrow—into the A&R department."

The king had spoken.

One day in 1956, King talent scout Ralph Bass had a visitor, a young black man named James Brown from Georgia who had just rolled into town with a vocal group called the Famous Flames. Brown had been making a name for himself as a loud and unearthly howler of rhythm and blues. King's reputation in that field had drawn Brown and the Flames to Brewster Avenue, but the operation itself looked unremarkable: the old icehouse next door was still banging out its cold crystals, and the halls at King were filled with throngs of odd characters, white and black, coming and going. This musical integration was by design. When the hillbilly sound temporarily plummeted in popularity in the early '50s, Nathan was not about to sit around and hope it would return to good health. He had already started signing many R&B singers, including Hank Ballard and the Midnighters (Ballard's song "The Twist" would first appear on King), organist Bill Doggett, Little Willie John, Otis Williams and the Charms, Wynonie Harris, Billy Ward and the Dominoes, and Nina Simone.

Hillbillies and black people, it was a strange combination, and as Ralph Bass showed Brown and his group around that day, it looked stranger. The bewildering maze of corridors and cubbyholes that passed for offices were lined with copies of King's growing list of hit records and albums. There were framed pictures of the label's stars—Earl Bostic, the black saxophonist; Copas, the hillbilly crooner; and long rows of famous, half-famous, and unknown faces, black faces out of the Deep South or the northern ghettos, white faces out of the hardscrabble mountains—a potpourri of race, talent, and unlikely ambitions.

In one studio, someone was wailing a wild R&B number, while a hillbilly singer wearing a wide cowboy hat smoked a cigarette and strummed a guitar in the corridor as he waited to go in next. Everything was a crazy juxtaposition—the music, the songs, the performers—and all of it held together by the loud voice of Sydney Nathan.

According to most accounts, Nathan was a terror in the studio. The black singers seemed to have the most difficulty making him understand their music. This was not hillbilly fare; no, this was rhythm, man. Over the years, Brown had to defend his projects against Nathan's tirades and on occasion even pay for the recordings himself to prove their worth. Nathan had unwavering opinions on what was good and not good in music. He was old style—hook line, strong melody. If he didn't like what was being recorded, he'd start yelling. He hated Brown's first hit, "Please, Please, Please" and threatened to fire Bass for making it with

Brown and the Famous Flames. Then suddenly the record sold—and sold and sold. Bass was a hero.

At the same time, Nathan supported his artists. He was not a folklorist, saving ethnic music for posterity. He was in show business, and he urged his new stars to cultivate a commercial sound to lengthen their careers. "Syd had a special insight, a way of seeing talent in people," said Ray Pennington, now retired from jobs as a Nashville record company president and staff producer at RCA. "I loved him. If he were still alive today, I'd probably still be working for him. He was one of the pioneers of the modern record industry. Funny, he couldn't play [well]; he couldn't sing. He could barely talk. But he had insight. It's sad to see a dynasty like King die, but I don't think anybody else was capable of keeping it going."

"Colonel" Jim Wilson, another Nashville record executive, began as a sales manager at King in 1949 and in one job or another lasted at the firm until 1965. "Mr. Nathan—I always called him that—used to say, 'All you need to get into the record business is a desk, a telephone, and an attorney.' Then he'd laugh. But he built a solid record company because he could do everything in-house. He didn't have to answer to a lot of other companies or people. King could do everything but make the shipping cartons."

Nathan knew the business from top to bottom. Wilson said the boss sold records through nontraditional outlets, such as general stores in rural areas and his own nationwide system of distributors, so often the nation's music charts didn't fully reflect King's sales. While on the road promoting hillbilly records in the 1940s, Nathan decided he should also start offering so-called race records—black music—on the same sales calls. So he returned to the office and started King signing black acts to contracts. He also opened his thirty-two sales branches in various cities, shunning the slow-paying independent distributors.

Nathan's offbeat operating procedures extended to the studio as well. Henry Glover, his chief producer, was a black man who wrote and recorded songs for all kinds of acts, from white pop singers to bluegrass pickers to black R&B vocalists. To Glover, a good song was a good song, regardless of what musical genre recorded it. Before the civil rights movement changed America, Glover was using black and white musicians on all kinds of sessions. "There was no color line at King," Jim Wilson said.

"Henry Glover was one of the first major African American executives in the record business," noted playwright KJ Sanchez, who interviewed dozens of former King employees in 2013. She said Nathan and Glover used to

> travel down South, scouting for talent and setting up accounts. Because they were going to the places where black people weren't allowed to go legitimately, except if they were working on a job or something, Henry Glover would go as Syd Nathan's driver, as his chauffeur. That's the only way he could get in. This is a man who today, [if] you go to BMI's [Broadcast Music Inc.] catalogue, [you will find] that Henry Glover owns over 400 songs in that catalogue alone. I mean, this is the man who is listed as the composer of "Drown in My Own Tears," a song that's been covered by Janis Joplin, Aretha Franklin, Stevie Wonder, scores of others—and in those days Glover had to pretend to be Syd's driver.

Obviously this couldn't have been healthy for Glover's self-esteem, but then he was used to the way things were in the South. No one knows exactly what Nathan thought of this arrangement, but he used to say he was familiar with discrimination's sting because he was a Jew. From the beginning he hired blacks and whites for all types of jobs and made sure they worked together. He believed that if people worked together, they would understand one another better, and tolerance would follow. So he mixed things up in every department and gave approval to hire more minorities if they could do the jobs. As a result, Sanchez said, King's A&R department was an incredible showcase of talented people of different races, "many of whom went on to run their own labels, many of whom were smart enough to get the rights to the songs they wrote."

Sanchez was impressed that he stood up and hired minorities at a time when most companies didn't. It wasn't that Nathan was committed to social justice in any obvious way, she said, "it just made good business sense to him—why shouldn't he have white and black musicians playing on the same records, if they were the best—and, of course, most affordable—musicians there were? . . . He was also promoting music of 'the folk'—what at the time was called 'race records' and the music of Appalachian immigrants of the area. He was promoting folk before folk was cool."

Nathan signed many doo-wop groups in the '50s, including the Platters and the Swallows. Some had been successful in the past, and he tried to resurrect their careers. Others, like eighteen-year-old Otis Williams of Cincinnati, were just starting out. Sometimes the black vocalists clashed with Nathan over royalty payments and song selection. Nathan was old school; he wanted songs that sounded familiar. Their battles sometimes lasted years, but the artists couldn't leave—they were under contract.

Williams, like James Brown, stood up to Nathan in the late 1950s and early 1960s. Williams maintained that he helped write songs but didn't receive credit. Yet he admitted, "He was one of the innovators. King had the best artists collectively. But he was shrewd. . . . It was one of those things. You either accepted it and went on with your work or . . ." Williams's group, the Charms, had several big R&B hits, including "Ivory Tower." Williams later went to court against Nathan to retain ownership of the name "Otis Williams and His Charms." "We started a [musical] revolution," he said of his generation's performers, "and didn't know it at the time. We were just there at the right time."

By 1967, Nathan's label was slowing down. Friends and family gathered at his home that July to honor him for his twenty-fifth year in the record business. Heart attacks had hit him hard over the last few years, and with them Nathan seemed to lose his way in the recording jungle. The King empire was already beginning to shrink. Nathan had closed his sales branches and had been forced to make do with the often unreliable independent distributors. The major labels had finally awakened to the country-western music market and descended on the hillbilly stars, fountain pens in hand. Race records had broken out of the ghetto and into mainstream America, and the big companies were now courting the singers.

So Nathan concentrated mainly on rhythm and blues. Although King continued to release many kinds of music, comedy, and other types of recordings, by the mid-1960s the label could be described in two words— James Brown. The self-proclaimed "Soul Brother Number One" was selling millions of records to both blacks and whites, just as he had predicted to Nathan in their studio shouting matches years before. "Cold Sweat," "It's A Man's, Man's, Man's World," "Papa's Got a Brand New Bag (Part One)," "I Got You (I Feel Good)," and dozens of other records poured out of the King pressing plant every day, from the same building where Brown recorded many of his hits.

Nathan had little time to savor his later successes, however. On March 5, 1968, he died of a heart attack in Miami, Florida, where he had been living six months of the year to take advantage of the warmer climate and local heart specialists. His death put the company's partners in a quandary. In the long term, they realized the kingdom could not exist without the king. So they decided to sell it. Over the next few years, the King companies were sold to other owners, a New York record label bought James Brown's contract, and other pieces of Nathan's kingdom were dispersed.

In Evanston, his dark factory sat empty. So did his recording studio. Employees scattered to New York, Nashville, Los Angeles, and other places. King Records—the heart of it anyway—was dead. There would be a new King, but nothing like the old one, for Nathan was King Records.

Today in Cincinnati, the name Sydney Nathan is rarely spoken, except by record collectors and historians. James Brown is dead, after a tumultuous end-of-life chapter that included prison and a crazy binge that led him there. The international record companies control the business now, and they have turned Nathan's "music of the little people" into a major industry. The name of their one-time king, the Pied Piper of Appalachia and of rhythm and blues, is a piece of music business trivia.

KJ Sanchez doesn't mourn its passing, but she knows what was lost in the company's demise. "King Records played a significant role in American music, and then, just as suddenly as it came, it went," she said. "The tragedy of the story is that the label was not able to live beyond Syd's lifetime, which makes the whole story rather Shakespearean in scope."

The king of King Records is dead, but not forgotten.

13

JOSEPHINE JOHNSON

Pulitzer Prize–Winning Author

Josephine Wilcox Johnson's life story is rather like one of her novels. The plot is evident, but the complexities take time and patience to unravel.

Becoming one of the youngest recipients of the Pulitzer Prize for fiction might have intimided some authors. Think of Harper Lee coming to a jarring halt after *To Kill a Mockingbird* or Margaret Mitchell producing just one gigantic, magnificent novel—*Gone with the Wind*. But Johnson—just twenty-four when she wrote *Now in November* and twenty-five when she won—was motivated by the recognition her book garnered. She knew she would continue to write, wherever life took her.

Johnson wrote the 1935 prizewinner in the attic of her mother's farmhouse in Missouri, but it was when she was a writer and parent in Clermont County, Ohio, that her vision matured and broadened. Whether she was writing about the crushing effects of the Great Depression or commenting on the horrors of the Vietnam War, nature was always a major character in her work. She was often lauded as a perceptive and lyrical observer of nature, but catagorizing Josephine Johnson as only a nature writer is like saying the same of Thoreau (to whom she has been compared). She saw the loveliness and pragmatic brutality of nature reflected in people, but she also examined how people respond to both everyday and extraordinary events.

Johnson's life began ordinarily enough. She was born on June 20, 1910, in Kirkwood, Missouri, a small town near St. Louis. As a child, she often visited her maternal grandmother's home, where the library was as filled and expansive as the gardens and grounds outdoors. Summers were spent with her three sisters visiting at a family dairy farm.

Josephine Johnson, circa 1936. (Courtesy of Terence Cannon for the Josephine Johnson Estate)

Although she wrote fondly of various family members and experiences in her partial memoir, *Seven Houses,* she concluded that her childhood was not particularly happy. "It was too full of a morbid and passionate sensitivity to both beauty and pain," she wrote. That double-edged sensibility would be replayed and examined in her writing as well as in her personal life.

She found her calling at age seven when she wrote her first poem, three lines inspired by a newspaper drawing celebrating the end of the Great War. Her only personal exposure to the war was watching her father go out once a week to train with the National Guard and once being taken to the Kirkwood train station to wave to a group of khaki-clad soldiers being sent off to duty. War, however, would be a recurring concern in her later writing.

When she was older, her father gave up a wholesale coffee company he had run for years in St. Louis and moved the family to a small farm near Webster Groves, Missouri. He farmed there for several years while Josephine began to write, as she would later reflect, "enormously, fulsomely" at a rolltop desk in the farmhouse attic.

A tall, handsome, green-eyed brunette, she was Josie—or Jo—to friends and family. She was a serious young woman, shy and rather introverted. But her talent and creativity were boundless; she was always reaching for new forms of expression. She attended art classes at Washington University in St. Louis, and although she did not complete a degree there, drawing and painting were lifelong joys for her.

When her father died of cancer—a devastating loss—her mother kept the farm. Josephine continued to live at home, writing steadily. She wrote in longhand, then sent her work out to be typed—a practice she followed throughout her career. Her short stories began appearing in various publications, including the *St. Louis Review, Hound and Horn, Atlantic Monthly,* and *Vanity Fair.* In 1934, she was awarded the first of what would be five O. Henry Awards for her short fiction.

Now in November was also published in 1934. The novel tells the harrowing story of the Haldmarne family trying to survive against nature and the economy on a hardscrabble farm during the Great Depression. The story is often grim, as a husband and wife and their three very different daughters concentrate on just surviving uncontrollable circumstances. Steady deprivation, unending backbreaking work, and mental and physical illness take heavy tolls on the family. Yet halfway through the tale, Marget, the daughter who is the narrator, finds some strength in the cycle of nature: "If anything could fortify me against whatever was to come . . . it would have to be the small and eternal things—the whippoorwills' long liquid howling near the cave . . . the shape of young mules against the ridge, moving lighter than bucks across the pasture . . . things like the chorus of cicadas, and the ponds stained red in evenings."

Despite tragedy and loss, Marget continues on, with life and with the land. Critics widely praised *Now in November* for Johnson's poetic writing style and beautiful use of language, although some later found her style at odds with the gritty subject matter. Sales of the novel, published by Simon & Schuster, were modest, but the positive reviews brought the book to the attention of the Pulitzer Prize fiction jury.

The jury, which consisted of three literary experts, had the job of sorting through dozens of novels to choose contenders. After reviewing their favorite books, they submitted titles to the advisory board for fiction, which chose the winner. Jury members did not always reach a consensus among themselves, and even when they did, the advisory board sometimes ignored their recommendation and rewarded a book of its own choice. That had happened with the 1934 Pulitzer Prize, and those involved were still fuming.

At first, it seemed as though the selection process for the 1935 fiction prize might be equally difficult. The jury could not find a truly outstanding novel, the chairman noted, although his comments about *Now in November* were the most positive in his report. The jury forwarded eight novels to the advisory board. Of these, perhaps only one title and author would be familiar to today's readers: *So Red the Rose*, by Stark Young, was a best-selling story of life following the Civil War.

The board chose Johnson's novel without any apparent dissent or fanfare. She learned of the prize through a newspaper reporter who called her at the farm. Her family was enormously proud of her, her eldest daughter, Annie Cannon would later report. She didn't recall her mother ever talking much about the prize, or whether the family celebrated it. As serious-minded as she was, Johnson probably realized that the honor was a double-edged gift. The Pulitzer certainly raised her stock with her publisher, but it would also raise expectations for all her future works and affect how people related to her personally. For the rest of her life—and even after her death—she would never be mentioned in a public context without the words "Pulitzer Prize." It would be up to her to forge an identity that encompassed more than the efforts of a twenty-four-year-old first-time novelist.

Hard at work on another novel and more short stories, Johnson concentrated on her craft rather than the prize. Ideas and themes that were important to her came bursting out in a variety of genres. Simon & Schuster took advantage of the narrow window of acclaim immediately following the Pulitzer win to publish as much as Johnson could provide. *Winter Orchard,* a thoughtful group of short stories, came out in 1935. A collection of poems, *Year's End,* followed in 1937. Her second novel, *Jordanstown,* published in 1937, did not receive the critical acclaim of her first work, but it did address one of her passions: social justice and workers' rights.

That passion was reflected in her life by her choice of first husband, Thurlow Smoot, an attorney for the National Labor Relations Board, whom she married in 1939. The union was relatively brief, and Johnson had little, if any, contact with Smoot afterward. But they did have a baby, a son she named Terence. Impending motherhood may have influenced her to write her first—and, as it turned out, only—children's book. *Paulina: The Story of an Apple-Butter Jar* was published in 1939. After *Now in November* was published, she had talked about wanting to write and illustrate children's books, "not for children, but a sort of nightmare collection such as has never been published."

Johnson's career would take another path, however. For a short time, she lectured on writing at the University of Iowa. She was becoming increasingly concerned with social issues, caring for baby Terry, and wanting to write full-time. It was a busy and exciting life, but there were more changes around the bend.

"Real life" began, Johnson wrote, when she met Grant Cannon, who would become her second husband and bring her to Ohio. Cannon, a Mormon and grandson of a livestock rancher, had grown up in Salt Lake City. He studied anthropology at Brigham Young University but left before earning a degree. Along the way, he separated from the Mormon faith and became involved with workers' rights. When he and Johnson met, he was working as a field examiner for the National Labor Relations Board, attending a case hearing in St. Louis.

The two young idealists married on Easter Day 1942 at her mother's home. "It was an extraordinary spring and from that hour I was married to an extraordinary man for thirty years," Johnson wrote in her memoir. "A man who built himself, faults, talents, wounds and virtues, into a work of amazing art. No, the word is *human.* Alive and mortal. Human without end."

Cannon adopted Terry as soon as possible; he was the only father the boy ever knew. Soon after the marriage, World War II separated the newlyweds. Cannon served as a combat intelligence officer with the Army Air Forces in the Pacific. He wrote "lovely" letters to little Terry while he was gone, recalled Annie Cannon. Terry and his mother waited out the war in Webster Groves. Her third novel, *Wildwood,* was published in 1945. The book examined the loss of idealism in the socialist movement and agnosticism. Its reviews and sales were modest.

After the war ended, Cannon moved his wife, Terry, and daughter Annie to Ohio. He went to work as a writer and photographer for an ambitious new national magazine, *Farm Quarterly,* published in Cincinnati. The family moved into an 1810 brick house on Round Bottom Road in Newtown in 1947. "And all those years, all those other places, do not seem as real as the Old House in Newtown," Johnson wrote. "It was the first house that either of us had ever owned." It was at the Old House that Johnson began to find her literary voice, not in the invention of fictional characters but in her own life and her observations of the world around here. Those experiences would form the second act of Johnson's writing career.

Motherhood marked the beginning of an almost twenty-year hiatus from book publishing for Johnson. The demands of a young family and the ever-in-need-of-attention Old House took precedence. But judging from the sharp memories and extensive details of her memoir, she must have kept a diary or journal during those years.

The Old House, situated on three acres just a half-mile from a noisy stone quarry, was a naturalist's dream. Old maple trees, a marshy area, a crumbling icehouse cloaked in ivy, and surrounding farm fields provided rich observation opportunities. The house, sprawling and drafty, was a character in itself. Stories of the Cannons' lives there over ten years comprise almost half of *Seven Houses.*

Life in Newtown was demanding, complex, and ever changing. Cannon's work on the *Farm Quarterly* figured large in the young family's life. The magazine was not content to just examine the latest type of fertilizer or seed corn on American farms; its writers approached farming as a science and an industry. Over the years, Cannon traveled as far as India and Pakistan to report on agriculture.

He pursued some of his own ideas at home. He made one cavernous room of the Old House into a laboratory, where he worked at turning corncobs into affordable, nutritious poultry feed. The entire homestead was a lab for Johnson. She watched her children grow, observed the constant cycles of nature, and thought much about the nature of human-kind. Motherhood had not given her a rose-colored view of life. If anything, it made her concerns and doubts more urgent as she considered the world her children would inherit.

Cannon dealt with his own doubts by embracing community and looking for ways to remain optimistic about life. Traveling and inter-viewing people for the magazine, joining professional groups, and attending meetings of the Society of Friends in Cincinnati helped him find balance. "Dad enjoyed people," Annie Cannon said in a 2013 interview. He once taught a janitor who worked in his office building to read. After the older children left home, he invited a teenager who didn't have any-place to work on his car to use the barn on the Cannon property.

Josephine, however, struggled with depression. "Her despair was a heavy burden for her," Annie said. Her concern over conditions in the world, as well as people's lack of care for nature, were persistent. At home with the children, she turned inward. In *Seven Houses,* she said that she had made a "lifelong truce with despair." Annie "learned to be an optimist just in reaction to gloomy people," Johnson wrote. That was not always easy, her daughter said. Johnson was not a joiner; she was not social, although she and Cannon were friends with a small group of Cincinnati-area writers.

But if despair was a lifelong acquaintance, so was Johnson's joy in her children, her husband, and the beauty of nature. Her husband was always coming up with a new project or pursuit. He earned a pilot's license, become a gourmet cook, made pottery, pursued photography, wrote a play. He also played the flute and sang, and Johnson loved to hear him sing the old hymns and Christmas carols she remembered from childhood.

When their second daughter, Carol, was born one April in the 1940s, Johnson's delight was immense. "The perfect packaging of a baby is more astounding than even the satin wrappings of the hickory and chestnuts buds," she wrote. "Carol came firmly packed and plump as a loaf of bread."

As the children grew, so did the couple's desire for more space and an even closer relationship with nature. In 1947 they moved to an abandoned farm of thirty-seven acres on Klatte Road, still in Clermont

County but further removed from neighbors, with no stone quarries nearby. It was about twenty miles east of Cincinnati. They resolved to let the place revert to a more natural state, with the goal of making it a nature preserve. Creeks, ridges, a meadow, and a pond provided rich habitats for multitudes of flora and fauna. Johnson came to think of the farm as her "inland island." But if the property separated her more from others, it brought her thoughts closer to the printed page. She began writing extensively in the early 1960s, working on a new novel.

It is significant that Simon & Schuster, who had published her first novel, came forward to publish the new one now, in 1963. Although none of Johnson's books had been best-sellers, the publishers must have believed in her talent and recognized that she was capable of writing thoughtful, meaningful fiction. She began working with Michael Korda, who would be that publisher's editor-in-chief for forty years as well as a best-selling author.

The Dark Traveler tells the story of a loving family of five who take in a troubled nephew, to whom the title refers. Paul is emotionally and psychologically unstable. His bullying, obnoxious father is a major source of his distress. That Paul's favored brother has been killed in the war strengthens his father's hatred for his surviving son. Although Johnson does not name the war or give it much prominence, it's reasonable to assume she is writing about Vietnam. At the time she would have been working on novel, American troops were beginning to be sent into the conflict. In some ways, *The Dark Traveler* is reminiscent of *Now in November*. Both stories focus on strong, yet troubled, families faced with personal conflicts. Nature is an important part of each—Paul's kindly uncle is a conservationist, as opposed to his father, a greedy developer. Societal problems—a war and the Depression—affect each family.

But the influence of a loving husband and children over the years tempers some of the harshness of the 1934 novel. The uncle in *The Dark Traveler* is described as a man with many of Cannon's characteristics. He is passionately concerned with the welfare of his family. He recognizes the evil in the world, but his decency and steadfastness bolster his loved ones, in particular his wife, who is more prone to melancholy.

Like her first novel, the book was praised for its poetic qualities. The book editor for the *Cincinnati Enquirer*, for instance, waxed poetic himself as he described Johnson. She was, he wrote, "a rare creature whose muse hovers with dark compassion and trembling." While the book received praise for taking on a familiar problem in an eloquent manner, sales remained modest.

While *The Dark Traveler* marked Johnson's return to the novel, she had never really been out of print. Numerous short stories she wrote in the 1940s and 1950s for *Harper's Bazaar* magazine and periodicals were reprinted regularly in anthologies. Many of the stories echo events or motifs from her life. "The Rented Room," written shortly after Cannon left for war, is a study of a woman and her young son waiting out her solider husband's orders in a boardinghouse occupied by other war wives and their children. "Penelope's Web" concerns a young mother living in a home much like the Old House. Throughout the day, the endless household work and her somewhat morbid thoughts wear her down. The arrival of her children from school cheers her and puts life into perspective. A demanding old country house much like the Newtown place also figures prominently in "The Glass Mountain," one of Johnson's more lighthearted stories. A young man desperate to court his dream girl is enlisted into helping her father make numerous repairs to the property.

Simon & Schuster reprinted many of her previously published stories, as well as a few new ones. *The Sorcerer's Son and Other Stories* remains an excellent primer to Johnson's themes and writing style. While the short-story collection was making its way into the world, Johnson was hard at work on what would become the most notable book of the second half of her career.

The 1960s would be the defining period in the lives of the immediate post–World War II generation in America. Political assassinations, the violation of the environment, and the horrors of the Vietnam War deeply affected people. To Johnson and her Quaker-influenced husband, the war was purely evil. Their children shared their beliefs as well as the philosophy that the individual must act on those beliefs. Terry became a conscientious objector. While living in San Francisco, he attended an antiwar demonstration that got out of hand. He ended up in jail with some of the protestors, where he wrote that police officers brutalized him and another man while in custody.

Johnson's own meditations on the war were included in her first nonfiction book, *The Inland Island,* which Simon & Schuster published in 1969. Her move from fiction was prompted by reading a book written under the New Journalism heading, where authors including Norman Mailer and Truman Capote injected personal opinion and conjecture into their factual nonfiction books.

"Mother was so excited by this," Annie Cannon remembered. "'He just wrote what *he* wanted to say,' she told my father." Grant encouraged his wife to do the same. She respected his opinions about writing and publishing. The couple sometimes read and edited each other's work, including Cannon's magnum opus, *Great Men of Modern Agriculture,* which Macmillan published in 1967.

The New Journalism approach was a liberating one for Johnson. She decided to write about what she knew: the natural life of the family's "island" on Klatte Road over twelve months and her feelings over the turmoil of the time. In *The Inland Island* Johnson writes exquisite, unflinching descriptions of nature and her interactions with it. But those experiences suddenly give way to her outrage over the war, racial injustice, and apathy in her fellow citizens.

Johnson turned fifty-seven as she was writing *The Inland Island.* She had lived through more than fifty years of war, uneasy peace, and rumors of war. Her loved ones of her mother's and grandmother's generations were gone. Most devastating of all, she learned her husband had cancer—still considered a death sentence in the 1960s. All the beauty of nature could not smooth over those deaths and the losses still to come. Chapter after chapter, her anger erupts sporadically—unexpectedly.

In one chapter, Johnson writes about coming face to face with a vixen guarding her three cubs on a quiet June evening. At first sight, the mother fox is "very beautiful . . . grey-red fur running down into red below and the plumed tail fringed in white." As author and fox engage in a staring contest, Johnson begins to notice more details: the vixen is plagued by gnats and ticks and one ravaged ear. Compelled to hunt for the cubs' food, she finally breaks her gaze and runs off.

"In the long looking," Johnson writes, "I had seen her as she really was—small, thin, harried, heavily burdened—not really free at all. Bound around by instinct, as I am bound by custom and concern." The following winter hunters killed off all the foxes for miles around. The fox tale soon gives way to discourse about the war. "Every woman of my generation is sick of war," she wrote, noting that it had touched each generation of her family since her childhood. "We who are opposed to war know what all the frustrated of the world must feel. . . . The opposition, the monolithic opposition, the misinterpretation, the prison sentences, and the silence. . . . And this is what the young black men feel, a thousand times over. This is where the fire and the gasoline bombs come from. The broken glass and the burning."

The year ends in conflict: she is intensely bitter about the stupidity of war, yet her heart instinctively gladdens when she feels the sun falling on her shoulders, causing "a curious hollow that is happiness." The book ends not with the dying year but with the dawn of a new one, beginning with "awesome clarity."

Johnson was able to step out of the role of fiction writer to share directly the personal philosophy she had been writing since the 1930s. "She was able to be herself in nonfiction," Annie Cannon said. The result was ragged, intimate, and beautiful. *The Inland Island* was perhaps the best-reviewed book of her career. "An awakening book for the quiet mind and insurgent spirit," was Edward Weeks's verdict in the *Atlantic*. He wrote that the book's principal strength came from Johnson injecting her abhorrence of the war amid her artistlike descriptions of nature.

"Her anger is noble, beautiful, pure," Edward Abbey wrote in the *New York Times Book Review*. He found her writing poetic in the contemporary sense: "terse and tense and starkly clear, the point of view tough, honest." When *Now in November* came out, some reviewers thought Johnson's lyrical writing masked a lack of substance. That was not the case with the new book. "There is hardly a prosaic line or a smoggy thought in the whole book," Abbey wrote.

The Inland Island reflects Johnson's whole life—living through wars, raising a family with a loving spouse, struggling with issues that concern us all. Things she had believed in and been moved by in her twenties were now experiences she had lived through or was going through as she wrote the book. In the *Saturday Review*, Granville Hicks compared her writing to that of Charles Dickens, William Wordsworth, and John Ruskin, all advocates of the importance of the individual and of a more humane society. Her writing was not merely beautiful, it was instructional: if society cannot stop itself from going to war, humanity will be destroyed, as will the natural world.

Although *The Inland Island's* reception was warm, Johnson's heart was heavy. Cannon—the person she loved most in the world and who had most shaped her adulthood—died in February 1969 at age fifty-eight. His death brought perhaps the most difficult transition she had to make.

Terry and Annie were young adults, off on their own, and she knew that Carol would soon be leaving too.

It's not surprising, then, that her next book should be a memoir, a "long looking" of her own at the places and loved ones who had shaped her life. Simon & Schuster published *Seven Houses: A Memoir of Time and Places* in 1973. Johnson wrote evocatively, sometimes sadly, about the houses and relatives of her youth. The book included old family photographs, among them some of her as a child. For an admittedly private person, it was quite personal. But still she did not share everything with the reader. Her growing-up years on the family's farm in Webster Groves were too painful to write about, even in middle age. "Growing up is a terrible time," she wrote. "A person lives with such intensity you wonder there is anything left to go with when it's over."

Her appreciation of nature is readily apparent in the book, as is her sense of humor—something that did not surface often in her writing. Describing her grandparents' vast library, she remembers seeing multiple copies of Victorian poet Robert Browning's works. She rhetorically asks her readers if they have read Browning recently, then notes, "The man's extraordinary. Full of dark horrendous scenes and tortures. I wonder what those ladies of the Browning Clubs were really up to."

The last quarter of the book, however, shows where Johnson's heart really was in those days. It chronicles—rather sketchily—Cannon's arrival in her life and the life they made together with Terry, Annie, and Carol at the Old House in Clermont County. She saw her husband as the center of the family's universe: "Sunlight streamed from Grant. We thought things were as they appeared to be. We had a past and a present and a future—all five of us. It was the high noon and the summer of our lives. Of all our five lives together."

Johnson dedicated *Seven Houses* to Cannon.

The publisher tried to market the book as a kind of companion piece to *The Inland Island,* by emphasizing its beautiful, attentive descriptions of nature. Sales were modest. It would be the last book she would publish with Simon & Schuster.

In 1974, Viking published *The Circle of Seasons,* which played off *The Inland Island*'s format of examining nature throughout the year. Johnson wrote the text, which was complemented by photographs by Dennis Stock.

The transition from fiction to nonfiction, which her husband had encouraged, gave Johnson an outlet that she might not have had otherwise.

In the 1980s, she turned to magazine writing. Only this time, instead of short stories, she wrote essays, mostly centered on her life on the "island." *Ohio* magazine began publishing her work semiregularly. John Fleischman, a Cincinnati writer and associate editor at *Ohio,* became her editor, and—very slowly—her friend.

He tried for a long time to convince Johnson to let him write about her—an idea she strongly resisted. Finally, in the spring of 1985, by which time Johnson was in her mid-seventies, she relented. Fleischman made several visits to the "island" that spring and summer. Johnson was sometimes lonely, still tangling with depression and upkeep of the property.

The children were living on either coast, all engaged in careers rooted in a Johnson-Cannon upbringing. Terence was writing political nonfiction, which later gave way to short stories. Carol was immersed in work related to anthropology. Annie was illustrating children's books and would eventually write the texts for them as well. Johnson never appeared to consider leaving Klatte Road to live with a child, move into a retirement community, or return to Missouri. "The land sustained her," Annie said. "That was more important to her than living near relatives."

Five years before Fleischman's visit, the county sewer district invaded her property to install a large concrete wastewater conduit next to the creek. In the installing of the line, work crews had opened up wooded areas, which then made the land accessible to trespassers and their vehicles, and occasional acts of vandalism. Still, Johnson persisted.

She remained on her inland island until just days before her death in 1990 at age seventy-nine. Her obituary in the *New York Times* noted that her writings were credited with helping to popularize ecological concerns. "I've never done anything too scientific," Johnson told Fleischman while looking over some plants during his 1985 visit. "I just watch."

And she wrote. And reminded the world of how nature and humanity are intertwined and why that matters so much.

BIBLIOGRAPHY

Caesar, Early Explorer

Baskin, John, and Michael O'Bryant. *The Ohio Almanac,* 3d ed. Wilmington: Orange Frazer Press, 2004.

Bogan, Dallas. "Naming of Caesar's Creek Is Still a Mystery." *Warren County Local History.* September 14, 2004. http://www.rootsweb.ancestry.com/~ohwarren//Bogan/bogan330.htm.

Dalton, Dennis. Interviews with Randy McNutt, April 4, 1996, and December 2, 2013.

Eckert, Allan W. *Blue Jacket: War Chief of the Shawnee.* Boston: Little, Brown, 1969.

———. *The Frontiersman.* Boston: Little, Brown, 1967.

Ewing-Gibbons, Vinnie. Interview with Randy McNutt, April 16, 1996.

Hall, Wade. "Black History Month." *Louisville Courier-Journal,* March 1, 1996.

"History and Culture." George Rogers Clark National Historical Park Web site. http://www.nps.gov/gero/historyculture/index.htm.

McNutt, Randy. "Et Tu, Apostrophe: Punctuation Betrays a Worthy Caesar." *Ohio* magazine, February 1997.

Robinson, George F. *A History of Greene County, Ohio.* Xenia: W. B. Chew, Printer, 1895.

Rowland, C. D., et al. "Was the Shawnee War Chief Blue Jacket a Caucasian?" *Ohio Journal of Science* 106, no. 4 (September 2006).

Benjamin R. Hanby, Christmas Composer

Brower, Barbara. Interview with Randy McNutt, December 3, 1987.

"Christmas Song Written Here." *New Paris Heritage.* New Paris: Sesquicentennial, 1967.

Combs, Mary. "Sing We Now of Christmas." *Franklin Chronicle,* December 17, 1991.

Crum, Carol R. "Just the Facts," letter to editor. *Ohio* magazine, February 1990.

Gilbert, Richard. "The Extraordinary Life of William Hanby: From Slave to Freedom Crusader." *Otterbein Towers* 83, no. 1 (Winter 2010).

Gilfillan, Merril C. *Wonderful World of Ohio.* Columbus: Ohio Department of Natural Resources, 1968.

Gross, Jeanne Bilger. "Notes on the Music of Benjamin Russel Hanby." Westerville: Westerville Historical Society, 1990.

———. "Time/Line: Chronology of the Life of Benjamin Russel Hanby." Westerville: Westerville Historical Society, 1990.

"Hanby House." Brochure. Westerville: Westerville Historical Society, 2009.

"Hanby House." Flyer. Columbus: Ohio Historical Society, 1960s.

"Hanby House." *Timeline,* April–June 2010.

Hart, Hugh. Interview with Randy McNutt, December 3, 1987.

McNutt, Randy. "Ohioan's Vision of Santa Still Timeless." *Cincinnati Enquirer,* December 25, 1987.

Miller, Millard J. *House of Brotherhood: Story of the Hanby House.* Westerville: Westerville Historical Society, 1990.

Sawyer, Sewall C. "Hanby Recognized as Writer of 'Up on the Housetop.'" *West Union People's Defender,* undated clipping.

Shoemaker, Dacia C. *Choose You This Day: The Legacy of the Hanbys,* edited by Harold B. Hancock and Millard J. Miller. Westerville: Westerville Historical Society, 1983.

———. "A Christmas Story." News release. Westerville Historical Society, December 10, 1941.

———. "Up on the House Top." *Columbus: Echoes* 2 (December 1963).

"Up on the House Top." *Cleveland Plain Dealer Pictorial Magazine,* December 25, 1949.

"Up on the House Top." *Otterbein Towers,* 1980.

James W. Denver, American Adventurer

Anderson, Nancy Scott, and Dwight Anderson. *The Generals: Ulysses S. Grant and Robert E. Lee.* New York: Vintage, 1989.

Austin, Henry. "Famous Duels—General James W. Denver and Hon. Edmund Gilbert." *Illustrated American* (1895).

"Biography of James William Denver." James William Denver Collection and Letters, 1846–65 Kenneth Spencer Research Library, University of Kansas, Lawrence. http://etext.ku.edu/view?docId=ksrlead/ksrl.kc.denver jameswilliamletters.xml.

"James William Denver (1817–1892)." *Biographical Directory of the United States Congress.* http://bioguide.congress.gov/scripts/biodisplay.pl?index =D000261.

Chamberlain, Ryan. *Pistols, Politics and the Press: Dueling in 19th Century America.* Jefferson, North Carolina: McFarland, 2008.

Connelly, William Elsey. *Quantrill & The Border Wars.* 1909. Reprint, New York: Konecky & Konecky, 1996.

Cook, Edward Magruder. *Justified by Honor: Highlights of the Life of General James William Denver.* Falls Church, Virginia: Higher Education Publications, 1988.

"Death of Gen. J. W. Denver." *Washington Star,* August 10, 1892.

Dullea, Mark, and Molly Dullea. "Welcome to the General Denver Hotel!" General Denver Hotel Web site. www.GeneralDenver.com.

"James W. Denver." *The Civil War Almanac,* edited by John S. Bowman. New York: Gallery, 1983.

Leslie, Edward E. *The Devil Knows How to Ride: The True Story of William Clarke Quantrill and His Confederate Raiders.* New York: Da Capo, 1998.

Martens, Barry. Interview with Randy McNutt, June 21, 1989.

Marvel, William. *Burnside.* Chapel Hill: University of North Carolina Press, 1991.

McNutt, Randy. "The Pride of Wilmington Makes a Comeback." *Tristate* magazine, July 23, 1989.

———. "The Real Denver." *Denver Post,* April 7, 1996.

Monaghan, Jay. *Civil War on the Western Border, 1854–1865.* New York: Bonanza, 1955.

Taylor, Edward T. "General James W. Denver: An Appreciation." *Colorado Magazine,* March 1940.

Thackston, Joyce. Interview with Randy McNutt, March 21, 1989.

David Harpster, the Wool King

Baumgartner, Celeste. "Ohio Novelist Highlights Changing Times on Farm." *Farm World,* May 14, 2008.

"A Calamity Howl from Columbus." *New York Times,* September 6, 1889.

Cayton, Andrew R. L. *Ohio: The History of a People.* Columbus: Ohio State University Press, 2002.

"Crossed Over: To the Eternal Shore Has David Harpster." Unidentified Wyandot County newspaper, November 3, 1898.

"Death of the Wool King." *Kansas City Journal,* November 6, 1898.

Dennis, Cecil W. Interview with Randy McNutt, June 1995.

Erickson, Fern. Interview with Cheryl Bauer McNutt and Randy McNutt, June 18, 1995.

Grove, Rick. Telephone interview with Randy McNutt, June 23, 2013.

Harpster, David. *Before the Ohio Wool-Growers' Association, Columbus, Ohio, January 24, 1888.* Cambridge: Cambridge Scholars Publishing, 2009.

The History of Wyandot County, Ohio. Chicago: Liggett, Canaway & Co., 1884.

Jones, Robert Leslie. *History of Agriculture in Ohio to 1880*. Kent: Kent State University Press, 1983.

Logsdon, Gene. "Harpster Unstrung." *Ohio* magazine, November 1991.

———. Interview with Randy McNutt and Cheryl Bauer McNutt, June 18, 1995.

———. *The Last of the Husbandmen*. Athens: Ohio University Press, 2008.

"Lonely Shepherds." *Ohio* magazine, November 1996.

"Ohio Wool Growers: The Ohio Wool Growers' Association Met in State Convention at Columbus on March 30—Steps toward the Formation of a National Wool Growers Association Made." *Perrysburg Journal*, April 6, 1883.

"Ohio Wool Growers: They Prepare an Address to the Wool Growers of the United States." *Maysville (Kentucky) Evening Bulletin*, November 27, 1889.

"The Questions of the Wool Tariff." *Salt Lake Herald*, August 24, 1890.

Sigler, Roberta. Telephone interview with Randy McNutt, November 5, 2013.

Untitled story on Columbus Delano, *Stark County Democrat*, September 25, 1890.

Untitled stories on John Stalter. *Winfield (Kansas) Courier*. August 4, 2013.

"Tales about Washington." *Anaconda (Montana) Standard*, September 29, 1890.

"Wool King." *Ohio Democrat*, January 31, 1891.

"Wool King Dead." *Reynoldsburg (Pennsylvania) Star*, November 2, 1898.

Lucy Webb Hayes, the Soldiers' Friend

Geer, Emily Apt. *First Lady: The Life of Lucy Webb Hayes*. Kent: Kent State University Press and Rutherford B. Hayes Presidential Center, 1984.

Hayes, Rutherford B. "Diary and Letters of Rutherford B. Hayes." Hayes Presidential Center Web site. www.rbhayes.org/hayes/diaries.

Hayes, Lucy. "Civil War Letters." Hayes Presidential Center Web site. http://www.rbhayes.org/hayes/onlinetexts/display.asp?id=300&subj=onlinetexts.

Perry, James M. *Touched with Fire: Five Presidents and the Civil War Battles That Made Them*. New York: Public Affairs, 2003.

Roberts, John B., II. *Rating the First Ladies: The Women Who Influenced the Presidency*. New York: Citadel, 2003.

Smith, Thomas A., comp. "Hayes of the 23rd Ohio Volunteer Infantry." Hayes Presidential Center Web site. March 9, 1995, http://www.rbhayes.org/hayes/civilwar/display.asp?id=311&subj=civilwar.

Trefousse, Hans L. *Rutherford B. Hayes*. New York: Times Books, 2002.

MOSES FLEETWOOD WALKER, WRITER-BALLPAYER

Achorn, Edward. *The Summer of Beer and Whiskey: How Brewers, Barkeeps, Rowdies, Immigrants, and a Wild Pennant Fight Made Baseball America's Game.* New York: Public Affairs, 2013.

Brown, Craig. Telephone interview with Randy McNutt, June 21, 2013.

Carter, Ulish. "Walker, Not Robinson, Was First Black into Majors." *Pittsburgh Courier,* September 21, 1974.

Dobson, Geoff. "Henry Flagler Brings Semi-Pro Baseball to St. Augustine." *Historic City News,* October 7, 2009, http://historiccity.com/2009/staugstine/news/florida/historic-city-memories-first-pro-baseball-team-1852.

"Fleet Walker." *Baseball-Reference.com,* http://www.baseball-reference.com/bullpen/Fleet_Walker.

Kirst, Sean. "Struggles of a Baseball Pioneer: In Syracuse, the Trials of Fleet Walker." *Syracuse (New York) Post Standard,* February 28, 1994.

"Moses Fleetwood Walker: Baseball's First African-American." *Jock Bio Legends.* 2004. http://www.jockbio.com/Classic/Walker/Walker_bio.html.

Murphy, Cait. *Crazy '08: How a Cast of Cranks, Rogues, Boneheads, and Magnates Created the Greatest Year in Baseball History.* New York: Smithsonian/Collins, 2008.

"Newark Little Giants." *Baseball-Reference.com.* December 12, 2013. http://www.baseball-reference.com/bullpen/Newark_Little_Giants.

Regan, Barry. "Moses Fleetwood Walker: The Forgotten Man Who Actually Integrated Baseball." *Bleacher Report.* April 16, 2012. http://bleacher report.com/articles/1147947-moses-fleetwood-walker-the-forgotten-man-who-actually-integrated-baseball.

Riley, James A. *The Biographical Encylopedia of the Negro Baseball Leagues.* New York: Carroll & Graf, 1994.

Walker, Moses Fleetwood. *Our Home Colony: A Treastise on the Past, Present, and Future of the Negro.* Cadiz: Weldy Walker, 1908.

Whirty, Ryan. "The First Jewish Baseball Superstar's Distinctive Mark on Reds History." *Cincinnati City Beat,* May 8, 2014.

Zang, David W. *Fleet Walker's Divided Heart: The Life of Baseball's First Black Major Leaguer.* Lincoln: University of Nebraska Press, 1995.

ZACHARY LANSDOWNE, AIRSHIP COMMANDER

"ZR-1 U.S.S. Shenandoah." *Airships.net: A Dirigible and Zeppelin History Site.* http://www.airships.net/us-navy-rigid-airships/uss-shenandoah.

"Colonel Mitchell on Witness Stand." *Columbus Evening Dispatch,* November 23, 1925.

"Fatal Voyage to Have Been Lansdowne's Last; Ordered to Report for Sea Duty." *Greenville Daily Advocate,* September 3, 1925.

"Greenville Bows with Grief for Her Noted Son." *Greenville Daily Advocate.* September 3, 1925.

Hauberg, Allen. "Zachary Lansdowne, Lt. Cdr. USN: A Greenville Native; The Story behind His Rise to Prominence, and His Fall to Earth." Leaflet. Greenville: Darke County Historical Society, 2010.

Keirns, Aaron. *Ohio's Airship Disaster: The Story of the Crash of the USS Shenandoah.* Howard: Little River Publishing, 2000.

"Loss of USS *Shenandoah* (ZR-1), 3 September 1925." Department of the Navy, Naval Historical Center. www.history.navy.mil/photos/events/ev-1920s/ev-1925/zr1-loss.htm. Accessed April 13, 2013 (story no longer online).

Magoto, Florence. Telephone interview with Randy McNutt, December 3, 2013.

"Many Citizens Greet Lieut. Lansdowne." *Greenville Daily News Tribune,* November 29, 1924.

Maurer, David. "Airship Drew Eyes to City's Skies." *Charlottesville (Virginia) Daily Progress,* August 21, 2011.

Nelson, Larry. "Disaster at Dawn." *Timeline,* December 1990–January 1991.

Roylance, Frank D. "In War, a Ring of Safety." *Baltimore Sun,* September 26, 1992.

"Shenandoah Crash Sites." *Aviation: From Sand Dunes to Sonic Booms: A National Register of Historic Places Travel Itinerary.* National Park Service. www.cr.nps.gov/nr/travel/aviation/she.htm.

"Shenandoah Is Destroyed; Fourteen Are Killed; Wilbur, Warned, Insisted on Flight, Is Charged." *Cincinnati Enquirer,* September 4, 1925.

Toland, John. "Death of a Dirigible." *American Heritage,* February 1969.

———. *The Great Dirigibles: Their Triumphs and Disasters.* New York: Dover, 1972.

"U.S.S. Shenandoah Service to Be Held Saturday." Uncredited newspaper clipping, September 2, 2010, Noble County, Ohio.

Walmsley, Nick. "Zachary Lansdowne: A Great American Airshipman." *Dirigible: The Journal of the Airship and Balloon Museum* 7 (Spring 1996).

Wheeler, Lonnie. "A Fall to Earth: Shenandoah." *Ohio* Magazine, September 1986.

"Wind Crashes Shenandoah; Commander Lansdowne, 12 Men, Killed." *Greenville Daily Advocate,* September 3, 1925.

Wood, Junius. "Seeing America from the 'Shenandoah.'" *National Geographic Magazine,* January 1925.

"Zachary Lansdowne: Lieutenant Commander, United States Navy." Arlington National Cemetery Web site. www.arlingtoncemetery.net/lansdown.htm.

BLANCHE NOYES, CHAMPION AVIATRIX

Adams, Jean, and Margaret Kimball. *Heroines of the Sky.* Garden City, New York: Junior Literary Guild and Doubleday, Doran & Co., 1942.

"Bendix and Thompson." *Time,* September 17, 1936.

Blair, Margaret Whitman. *The Roaring Twenty: The First Cross-Country Air Race for Women.* Washington, D.C.: National Geographic, 2006.

"Blanche Noyes." *Ninety-Nines Newsletter,* May 1939.

"Blanche Noyes Dies, Pioneer in Aviation." *Cleveland Press,* October 9, 1981.

"Blanche Noyes, Ohio's First Licensed Woman Pilot, First Woman to Win Bendix Trophy." *Toledo Blade,* October 8, 1981.

"Blanche Noyes Spreads Air Markers Across U.S. as Her Job With CAA," Associated Press dispatch, 1948. Blanche Wilcox Noyes Collection. International Women's Air and Space Museum, Cleveland.

"Blanche Noyes Was Pioneer in U.S. Aviation." *Washington Post,* October 9, 1981.

Caidin, Martin. *Barnstorming: The Great Years of Stunt Flying.* New York: Duell, Sloan, & Pearce, 1965.

Culbertson, Shawnee, "Ohio's First Licensed Woman Pilot Still Flying." *Middletown Journal,* October 31, 1976.

"Deletes Markers She Set for Pilots." *New York Times,* August 20, 1942.

"Dewey Noyes Dies as Plane Crashes." *Cleveland Plain Dealer,* December 12, 1935.

"Dewey Noyes Dies in Crash." *Youngstown Vindicator,* December 12, 1935

Dwiggins, Don. *They Flew the Bendix.* Philadelphia: Lippincott, 1965.

Earhart, Amelia. Letter to Eugene L. Vidal, May 8, 1936. Blanche Wilcox Noyes Collection.

"First Woman Pilot Enters Races Here." *Cleveland Plain Dealer,* April 6, 1929.

"Girl Flier Fights Blaze in Air." *Pittsburgh Press,* August 22, 1929.

Jablonski, Edward. *Ladybirds: Women in Aviation.* New York: Hawthorn, 1968.

Jones, Jack. "Lovebug Bit Pioneer Woman Pilot." *Dayton Daily News,* May 5, 1978.

Maxim, Edie. "Blanche Noyes," undated notes. Blanche Wilcox Noyes Collection.

Nobles-Harris, Ellen. "The Ninety-Nines: Marking the Way." *99 News Magazine,* March–April 2002.

Noyes, Blanche Wilcox. Letter to Mrs. Elden Bayley, June 20, 1948. Blanche Wilcox Noyes Collection.

———. Speech to the American Institute of Aeronautics and Astronautics, Dayton, Ohio, April 27, 1978. Blanche Wilcox Noyes Collection.

"One-Time Actress Becomes a Flier." *Saskatoon (Washington) Star-Phoenix,* August 10, 1939.

Sammon, Helen. Telephone interview with Cheryl Bauer McNutt, February 1, 2013.

Rickman, Sarah Byrn. Telephone interview with Cheryl Bauer McNutt, February 1, 2013.

Thaden, Louise McPhetridge. "Five Women Tackle the Nation." *N.A.A. Magazine,* August 1936.

———. *High, Wide, and Frightened.* 1938. Reprint, Fayetteville: University of Arkansas Press, 2004.

"Woman Battles Fire in Plane." *St. Petersburg Times,* August 22, 1929.

"Woman Will Try World Flight." *Miami News,* August 28, 1933.

CLAYTON BRUKNER, AVIATION TYCOON

"Airplane Concern Holds Option on Troy Building." *Troy Daily News,* March 28, 1923.

Associated Press. "Rebels Try to Destroy Planes." *New York Times,* August 30, 1932.

Bayne, Walter J. *The Aircraft Treasures of Silver Hill.* New York: Rawson, 1982.

Brandley, Raymond H. *The Authentic History of WACO Airplanes.* N.p.: Raymond H. Brandley, 1979.

Dahlem, Valentine. Interview with Cheryl Bauer McNutt, August 24, 2013.

Drummond-Hay, Grace. "Goering, Hitler's Chief Minister, Sees 'Bloodless Revolution' in Germany." *Milwaukee Sentinel,* April 2, 1933.

"Lady Hay Vividly Pictures Greatest Air Adventure." *Toledo News-Bee,* August 9, 1929.

Francis, Dale. "Today's Troy Owes Much to Clayton Brukner." *Troy Daily News,* January 13, 1978.

Heithaus, Harriet Howard. "Clayton J. Brukner." *Troy Daily News,* December 28, 1977.

"Industrial Situation of Troy Is Taken Up by City Councilmen." *Troy Daily News,* March 20, 1923.

Junkin, Hattie M. W. *Mrs. WACO: The Early Days of the WACO Aircraft Company.* Troy: WACO Historical Society, 1996.

Moffitt, Charles. Interview with Dick Francis, April 14, 1979, Troy, Ohio. Transcript, WACO Historical Society and Museum.

Schreiner, Herm. "The WACO Story." *American Aviation Historical Journal* 25, no. 4 (Winter 1980).

Willis, Don. Telephone interview with Cheryl Bauer McNutt, June 27, 2013.

MILDRED GILLARS, TRAITOR AND TEACHER

Associated Press, "Axis Sally's Nabbed; Faces Treason Charge." *Ellensburg (Washington) Daily Record,* March 21, 1946.

"'Axis Sally' Graduates from Ohio Wesleyan." *Columbus Dispatch,* June 11, 1973.

"Axis Sally Leaves Prison." *Milwaukee Journal,* July 9, 1961.

"Axis Sally Paid Well, Nazi Says." *Pittsburgh Press,* January 25, 1949.

Barden, Judy. "Axis Sally Brazenly Says Conscience Clear." *Calgary Herald,* March 25, 1946.

Davis, Jack. "'Axis Sally' Out after 11 Years." *Charleston Daily Mail,* July 10, 1961.

Edwards, John Carner. *Berlin Calling: American Broadcasters in Service to the Third Reich.* New York: Praeger, 1991.

Horten, Gerd. *Radio Goes to War: The Cultural Politics of Propaganda during World War II.* Los Angeles: University of California Press, 2002.

Lucas, Richard. *Axis Sally: The American Voice of Nazi Germany.* Philadelphia: Casemate, 2010.

McGarey, Mary, "'Axis Sally' Wants to Forget Past." *Dover Daily Reporter,* August 18, 1961.

"Pleased." *Delaware Gazette,* June 11, 1973.

Trilly, Andrew. "Now She's Treasonous Sal, a Nazi-Kind of Gal." *Pittsburgh Press,* January 26, 1949.

Van Dyne, Edward. "No Other Gal Like Axis Sal." *Saturday Evening Post,* January 15, 1944.

Yee, Greg. "Veteran Shares Story during 90th Birthday Celebration." *Farmington (New Mexico) Daily Times,* January 21, 2013.

Lloyd Copas, Cowboy Singer

Blasé, Darren. "The Lonesome Ballad of Cowboy Copas." *Cincinnati Magazine,* August 2013.

Boehme, Stephen. "Concert Celebrates Cowboy Copas' Legacy." *West Union People's Defender,* August 13, 2013.

Cooper, Peter. "Patsy Cline, Cowboy Copas, Hawkshaw Hawkins, Randy Hughes Remembered, 50 Years after Plane Crash." *Nashville Tennessean,* March 2, 2013.

"Cowboy Copas Makes His Film Debut in 'Square Dance Jubilee.'" *West Union People's Defender,* November 10, 2004.

"Cowboy Copas' Career Has Its Ups and Downs." *West Union People's Defender,* November 24, 2004.

Delmore, Alton. *Truth Is Stranger Than Publicity.* Nashville: Country Music Foundation Press, 1977.

Jones, Louis M., with Charles K. Wolfe. *Everybody's Grandpa: Fifty Years behind the Mike.* Knoxville: University of Tennessee Press, 1984.

Kelley, Stephen. "Copas' Talent and Drive Takes Him to the Big City." *West Union People's Defender,* October 20, 2004.

———. Interview with Randy McNutt, April 20, 2003.

Kessel, Howard. Interview with Randy McNutt, December 19, 1999.

"Local Musicians Leave Mark on National Scale." *West Union People's Defender,* October 13, 2004.

McNutt, Randy. *We Wanna Boogie: An Illustrated History of the American Rockabilly Movement.* Hamilton: HHP Books, 1988.

Stanton, Scott. *The Tombstone Tourist*, 2d ed. New York: Pocket Books, 2003.

"Wedding Bells Ring for Cowboy Copas." *West Union People's Defender*, December 1, 2004.

Weyrich, Carleta. "Memorial Honors Music Legend." *West Union People's Defender*, November 17, 2004.

Whitburn, Joel. *Top Country Singles 1944–1988*. Menomonee Falls, Wisconsin: Record Research, 1989.

SYDNEY NATHAN, MUSIC MAN

Brown, James, and Bruce Tucker. *James Brown: The Godfather of Soul*. New York: Macmillan, 1986.

Delmore, Alton. *Truth Is Stranger Than Publicity*. Nashville: Country Music Foundation Press, 1977.

Gillett, Charlie. *The Sound of the City: The Rise of Rock and Roll*. New York: Pantheon, 1983.

Halper, Dorothy. Telephone interview with Randy McNutt, January 13, 1981.

Herzog, E. T. "Bucky." Interview with Randy McNutt, June 21, 1989.

"The Influx of Independents." Clipping, unknown magazine. Collection of Zella Nathan.

Jones, Louis M., with Charles K. Wolfe. *Everybody's Grandpa: Fifty Years behind the Mike*. Knoxville: University of Tennessee Press, 1984.

Kessel, Howard. Interview with Randy McNutt, July 21, 1995.

McNutt, Randy. "King Records: The Country Side of a Rhythm and Blues Label." *Goldmine*, February 9, 1990.

———. *King Records of Cincinnati*. Charleston: Arcadia Publishing, 2009.

———. "Sydney Nathan," Ohioans. *Ohio* magazine, September 1990.

Pennington, Ray. Interview with Randy McNutt, July 10, 1987.

Ramey, Jack. "Jukebox Operator." *Cincinnati Enquirer*, February 6, 1949.

Ruppli, Michel. *The King Labels: A Discography*, 2 vols. Westport, Connecticutt: Greenwood, 1985.

Sanchez, KJ. E-mail interview with Randy McNutt, July 18, 2014.

"Soul Brother No. 1." *Billboard*, September 25, 1971.

Williams, Otis. Interview with Cheryl Bauer McNutt and Randy McNutt, May 18, 2008.

Wilson, Jim. Interviews with Randy McNutt, May 8 and September 18, 1990.

York, Rusty. Interview with Randy McNutt, June 18, 1986.

JOSEPHINE JOHNSON, PULITZER PRIZE–WINNING AUTHOR

Abbey, Edward. "The Inland Island." *New York Times Book Review,* March 2, 1969.

Cannon, Annie. Telephone interview with Cheryl Bauer McNutt, October 10, 2013.

Darack, Arthur. "Tender Is the Novel Today." *Cincinnati Enquirer,* April 20, 1963.

"Electronic Writing 'Gadgets' Serve Grant Cannon Well." *Cincinnati Enquirer,* May 28, 1967.

Fleischman, John. "News from the Inland Island." *Audubon,* March 1986.

Fraser, C. Gerald. "Josephine Johnson, Nature Writer, Poet, and Novelist, 79." *New York Times,* March 2, 1990.

Fuller, Edmund. "The Bookshelf: Wilderness and Animals." *Wall Street Journal,* March 31, 1969.

"G. G. Cannon, Editor of National Magazine." *Cincinnati Enquirer,* February 23, 1969.

Hicks, Granville. "Literary Horizons." *Saturday Review,* February 15, 1969.

Hohenberg, John. *The Pulitzer Prizes: A History of the Awards in Books, Drama, Music, and Journalism, Based on the Private Files over Six Decades.* New York: Columbia University Press, 1974.

Johnson, Josephine W. *The Inland Island.* New York: Simon & Schuster, 1969.

———. *Seven Houses: A Memoir of Time and Place.* New York: Simon & Schuster, 1973.

McFadden-Gerber, Margaret. "Josephine Winslow Johnson." *American Women Writers,* edited by Lina Mainiero. New York: Frederick Ungar, 1980.

Stuckey, W. J. *The Pulitzer Prize Novels: A Critical Backward Look.* Norman: University of Oklahoma Press, 1981.

Weeks, Edward. "The Peripatetic Reviewer." *Atlantic,* May 1969.

INDEX